Islam in der Gesellschaft

Reihe herausgegeben von

Rauf Ceylan, Universität Osnabrück, Düsseldorf, Nordrhein-Westfalen, Germany

Naika Foroutan, Institut für Sozialwissenschaften, Humboldt-Universität zu Berlin, Berlin, Germany

Michael Kiefer, Institut für Islamische Theologie, Universität Osnabrück, Osnabrück, Germany

Andreas Zick, Institut für Konfliktforschung, Universität Bielefeld, Bielefeld, Germany

Die Reihe *Islam in der Gesellschaft* publiziert theoretische wie empirische Forschungsarbeiten zu einem international wie national aktuellem Gegenstand. Der Islam als heterogene und vielfältige Religion, wie aber auch kulturelle und soziale Organisationsform, ist ein bedeutsamer Bestandteil von modernen Gesellschaften. Er beeinflusst Gesellschaft, wird zum prägenden Moment und erzeugt Konflikte. Zugleich reagieren Gesellschaften auf den Islam und Menschen, die im angehören bzw. auf das, was sie unter dem Islam und Muslimen verstehen. Der Islam prägt Gesellschaft und Gesellschaft prägt Islam, weil und wenn er in Gesellschaft ist. Die damit verbundenen gesellschaftlichen Phänomene und Prozesse der Veränderungen sind nicht nur ein zentraler Aspekt der Integrations- und Migrationsforschung. Viele Studien und wissenschaftlichen Diskurse versuchen, den Islam in der Gesellschaft zu verorten und zu beschreiben. Diese Forschung soll in der Reihe *Islam in der Gesellschaft* zu Wort und Schrift kommen, sei es in Herausgeberbänden oder Monografien, in Konferenzbänden oder herausragenden Qualifikationsarbeiten.

Die Beiträge richten sich an unterschiedliche Disziplinen, die zu einer interwie transdisziplinären Perspektive beitragen können:

- Sozialwissenschaften, Soziologie
- Islamwissenschaft
- Integration- und Migrationsforschung
- Bildungswissenschaft
- Sozialpsychologie
- Kulturwissenschaften
- Geschichtswissenschaft und
- weitere Wissenschaften, die Forschungsbeiträge zum Thema aufweisen

Rauf Ceylan · Marvin Mücke
Editors

Muslims in Europe

Historical developments, present issues, and future challenges

Editors
Rauf Ceylan
Institute for Islamic Theology
Universität Osnabrück
Osnabrück, Germany

Marvin Mücke
Institute for Islamic Theology
Universität Osnabrück
Osnabrück, Germany

ISSN 2569-6203   ISSN 2569-6211 (electronic)
Islam in der Gesellschaft
ISBN 978-3-658-43043-6 ISBN 978-3-658-43044-3 (eBook)
https://doi.org/10.1007/978-3-658-43044-3

© The Editor(s) (if applicable) and The Author(s), under exclusive license to Springer
Fachmedien Wiesbaden GmbH, part of Springer Nature 2024

This work is subject to copyright. All rights are solely and exclusively licensed by the Publisher,
whether the whole or part of the material is concerned, specifically the rights of translation, reprint-
ing, reuse of illustrations, recitation, broadcasting, reproduction on microfilms or in any other
physical way, and transmission or information storage and retrieval, electronic adaptation, computer
software, or by similar or dissimilar methodology now known or hereafter developed.
The use of general descriptive names, registered names, trademarks, service marks, etc. in this
publication does not imply, even in the absence of a specific statement, that such names are exempt
from the relevant protective laws and regulations and therefore free for general use.
The publisher, the authors, and the editors are safe to assume that the advice and information in this
book are believed to be true and accurate at the date of publication. Neither the publisher nor the
authors or the editors give a warranty, expressed or implied, with respect to the material contained
herein or for any errors or omissions that may have been made. The publisher remains neutral with
regard to jurisdictional claims in published maps and institutional affiliations.

This Springer VS imprint is published by the registered company Springer Fachmedien Wiesbaden
GmbH, part of Springer Nature.
The registered company address is: Abraham-Lincoln-Str. 46, 65189 Wiesbaden, Germany

Paper in this product is recyclable.

About this Volume: A Brief Overview

Since the migration movements of migrants from Islamic-influenced countries, a Muslim diaspora has developed in many Western societies. While in classical Islamic theology residence in non-Muslim countries has always been a controversial issue, in the course of globalization and internationalization processes the classical division into "Islamic world" and "non-Islamic world" has long been relativized. In the meantime, nearly 30 million Muslims live in Europe alone. This has created facts that entail both challenges and opportunities for the countries of origin and host countries. In the context of the countries of origin—the initially often temporary intended stay on the part of Muslims—the migration of their Muslim citizens meant a transfer of foreign exchange and thus economic interests. In this context, it was also hoped that qualified personnel would return to their countries of origin. At the beginning of the migration waves, the host countries also focused primarily on economic goals without long-term social consequences. With the permanent residence or settlement of the first generation of Muslim migrants and new forms of migration (chain migration, family reunification, refugee migration), the situation has changed completely. For the countries of origin, this settlement means that an increasingly emancipated Muslim community is forming in Western societies. They often take on the citizenship of their new homeland and have created their own Islamic infrastructure. Because of the diaspora situation, new theological questions are also increasingly being raised that correlate with the realities of life in these Western host countries. For the host societies, the permanent presence of Muslims also raises numerous new questions. In addition to the classic integration questions concerning the world of work, the housing market or the education system, the question of the relationship between state and religion is also being reactualized. It is true that European countries have taken different paths on this issue with their specific political systems (secularism, state church, secularism under the rule of law). However, the role of the church in politics and the state is clearly regulated. With the presence of Islam, this question is now being revisited. In the process, it becomes clear, as in Germany, for example, that the question of religion in the public sphere is still an indication of latent and manifest conflicts. In Germany, for example, there is an ongoing debate about whether crucifixes may be hung in school classrooms, as is the case in Bavaria, or whether religious symbols are contrary to the ideologically neutral orientation of the German state? This debate has been largely dominated in recent years by the legal question of whether Muslim teachers wearing headscarves should be allowed to teach in state schools. Often, these debates about the role of Islam in the public sphere suggest that unresolved issues in the context of Christianity and the public sphere are being addressed vicariously through the discourse of Islam.

Against the backdrop of the numerous challenges facing the Muslim community as well as the respective Western host countries, this book aims to address historical, current, and future developments in Europe. Selected European countries are examined, each with a different emphasis, to provide an insight into the situation there.

The first focus is on Western Europe. Frank Fegosi opens with his contribution on Muslim life in secular France. A state that, compared to other European countries, has most strictly enforced the separation of state and religion. In his contribution, Fregosi analyzes on the one hand the different Muslim currents, and on the other hand the question of how the state deals with the numerous Muslim actors. The second article by Corinne Torrekens focuses on developments in Belgium. There, the Muslim minority—predominantly immigrants from Morocco and Turkey—obtained Belgian citizenship relatively early, and in this respect Muslims there look back on a longer history of the institutionalization of Islam. Again, the question of the representation of Islam arises for the very heterogeneous Muslim-Belgian population. Seamlessly, the question of representation runs like a thread through the third article by Thijl Sunier. Using a phase model for the Netherlands, Sunier shows the development of the Muslim community in interaction with Dutch integration policy. In striving for recognition and equality, Sunier identifies two factors in particular: the Muslim educational upstarts and the increasingly engaged Muslim women. Developments in Germany are analyzed by Rauf Ceylan in the fourth essay. The focus is on the structural integration of Islam at universities. Since the German Islam Conference in 2006, a Muslim academic community has emerged in Germany to compete with orthodox Muslim organizations in the Islamic religious field. In the fifth article, Marvin

About this Volume: A Brief Overview

Mücke and Sören Sponick continue the analyses in Germany with their investigation on converts. Drawing on several publications and research on this topic, they critically analyze the different research designs. One result of this analysis is the lack of epistemic connectedness between these publications. The last two articles are also devoted to developments in the German-speaking world. For Switzerland, Mallory Schneuwly Purdie shows the historical development that led to the multiethnic constellation of Muslims. Also discussed is the merging of the migration discourse with the Islam discourse (politics, media). Paradoxically, this very discourse to stop "Islamization" has fostered the genesis of Islamic militancy rooted in the Swiss. Finally, the first focus of the book is concluded with the contribution of Hüseyin Cicek. In his article, Cicek lays out the long history of Muslims in Austria, which does not begin with the migration movements. The focus of his interest is the so-called Islam Law, which is based on a political tradition in dealing with Muslims in Austria and has been updated. Turkish-Muslim organizations as well as Alevi organizations benefit in different ways from this legislation, which aims at a long-term integration of Islam.

The second focus of this publication analyzes developments in Southern Europe. The first contribution by Ana I. Planet and Johanna M. Lems continues the red, thematic line on the question of the relationship between the state and Islam. Using Spain as an example, the two authors show how the Muslim community has been struggling for legal equality for years. The tension in Spain revolves around the question of who is the central Muslim interlocutor vis-à-vis the state and how the deficit in legal issues (citizenship law, anti-Muslim racism, Islamic everyday life, etc.) can be resolved constructively. The second essay, by Stefano Allievi, deals with developments in Italy. There, as in Spain, Islam looks back on a centuries-old history. Likewise, Italy's more recent history has been shaped by Islam as a result of migration processes. In the course of their attempts to gain recognition, the now two million Muslims are experiencing various transformation processes, which are particularly evident in the contrast between the first and second generations.

In the third thematic focus, the southern European region is examined using the example of Muslims in Croatia and Greece. In the first article, Dino Mujadžević analyzes the historical and recent discourse on Islam in Croatia. Based on a source analysis in the period between 1500 and ca. 1990, ruptures and continuities corresponding to the different political eras in the collective archive of stereotypes are elaborated. The second article by Konstantinos Tsitselikis focuses on Islam in Greece. Specifically, he focuses on the theological and legal reference of the muftis for the Muslim minority there. In this article, too, the common thread of the entire book becomes clear when it comes to the relationship between the state and Muslims. In this context, it is about the struggle over interpretive sovereignty on Islam when the state and Muslims are at odds over the selection of muftis as well as over the substantive areas of authority.

Finally, the last focus deals with the situation in Northern Europe, using Sweden as an example. By analyzing the history of Muslims in Sweden and evaluating the publications on Muslims in Sweden, Göran Larsson and Simon Sorgenfrei not only provide an overall view, but also point out desiderata for further research on the situation of this religious minority.

Contents

Part I   Western Europe

1   Being Muslim in a Secular State: History, Sociological Realities, and Institutional Issues—the French Case 3
Franck Frégosi

2   Muslims in Belgium: From Immigrant Guestworkers to a Polymorphic and Contested Minority 23
Corinne Torrekens

3   Islam in the Netherlands: Denominational Pillar or 'Fifth Column'? 39
Thijl Sunier

4   The Academization of Islam in Germany—Structural Integration and Competitive Struggles Over Interpretive Authority in the Religious Field 59
Rauf Ceylan

5   Research on Conversion to Islam in Germany Between 1995 and 2022 75
Marvin Mücke and Sören Sponick

6   Islam and Muslims in Switzerland Through the Prism of Religious Visibility and Islamic Militancy 97
Mallory Schneuwly Purdie

ix

x   Contents

7   Alevis and Turkish-Muslims in Austria: History and Current
      Developments 113
      Hüseyin Çiçek

Part II   Southern Europe

8   Religious Freedom, Civil Rights, and Islam in Spain 133
      Ana I. Planet and Johanna M. Lems

9   An Unacknowledged Presence—Islam in the Italian Public
      Space: History, Reactions, Perspectives 149
      Stefano Allievi

Part III   Southeast Europe

10   Islam and Muslims in the Perspective of Croatian
      Historiography 167
      Dino Mujadžević

11   The Position of the Mufti in Greece. New and Old Ambiguities ... 185
      Konstantinos Tsitselikis

Part IV   Northern Europe

12   Muslims in Sweden: Historical Developments, Present Issues,
      and Future Challenges 201
      Göran Larsson and Simon Sorgenfrei

Editors and Contributors

About the Editors

Rauf Ceylan has been Professor at the University of Osnabrück/Institute of Islamic Theology (IIT) in Germany since 2009. He was a Visiting Professor in 2018 at the University of Zürich. His research focuses on the Sociology of Migration and Religion based on the study of the Turkish community in the Diaspora. He is a member of the Institute for Migration Research and Intercultural Studies (IMIS) and the Council for Migration (RfM eV).

Marvin Mücke, M.A. is research assistant at the Institute for Islamic Theology at the University of Osnabrück and currently a Ph.D. candidate. His research interests lie in conversion to Islam, radicalization, and the prevention of radicalization. He holds a Master's degree in Arabic and Middle Eastern Studies from the University of Edinburgh.

Contributors

Stefano Allievi Università di Padova – FISPPA, Padova, Italy

Rauf Ceylan University of Osnabrück, Osnabrück, Deutschland

Priv.-Doz. Dr. Hüseyin Çiçek Department of Religious Studies, University of Vienna, Vienna, Austria

Franck Frégosi CNRS, Apt, France

Göran Larsson Faculty of Humanities, Department of Literature, History of Ideas, Religion, University of Gothenburg, Gothenburg, Sweden

Johanna M. Lems Assistant Professor, Universidad Complutense de Madrid, Madrid, Spain

Dino Mujadžević Hrvatski institut za povijest, Zagreb, Croatia

Marvin Mücke M.A. University of Osnabrück, Osnabrück, Germany

Ana I. Planet Professor, Universidad Autónoma de Madrid, Madrid, Spain

Mallory Schneuwly Purdie Swiss Center for Islam and Society, University of Fribourg, Fribourg, Switzerland

Simon Sorgenfrei Historical and Contemporary Studies, Södertörn University, Huddinge, Sweden

Sören Sponick M.A. University of Osnabrück, Osnabrück, Germany

Thijl Sunier Vrije UniversiteitNetherlands, Amsterdam, Netherlands

Corinne Torrekens ULB, Université libre de Bruxelles, Brussels, Belgium

Konstantinos Tsitselikis Professor, University of Macedonia, Thessaloniki, Greece

Part I

Western Europe

Being Muslim in a Secular State: History, Sociological Realities, and Institutional Issues—the French Case

1

Franck Frégosi

Abstract

This chapter points out the original situation of Muslims in France, settled and established in a deeply secularized society, and facing one of the more secular European states. Different ways of being Muslim within the society are analyzed as well as the different religious currents observed in France. Finally, we focus on the main issue of governing Islam in the specific context of a state supposed to be neutral, protecting both freedom of religion and being separated from religious institutions.

Keywords

French Colonial Empire • French secularism • Migrations • Muslim Diaspora • Islamic federations • Governing Islam • Muslim religious currents • Conservative Islam • Reformed Islam • Imams • Radicalization • Islamophobia

1 Introduction

Islam in France covers a demographic, social, and religious reality that is resolutely plural. Its historical roots go back to the genesis of the French colonial empire (Luizard 2006; Vermeren 2016), while its contemporary extensions largely

---

F. Frégosi (✉)
CNRS, Apt, France
e-mail: fr.fregosi@gmail.com

© The Author(s), under exclusive license to Springer Fachmedien Wiesbaden GmbH, part of Springer Nature 2024
R. Ceylan and M. Mücke (eds.), *Muslims in Europe*, Islam in der Gesellschaft, https://doi.org/10.1007/978-3-658-43044-3_1

echo the history of migratory cycles, particularly from the southern Mediterranean countries, and their progressive sedentarization. If Islam is now part of the religious landscape of contemporary France, its presence still fuels many controversies and also questions the way in which the French regime of secularism takes note of this religious reality.

In this chapter, we will review the situation of Islam as a religious community in a deeply secularized French society (Portier and Willaime 2021), the place of Muslims as a minority demographic (Bucaille and Villechaise 2020) component of the French population, and the institutional and political issues raised by this Muslim presence within the framework of a secular state.

2 Genesis of the Muslim Presence in France and Demographic Data

Continental Europe today has more than 44 million people of Muslim culture (Pew Research 2011) which represents 6% of its overall population, but only 3% of Muslims worldwide.

This socio-demographic reality constitutes, along with the loss of social control by churches (unchurching), one of the major characteristics of the European religious landscape compared to other more religious societies such as the United States (Berger and Fokas 2008).

With an estimated 8,8% of the population, France is the European country with the largest number of Muslims in terms of volume, after Sweden (8,1%), Belgium (7.6%), the Netherlands (7,1%) and Austria (6,9%), United Kingdom (6,3%), Germany (6,1%), Greece (1.5%), Italy (4,8%) and Spain more than 2% (Pew Research Center, 2017).

2.1 The Colonial Episode and Migration Cycles

If the first moment of the Muslim history of Western Europe coincides with the beginning of the Muslim presence in Spain between 711 and 1492, and in various other points of settlement, in Italy (Sicily) as in the South-East of France, the second strong moment of the meeting between Islam and the European continent will be carried out via the European expansion of the Ottoman Empire. This expansion took place from 1402 (the beginning of the expansion of the Ottoman power towards the Danube, the Aegean Sea and the foothills of the Balkans) to

1 Being Muslim in a Secular State … 5

the first third of the twentieth century (1919–1923), with the birth of the Turkish Republic of Mustapha Kemal.

The confrontation with the Muslim world, also occurred in reverse, from the West to the Muslim world, via the colonial empires (Maréchal 2002).

From the end of the nineteenth century until the very beginning of the twentieth century, it was through the expansion of certain European powers outside the Old Continent that Islam made its return to European history through its colonial side. This was of course the case for France, notably through its expansion in the Maghreb and in West and Sub-Saharan Africa.

In the case of France, this colonial experience, particularly in Algeria, proved to be foundational in that it was to have a lasting influence on the way in which the Republic intended to manage its relations with Islam as a religion in metropolitan France (Luizard 2019).

Finally, Europe's relationship with Islam interferes with the more recent history of different waves of migration, in other words, with the movement of populations between the two shores of the Mediterranean.

Thus, the first arrivals of Muslims in France, on the metropolitan territory, were first in the form of military contingents, soldiers, on the occasion of the Franco-Prussian war of 1870, then during the First World War between 1914 and 1918. Among the 800,000 colonial subjects from the Colonial Empire who arrived in France between 1914 and 1918, nearly half were Muslims (Katz 2018).

This war-related immigration was also coupled with a first labor immigration. This immigration from colonized Muslim societies developed especially from the 1920s. It increased with the end of the Second World War and continued until the mid-1970s. The government then tried to progressively limit immigration by setting up a policy of family reunification.

These waves of labor migration contributed to the creation of the first Muslim populations throughout Western Europe, and particularly in France.

2.2 From Silent Islam to the Claimed Islam

The installation of these immigrant populations from Muslim societies, in the French case, coming mainly from North African societies (Algeria, Morocco, Tunisia) and from sub-Saharan Africa, then from 1970 onwards, from Turkey, was to take place in different stages. Each of these stages was to result in different types of presence and different ways of declining to belong to Islam.

Thus, the decade of the 1960s was characterized in France by an Islam so called as "Silent Islam" in the sense that it did not show itself (invisible Islam), and did not leave the closed and private space of immigrant workers' homes. Moreover, it was lived in a transitory mode (transplanted Islam) with the ultimate perspective of returning to and settling in the country of origin.

From the mid-1970s onwards, with the implementation of family reunification policies, the logic of sedentarization gradually took precedence over that of displacement. Islam was lived in a more family mode, but in the intimacy of the home.

It is from the beginning of the 1980s that we witness the emergence of Islam as a collective religious reality and no longer as an individual one that remains limited to the family. Islam then left the circle of families and groups of practitioners began to request and obtain the opening of prayer rooms in their places of work and residence. An Islamic association fabric began to be structured, largely supported financially by Gulf States. It was also during this decade that some of the major Islamic federations in France were created. In 1983, the Union of Islamic Organizations in France was founded, which later became the Union of Islamic Organizations of France (UOIF), and then Musulmans de France (MdF), reputed to be close to the religious and ideological movement of the Muslim Brotherhood and the conservative Gulf monarchies (Maréchal 2009). The National Federation of Muslims of France (FNMF) was created in 1986, at the instigation of a French convert and with the support of the World Islamic League (WIL). This originally multi-ethnic federation sought to counter the Algerian influence of the Grand Mosque of Paris on the French Islamic landscape. This federation was to undergo various splits over the course of its history and became, particularly from the 1990s onwards, the main channel of expression in France for official Moroccan Islam (Frégosi and Tozy 2017).

The decade of the 1990s was more clearly marked by an increased visibilization of Islam, which among the youngest elements will sometimes take the form of a reislamization. This was manifested, for example, through the development of gestures, language and clothing practices considered Islamic (*hijab, niqab*, etc.), and through the insistence on combining scrupulous fidelity to religious teachings with the demand for a more active citizenship.

Islam has thus become, in France, as in the rest of Europe, for the younger generations a privileged mode of self-affirmation, the expression of an identity that is both individual, the fruit of a personal belief, and at the same time collective, in its relationship to political citizenship and to the community of believers.

With the decade starting in 2000, we entered a new stage in the history of Islam in France. As in the rest of the European continent, we witnessed the gradual emergence of an indigenous Islam that thinks of itself more European.

This Islam in the process of taking root directly challenges the States and, through them, the different classical modes of regulation of religious pluralism in force in the European space (Bastian and Messner 2007).

3 The Religiosities of Islam at the Heart of Controversies and Recompositions

The visibility of certain practices such as wearing the simple (*hijab*) or full veil (*niqab*) and demands for the organization of hours reserved for women in public swimming pools, or the development of businesses that are supposed to sell legal products (*halal*), often make headlines and are a source of numerous controversies.

3.1 Controversies Around Islam

The historical sequence we are going through has also been punctuated by mobilizations of an islamophobic type (Goldman 2012). This is notably carried in France by political parties such as the Rassemblement National (RN), and more recently, by the Reconquest movement created by the far-right journalist Éric Zemmour. This climate of obsessive fear and moral panic against Islam (Marwan and Hajjat 2013) is maintained and fed by certain intellectuals and essayists (Geisser 2003). It also feeds on the political exploitation of jihadist attacks committed in France during the last decade (2012, 2015, 2020), as well as more recently on the crisis of refugees fleeing conflict zones (Syria, Iraq, Afghanistan...), and misery (sub-Saharan Africa, Horn of Africa...). A interpretative framework is gradually spreading among certain political elites that tends to associate the two phenomena, maintaining the amalgam between the terrorist threat, the presence of rooted Muslim communities and migration.

Controversies about Islam are legion (Göle 2015). These, most of the time in France, concern the points of divergence, of tension between certain intensive practices of the religion and the rule of secularism, such as the question of the veil. The controversy around the veil has thus led to the vote of two laws limiting the visibility of this type of clothing, on the one hand the law of March 15, 2004, which banned the simple veil from public school-space of elementary schools, colleges and high schools, then the law of October 11, 2010, which prohibits any full veil in the public space.

More recently, since the attacks of 2020, the controversies have focused more on the reputedly dominant place within the Islam of France of the most conservative Muslim currents (Rougier 2021). These are suspected of being at the origin of a multiform process of promotion of the Islamic reference (wearing the veil, Islamic schools, halal butcheries…) and are also denounced for their supposed ideological complicity, and the links maintained with the most radical currents, following the example of the jihadist movement which sanctifies the recourse to violence within the French society (Kepel 2015).

The prevailing perception of Muslims in France is therefore most often that of a human group supposedly growing in population on the one hand, and that is sometimes denounced as a tyrannical minority (Zarka 2004), apprehended through the prism of religion alone and regularly asked to renounce certain forms of visibility in the public space and to reform their approach to Islam on the other.

3.2 Muslim Religiosities in Question

A resolutely sociological analysis of contemporary Muslim belonging in France, far from referring to a monolithic and homogeneous religious reality, invites us to specify that the people perceived as Muslims in France by the rest of society are not only Muslims. Their religious identity is only one of the components of their overall social identity. They are women and men, young and old, students, employees, and workers, unemployed and members of the middle classes, French descendants of immigrants, converts or foreigners, etc. … Their objective relationship to religion refers to a contrasting universe and to different understandings of this Islam that is supposed to characterize them exclusively.

It is preferable to reason in terms of Muslim religiosities, by putting forward differentiated modes of affiliation to Islam, of mobilization of Islamity (modes of being a religious, cultural, secular, political Muslim…) and of contrasting religious experiences in the space of the city. The polymorphism that is materialized by the plurality of the modes of being Muslim is prolonged by a no less astonishing polyphony, by a plurality of readings made of Islam and of the enunciations of the Islamity by the interested parties themselves.

Like Christianity (Lagroye 2009) or Jewishness (Memmi 2010; Guland and Zerbib 2000; Podselver 2004), Islamity, the fact of being Muslim and of considering oneself as such, cannot refer to an essence, nor can it be reduced to the only religious belonging or affiliation. Far from it!

In spite of the commonplace that would like Islam to be "one" in the same way that "God" is supposed to be "One", there are in reality different ways of calling oneself Muslim, of living (positively, negatively or in a more contrasted way) one's relationship to this religion, and to its history, which has espoused very different cultural, political and social contexts.

This issue of belonging and affiliation to Islam is particularly topical in France, at a time when people of Muslim culture are sometimes the subject of prosecutions (alleged incompatibility between their membership in Islam and some of their practices with a set of principles such as equality between women and men, freedom of conscience or the secular conception of the State).

The question of Islamic belonging is also relevant from an intra-Islamic perspective. This is the case if one observes the deployment of literalist currents of the neo-Salafist type (Adraoui 2013), which cling to an exclusivist and standardized vision of belonging to Islam and use anathema against other Muslim religious currents castigated as heterodox and deviant from an orthonormal (orthodox and orthoprax) conception of Islam, not to mention violent and armed currents (Jihadism).

The acuteness of this question also stems from the emergence of claims and demands for recognition of pluri-membership at the very heart of Islam, such as that carried by the gay Muslim movement which is beginning to emerge in France[1] and in the rest of Europe via the CALEM[2] confederation. It is the same with the structuring of a Muslim movement that promotes the accession of women to the imâmat. Since January 2017, two projects of so-called inclusive mosques and carried by three women have thus emerged in France. The first project called the Fatima Mosque (Bahloul 2021) was initiated by the French-Algerian Kahina Bahloul, the second, the Sîmorgh Mosque, is carried by two converts, Eva Janadin and Anne Sophie Monsinay (Janadin and Monsinay 2019). These two projects clearly raise both the question of the effective mixing of prayers in mosques (without spatial separation) and that of the legitimate accession of women to the imâmat. The preaching can be provided alternatively by a male imâm and a female imâm. On Saturday, September 7, 2019, Eva Janadin and Anne Sophie Monsinay led for the first time a mixed prayer time in front of eighty faithful and received the support of other women imâms from the USA and Germany and the reinforcement of a homosexual imâm who had been the first to open an inclusive mosque welcoming anyone regardless of gender, sexual orientation, religious beliefs (etc.…) in 2012 in Paris.

---

[1] http://www.homosexuels-musulmans.org.

[2] http://www.calem.eu/francais/home.html. Accessed: 29 November 2022.

3.3 Various Ways of Being Muslim ...

In France, all the studies related to Islam, whether it is the 1992 study conducted within the National Institute of Demographic Studies (INED) which focused on the integration of immigrant populations, or the 2008 study on *Trajectories and Origins* (TEO) (Tiberj and Simon 2010), as well as regular surveys conducted between 1989 and 2011 by IFOP for the daily newspapers *Le Monde, Le Point* and *La Croix*, as well as monographs targeted at certain components of the Muslim population (young people, women ...) provide us with some useful information on the forms of identification with Islam among Muslims in France (Tribalat 1995).

All these surveys on Muslim populations confirm the multiple contours of the identity of Muslims in France (Khosrokhavar 1997; Flanquart 2003; Venel 2004; Hajji and Marteau 2005; Kakpo 2007) and the fact that secularization in terms of the weakening of religious practice is far from being uniform among them. It even seems that certain components of the Muslim population present more observant profiles against a background of identity recomposition (Lagrange 2014).

No more than they rigorously observe all of its religious precepts (five daily prayers, fasting during the month of Ramadan, dietary prohibitions, rules of dress...), they do not agree on the content of what Islam covers.

The Muslim world in France is a heterogeneous human, social, cultural, and religious reality that includes the intimate Islam of simple believers, the external-ized Islam of practicing believers, the more "virtual" Islam of people of Muslim culture, and finally, the "rejected" Islam of those who declare that they have broken with this religion while continuing to refer to it negatively.

Thus, the IFOP survey for the daily newspaper La Croix published in July 2011 (La Croix 2011) in the form of an opinion poll conducted among a sample of 537 people from a Muslim family living in France shows a significant evolution (in percentage) of the trends between the different ways of belonging to Islam in France.

The increase observed for several years in the indices of religiosity (daily prayers, prayers at the mosque, observance of the fast, *halal fooding...*) has resulted in a significant increase in the percentage of regular practitioners, esti-mated today at 41% compared to 33% in 2007. This increase in religiosity varies in intensity and time depending on whether one considers the daily prayer or the Friday prayer or the five daily prayers. According to this survey, the five daily prayers concern 39% of Muslims, which represents a significant increase of 6 points over a short period of time, between 2001 and 2007. As for the Friday community prayer (at the mosque), it is currently around 25%. Unlike the daily prayer, its increase is staggered over time: over a sequence of twenty years it has only increased by 9 points!

This survey also shows that if 41% of Muslims recognize themselves as practicing believers, 34% declare themselves simply believers, 22% define themselves as of Muslim origin or culture, and finally 1% would have opted for another religion and 3% would have renounced any religion.

3.4   …and to Mobilize in the Name of Islam

Islam in France is in fact today crossed by five dynamics that translate the multiple possible readings of Islamity.

Most Muslim religious currents tend to promote a resolutely ritualistic and normative reading of Islam. This leads to a total refocusing of Islamic belonging on the ritual sphere alone, to an over-coding of all acts of daily life, and even to a withdrawal into the doctrinal sphere in terms of exclusivist orthodoxy. This religious declension tries to ward off the dissolving effects of secularization by overvaluing the ritual device and reinforcing the doctrine.

The other religious alternative consists in a reinforced spiritualization of the reference to Islam. It tends to affirm the primacy of an Islam of the interior against any attempt to reduce Islam to a system of normativity dominated by the sole logic of *halal* and *haram*, licit and illicit. This spiritualization of Islam corresponds to the mystical path (Sufism), a plural expression of an individualization of belief within a restricted elective and emotional group based on an interpersonal attachment to the person of the *sheikh*. But it can also take the form of an ethicization of Islam which could lead to a liberal or reformed Islam similar to what liberal Judaism represents in the Jewish world. This approach is part of a logic of self-centered development that tends to relativize any externalization, any excessive effusion of religion in the century in favor of spiritual self-realization or the return to an ethical and intellectualized (rational) version of the Islamic faith.

But Islam in France is also expressed through currents structured around a resolutely political understanding of belonging to Islam. For them, being Muslim is not limited to praying within the narrow walls of mosques, but to engaging in the city in the name of values and principles supposedly derived from their understanding of Islam. A first dynamic is then emerging which promotes a citizen religiosity. This is what is notably carried by the young French (and European) Muslim associative fabric in the form of a claim of belonging to Islam in a non-Muslim and religiously pluralist environment combining the act of believing and a determined social action (link between faith and social justice, liberation from consumer society, reopening the question of meaning in secularized societies…). This more socio-centered logic leads to the claim of a civic Islam, for which there can be no Islamic consciousness without social consciousness and therefore a political consciousness (Ramadan 2003).

The other political alternative in the name of Islam is carried by currents directly linked to Islamic movements active in Muslim societies, which are often in direct confrontation with the regimes around the conquest of power by legal means, or on the contrary, on the basis of armed mobilizations.

Finally, one of the effects of the secularization of Islam in France could be the "exit from religion" through the ethnicization of the Islamic referent, which becomes a substitute for identity (nominal Islam), the equivalent of a community marker that social actors mobilize according to circumstances, depending on local or international issues, independently of any actual practice. This is the case with the "virtual Islam" of certain young people in the suburbs who express themselves rhetorically and by adopting coded gestures (hand on heart) and episodically in a vindictive mode (provocative Islam) in the form of slogans referring to Iraq, Palestine, or Bin Laden. This category also includes the "minimal" or "residual" Islam of secular Muslim elites who do not give up emphasizing their Islamic origins in order to better distinguish themselves from all radical contemporary Islamic expressions. Finally, another variant can be found in certain types of intellectual discourse that do not want to be associated with religious classical Islam. According to this view "religious normality" today resides in a necessary distancing from any practice, any attitude and any claim using religious vocabulary (Bidar 2004). What amounts to postulate, as far as Islam is concerned, that by ricochet, the "deviant" religious form, the religion out of the norm, would paradoxically be the various expressions of orthonormed if not orthodox Islam.

It is around this delicate question of the redefinition of the contours of Muslim communities in France that the future of the reference to Islam in the north of the Mediterranean basin is at stake.

While literalist currents consider that Islam must be observed to the letter in all its normative dimensions without taking into account the local or national environment, without even tolerating other readings of the same tradition in the name of a supposed original purity, others consider it necessary to cut back the horizontal, normative and constraining dimension that Islam comprises in favor of its inner dimension, of the spirituality of questioning, or even to bring about the emergence of a new Muslim consciousness (Geoffroy 2009).

Some religious leaders believe that the progressive integration of Muslims passes by the production of an adapted Islamic normativity which guarantees a minimal orthodoxy in a secular society (sharia of minority! Oubrou 2019), while others believe that the faith, in Islam, passes by an immersion in the social.

Finally, secular intellectuals speak out against any overly religiocentric approach to Islam and boldly call for the liberation of Islam from any logic of submission (Bidar 2006, 2008).

These Muslim religiosities in France, as elsewhere in the world, are there to remind us how much Islam, under the guise of a call for communal unanimity, is indeed a bearer of plural singularities.

4 Governing Islam in France?

It should be noted that one of the specificities of Islam in France is also that this religion has developed within the framework of a secular system, without any real equivalent in the rest of Europe.

In this system, the State is supposed to be religiously neutral, and no public support, notably in the form of compulsory public funding, applies to religions, which are supposed to organize themselves freely according to their own rules and customs (Messner et al. 2013).

As far as the situation of the Muslim religion is concerned, it must be noted, however, that we are faced with a secular state which, for the past thirty years, has regularly intervened to forge an official representation of this religion, and still seems reluctant to consecrate in practice the autonomy of Islam in relation to the public authorities (Frégosi 2012).

4.1 The Colonial Moment and the Pursuit of the Institutional Fabrication of the Islam of France

In a pioneering study on colonial Algeria, the historian Oissila Saadia (Oissila 2015) describes the different stages and motivations that presided over the invention of the Muslim cult from 1851. This was mainly summarized in the production of a classification of Muslim religious buildings, the establishment of a hierarchy of personnel serving these religious spaces and a process of appointment by the colonial administration, without forgetting the establishment of direct financial links at the end of which the servants (imâms, readers of the Koran, guardians...) were salaried by the administration to whom the said buildings belonged from then on in place of the traditional system of pious foundations. Beyond this process of concordatization without a real Concordat of Islam in Algeria, which was to survive the vote of the law of 9 December 1905 on the separation of religions and the State (never extended to the three Algerian departments!), a public logic of surveillance and systematic control of the public exercise of the Muslim religion was deployed. This process was accentuated as the Algerian national movement developed (Achi 2007).

This dynamic of governance of Islam found its metropolitan extension with the erection of the Muslim Institute of the Great Mosque of Paris (IMMP) in the 1920s. This building, which was initially intended to honor the memory of the soldiers of the colonial armies, was to serve as a showcase for France's colonial enterprise, which was presented as respectful of the religious needs of its Muslim subjects, while at the same time being resolutely in line with a policy of control and surveillance of the population through the religious sphere in the metropolis, even though religious life there was most often embryonic (Sellam 2006).

It is not insignificant to also note that, once it came under the control of the Algerian authorities during the 1980s, the Great Mosque of Paris retained this implicit social function of a religious authority in charge of regulating the Muslim religious services offered to the Algerian diaspora in France, while at the same time ensuring its loyalty to the regime in Algiers.

4.2 Top-Down Organization Policies of Islam Today

From the 1990s onwards, all successive governments in France have implemented particularly proactive policies towards Islam. The secular state thus took an active part in the process of institutionalization of Islam, to the point of making the public authorities themselves the main architects of the representation of the Muslim faith.

This is how the Conseil de Réflexion sur l'Islam en France (CORIF) was created in 1990, the Charte du culte musulman en France (*Charter of the Muslim Faith in France*) in 1995, and la Consultation des musulmans de France (*al istishâra*) in 1998, from which the Conseil Français du Culte Musulman (CFCM) was created in 2002, following a process that combined state voluntarism and consultation with the various Muslim federations, not to mention the consultation of foreign chancelleries and experts.

The CORIF, created at the initiative of the socialist minister Pierre Joxe, was a simple ad hoc para-ministerial body, acting both as a collegial consultative body providing the minister with advice on practical aspects of the cult that might concern the administration (the setting of the beginning of the Ramadan fast, ritual slaughter, Muslim squares in cemeteries, etc.) and as a body responsible for thinking about the contours of a future representative organization of the Muslim cult. The Charter of the Muslim faith in France promoted by the Great Mosque of Paris was endorsed by Charles Pasqua, the Gaullist Minister of the Interior. This document was supposed to regulate the different sensitivities and currents crossing the Islamic communities in France and to define the relations between the State and the Muslim cult. The said charter, which was presented as the expression of the contractual character marking the situation of Islam outside the Muslim world, provided for the creation of a Representative Council of Muslims in France. Presented as the founding act of an Islam passing from the social status of a tolerated religion to that of an accepted religion, this charter was only ratified by a limited number of Muslim organizations. In reaction, a short-lived High Council of Muslims of France (HCMF) was created, which was at the origin of the constitution of a National Council of Imams of France (CNIF) whose only symbolic measure was to publish a fatwa (legal opinion) condemning the kidnapping in Algeria of the Trappist monks of the monastery of Tibéhirine in May 1996.

In November 1998, on the initiative of the socialist minister Jean Pierre Chevènement, an official consultation (al istishâra) was launched with the five main Muslim organizations of France with a religious orientation and reflecting the various sensitivities and ethnic components of the Muslim populations of France,[3] to which various Muslim personalities[4] and six major mosques and regional Islamic centers[5] were also invited. This consultation had a double objective: on the one hand, to complete the integration of the Muslim faith within the framework of the principles and rules of the law of December 9, 1905, and on the other hand, to create a central and confederal body for the Muslim faith. A framework agreement signed on July 3, 2001 set out the terms and conditions for the election of members of the French Council of the Muslim Faith by the places of worship. Nicolas Sarkozy took up this approach and made a few modifications (appointment of a good part of the members of the body by co-optation,

---

[3] Union des Organisations Islamiques de France (UOIF), Institut Musulman de la Mosquée de Paris (IMMP), Fédération Nationale des Musulmans de France (FNMF), *Tabligh*, and *Diyanet* (Turkish State Official Islam).

[4] They were Saada Mamadou Bâ CNRS ethnologist, Soheib Bencheikh Grand Mufti of Marseille, the scholar and editor Michel Chodkiewicz (replaced by Eric Geoffroy), Khaled Bentounès *cheikh* of the *Alawiyya Brotherhood*, the theologian Mohsen Ismaïl and Bétoule Fekkar Lambiotte director of the association " Terres d'Europe".

[5] The *Ad da'wa* Mosque in Paris (declined the invitation), the Islamic center of Évry-Couronnes, Mantes-la-Jolie Grand Mosque, Lyon Grand Mosque, and *Islah* Mosque in Marseille and the Grand Mosque of Saint-Denis de la Réunion.

nomination of a woman within it…) before the first CFCM was created in 2003. While failing to regulate the practice of Islam in France, this council was above all intended to spare the egos of Muslim notables, while at the same time ratifying the interests of foreign powers (Algeria, Morocco in particular) wishing to influence the governance of Islam, without offending the proponents of religious conservatism and their hexagonal relay (the UOIF). Algeria was to hold the presidency of the future council, its Moroccan rival and the more conservative Muslims two vice-presidencies, and the secretariat was to be provided by the representative of Turkish State Official Islam from Ankara.

The process of elaboration and consecration of the CFCM as the sole representative body of the Muslim faith in France turned out to be a process of selection of Muslim interlocutors deemed legitimate with whom the public authorities intended to dialogue and negotiate. In return, this meant formally disqualifying all the others who were kept on the sidelines, or who refused to participate in this original mechanism of production of an official Islam in a secular State. This was the case of the associations of young Muslims, critical of the Muslim notables chosen as partners by the public authorities, and of certain organizations grouping foreign Muslims, relaying in France political opposition movements such as the Turkish *Millî Görüs*, to which was preferred the official Islam of the *Diyanet* (Akgönül 2005).

4.3 A Governance in Crisis

Since its creation, the CFCM has seen its community legitimacy regularly and seriously weakened with each election. Some of the federations that participated in its foundation, such as the UOIF, the Muslim Institute of the Mosque of Paris and the Grand Mosque of Lyon, boycotted it, demanding a complete overhaul of its mode of designation. Most of the claims were in fact more about a rebalancing of the CFCM's membership in favor of co-opted personalities and about a reworking of the very principle of calculating the number of delegates in proportion to the floor space of places of worship, than about soliciting the direct vote of the faithful. A reform finally took place in February 2013 that reinforced the principle of collegiality by setting up a rotating presidency of the CFCM every two years, between the different federations participating in the elections.

This focus on the issue of the emergence driven by the public authorities of a body representing the Muslim faith is still relevant, as evidenced by the initiatives around the creation of a body for dialogue with Islam in 2013 at the initiative of the Minister of the Interior Bernard Cazeneuve, the more recent developments around the publication of the Charter of the Imam in France published in March 2017 by the CFCM, or the generalization of diploma training civil and civic for Muslim clerics (Bobineau 2010) and then expanded to other faiths. In July 2019, a circular from the Ministry of the Interior had been sent to all prefectures (state administration within a French department) to invite local Muslim associative leaders (in charge of mosques or simple Muslim collectives...) to participate in local dialogue instances and to reflect on a redesign of the organization of the Muslim cult from a departmental logic.

The development of jihadism in which young French people are involved (Truong 2017) has also contributed to giving the question of the administration of religion a strong security resonance. As various parliamentary reports attest (Feret et al. 2016; Ciotti and Menucci 2015; Goulet et al. 2015), the time has come to mobilize all public state actors, and their private Muslim partners, in the fight against radicalization using an Islamic frame of reference. Muslim leaders, as well as imâms, are often invited to become auxiliary forces of public authorities in their fight against the supporters of radical violence using an Islamic frame of reference (Mamoun 2017).

The governance of Islam in France reached a new stage in 2021, with the end of the French Council of the Muslim Faith (CFCM), announced by Gérald Darmanin, Minister of the Interior in charge of religious policies, and the announcement by the government of the creation in February 2022 of a Forum of Islam in France (FORIF), promoted as a new channel of expression of the relations between the public authorities and Islam. The CFCM during the last twenty years paradoxically embodied the official Islam of a secular state, enjoying the official recognition of all governments. In spite of this, it has not succeeded in gaining legitimacy, especially among the main people concerned, namely French Muslims.

As a showcase for an Islam of notables linked to the major federations of foreign states or embodying various transnational currents of Islam (pietism, Muslim Brotherhood, etc.), the CFCM has not taken up some of the expected challenges, such as the financing of the cult, the training of imâms, and the fair representation of all components of Islam and of Muslim generations (etc.). The initiative taken by the associative leader Marwan Mohammed (former president of the Council Against Islamophobia in France) in April 2019 to launch a vast online questionnaire relays this state of affairs. Internet users will criticize the CFCM, the interference of foreign states while pointing to the involvement deemed disproportionate public authorities in the organization of Islam in France (Doucouré and Trinh Nguyen 2018).

The national body has often become a recording chamber for the expectations of the public authorities, drafting various solemn texts, the latest being the Charter of the Principles of Islam in France in January 2021, at the express request of the Head of State. It was above all the permanent theater of quarrels of egos, of precellence between members who considered themselves to be all indispensable and representative and striving to compete in loyalty to the public authorities, against a background of rivalries maintained by various foreign financial backers. This CFCM was too pyramidal, giving too much room to individuals co-opted by the founding members, without the ordinary faithful or even the imâms having any say, under the interested gaze of foreign chancelleries. Everyone, starting with its historical members, have taken note of its demise, those who have greatly contributed to its disgrace and those who have hastened its decay.

Today, FORIF is about breaking away from the verticality of large federations, emanating from the Algerian, Moroccan or Turkish governments, or from conservative transnational religious currents, and making room for more horizontality. The forum is made up of about 100 people chosen by the authorities from lists provided by the prefectures. These personalities are divided into four working groups: the first one is focused on the elaboration of a future status for imâms in France (and their training), the second one is concerned with the issue of chaplaincies in public services, the third one with the securitization of places of worship and the fight against anti-Muslim acts, and the last one has to watch over the application of the law of August 24, 2022, reinforcing the principles of the Republic, which modified the legal regime of religions in France.

The public authorities, who had brought the CFCM to the baptismal font, are today pronouncing its political excommunication, and agreeing to new interlocutors deemed to better reflect the Islam of the territories.

But is there not a risk that the public authorities are once again preparing to select upstream the Muslim actors deemed most likely to correspond to their expectations, in terms of independence from foreigners or from conservative Islam? At no time was the idea of letting the Muslim faithful, following the example of the French Jews and Protestants, choose by way of elections those who will have the function of governing the community bodies from the bottom up, seriously considered.

At the end of this chapter, several challenges condition the future of Islam in France.

-The first challenge is that of radicalization. What happened in January 2015 (attacks against Charlie-Hebdo and the Hyper Cacher at Porte de Vincennes), then in November (shootings at the Bataclan and on restaurant terraces in Paris), and again in 2020 (the murder of Samuel Paty and three people in a church) leads

1 Being Muslim in a Secular State ...

us to reflect further upstream on the articulation between social and psychological data, context and various clues that mark out the paths of radicalization of certain young Muslims. In short, it is a question of trying to identify the type of demographic, social, even cultural, and psychological soil, the types of social and human distress; on which certain radical discourses instrumentalizing religion take root. The idea is not simply to identify possible religious currents supposed to be sectarian, but not to lose sight of the fact that what makes these currents attractive is both their capacity to surf on frustrations and social distress and their claim to produce meaning, to put words on the evils experienced or felt subjectively by individuals who are fragile, mistreated or simply lacking strong reference points. The question cannot be reduced to its exclusively security aspect (which remains indispensable!), it is also necessary to provide a social, political, and even religious response.

-The other challenge concerns secularism. We have observed that what is taking shape today is also the tendency, in the belief that we are responding to the process of increased visibility of the religious phenomenon in the public space, to react by reinforcing the secular legislative system through the vote of new restrictive laws on religious expression (with Islam as an implicit target!). The risk of deviating the secular ideal into a punitive device against religious minorities is real and risks feeding in return the machine to manufacture self-victimization among some French people of Muslim faith.

Finally, everyone today seems to agree on wanting, for example, that imâms be listened to more, and that they take an active part in the fight against radical temptation, and that they benefit from civil training in France. They should have been involved in the governance of Islam at a much earlier stage, and not confined to the role of extras, spectators or, worse, the source of all the problems.

The same goes for the believers and users of the places of worship that are the faithful. Any reorganization of Islam in France cannot escape a re-evaluation of the role of the faithful, regular, or occasional users of the places of worship, and main financiers of the cult.

The government of Islam in a secular regime would gain in legitimacy if it were rethought in close association with the main interested parties who are the faithful on the one hand, and their imâms on the other.

References

Achi, R. 2007. Laïcité d'empire. Les débats sur l'application du régime de séparation à l'islam impérial ; In *Politiques de la laïcité au XXe siècle*, Hrsg. P. Weil, 237–263. Paris : PUF.

Adraoui, M-A. 2013. *Du Golfe aux banlieues. Le salafisme mondialisé*. PUF. Coll. Proche-Orient.

Akgönül, S. 2005. Islam turc, islams de Turquie : acteurs et réseaux en Europe, *Politique étrangère*, 2005/1 Printemps, 35–47.

Bahloul, K. 2021. *Mon islam, ma liberté*. Paris: Albin Michel.

Bastian, J.-P., and Messner, F (2007). *Minorités religieuses dans l'espace européen. Approches sociologiques et juridiques*. Paris: PUF.

Berger, P., Davie, G., and Fokas, E. 2008. *Religious America, secular Europe? A theme and Variations*. Farnham: Ashgate.

Bidar, A. 2008. *L'islam sans la soumission. Pour un existentialisme musulman*. Paris : Albin Michel.

Bidar, A. 2006. *Selfislam*. Paris :Seuil.Coll. Non-conforme.

Bidar, A. 2004. *Un islam pour notre temps*. Paris : Seuil. Coll. La couleur des idées.

Bobineau, O., Ed. 2010. *Former des imams pour la République. L'exemple français*.Paris :CNRS Éditions

Bucaille, L., and Villechaise, A. 2020. *Désirs d'islam .Portraits d'une minorité religieuse en France*. Paris: Sciences Po, Les Presses.

Ciotti, E., and Mennucci, P. 2016. *Rapport de la Commission d'enquête de l'Assemblée Nationale sur la surveillance des filières et des individus djihadistes*, Paris, Assemblée Nationale de la République Française, rapport n° 2828, (Juin 2016).

Doucouré, S., and Trinh Nguyen, H. 2018. Consultation initiée par Marwan Muhammad: des chiffres … et des luttes. https://www.saphirnews.com/Consultation-initiee-par-Marwan-Muhammad-des-chiffres-et-des-luttes_a25638.html. Accessed: 29. Nov. 2022.

Féret, C., Goulet, N., and Reichardt, A. 2016. *Rapport sénatorial sur l'organisation, la place et le financement de l'islam en France et de ses lieux de culte*, Sénat de La République française, rapport n° 757 (Juillet 2016).

Flanquart, H. 2003. *Croyances et valeurs chez les jeunes Maghrébins*. Bruxelles: Éditions Complexe. Coll. «Les dieux dans la Cité».

Frégosi, F., and Tozy, M. 2017. *Regards sur l'islam marocain en France. Mosquées, imâms, fédérations*. Aix-en-Provence.Étude réalisée pour le CCME. Sciences Po Cherpa.

Frégosi, F. 2012. *L'islam dans la laïcité*. Paris: Pluriel Hachette.

Geisser, V. 2003. *La Nouvelle islamophobie*. Paris: La Découverte.Coll. «Sur le vif».

Geoffroy, E. 2009. *L'islam sera spirituel ou ne sera plus*. Paris: Seuil. La couleur des idées.

Göle, N. 2015. *Musulmans au quotidien. Une enquête européenne sur les controverses autour de l'islam*. Paris: La Découverte.

Goldman, H. 2000. *Le rejet français de l'islam. Une souffrance républicaine*. Paris: PUF.

Goulet, N., Reichardt, A., and Sueur, J.-P. 2015. *Rapport sénatorial sur l'organisation et les moyens de lutte contre les réseaux djihadistes en France et en Europe*, Sénat de la République française, rapport n° 388 (Avril 2015).

Guland, O., Ml., and Zerbib, Eds. 2000. *Nous, Juifs de France*. Paris: Bayard.

1 Being Muslim in a Secular State ...

IFOP pour *La Croix, Enquête sur l'implantation et l'évolution de l'Islam en France, juillet 2011.*

Janadin, E., and Mosinay, A.-S. 2019. *Une mosquée mixte pour un islam spirituel et progressiste.* Paris: Fondation pour l'Innovation Politique.

Hajji, S., and S. Marteau. 2005. *Voyage dans la France musulmane.* Paris: Plon.

Katz, E.-B. 2018. *Juifs et musulmans en France. Le poids de la fraternité.* Paris: Belin.

Kepel, G. 2015. *Terreur dans l'hexagone. Genèse du djihad français.* Paris: Gallimard.

Kakpo, N. 2007. *L'islam, un recours pour les jeunes.* Paris: Sciences Po. Les Presses. Coll. Sociétés en mouvement.

Lagrange, H. 2014. Le renouveau religieux des immigrés et de leurs descendants en France. *Revue Française de sociologie* 55(2):201–244.

Khosrokhavar, F. 1997. *L'islam des jeunes.* Paris: Flammarion Coll. Essais.

Lagroye, J. 2009. *Appartenir à une institution. Catholiques en France aujourd'hui.* Paris: Économica. Coll. Études politiques.

Luizard, P.-J. 2019. *La République et l'islam. Aux racines du malentendu.* Paris: Taillandier. Coll. Essais.

Luizard, P.-J., Eds. 2006. *Le choc colonial et l'islam. Les politiques religieuses des puissances coloniales en terres d'islam.* Paris: Éditions la découverte, Coll. Textes à l'appui/ histoire contemporaine.

Mamoun, A. 2017. *L'islam contre le radicalisme : manuel de contre-offensive.* Paris: Cerf.

Maréchal, B. 2009. *Les frères musulmans en Europe. Racines et discours.* Paris: PUF.Coll Proche-Orient.

Maréchal, B. Eds. 2002. *L'Islam et les Musulmans dans l'Europe élargie : radioscopie. A Guide Book on Islam and Muslims in the Wide Contemporary Europe.* Bruxelles: Academia Bruylant.

Portier, Ph., and Willaime, J.-P. 2021. *La religion dans la France contemporaine. Entre sécularisation et recomposition,* Paris: Armand Colin, Coll. U.

Marwan, M., and A. Hajjat. 2013. *Islamophobie : Comment les élites françaises fabriquent le problème musulman.* Paris: La Découverte.

Memmi, A. 2010. *L'homme dominé.* Paris: Folio Actuel.

Memmi, A. 2003. *Portrait d'un Juif.* Paris: Folio Actuel.

Messner, F., Prélot, -P. H., and Woehrling, J.-M., Eds. 2013. *Traité de droit français des religions.* Paris: LexisNexis.

Oissila, S. 2015. *Algérie coloniale. Musulmans et chrétiens: le contrôle de l'État (1830–1914).* Paris: CNRS Éditions.

Oubrou, T. 2019. *Appel à la réconciliation ! Foi musulmane et valeurs de la République française.* Paris: Plon. Coll. Tribune libre.

Podselver, L. 2004. *Fragmentation et recomposition du judaïsme. Le cas français.* Genève: Labor et Fides.

Ramadan, T. 2003. *Les musulmans d'Occident et l'avenir de l'islam.* Paris: Sindbad Actes sud.

Rougier, B., Ed. 2021. *Les Territoires conquis de l'islamisme.* Paris: PUF. éd. augmentée.

Sellam, S. 2006. *La France et ses musulmans : Un siècle de politique musulmane (1895–2005).* Paris: Fayard.

Tiberj, V., and Simon, P. 2010. «Religions», INED (Eds.) *Trajectoires et Origines : enquête sur la diversité des populations en France.* Chapitre 6 (document de travail).

Tribalat, M. 1995. *Faire France. Une enquête sur les immigrés et leurs enfants.* Paris: La Découverte.

Truong, F. 2017. *Loyautés radicales. L'islam des 'mauvais garçons' de la Nation.* Paris: La Découverte.

Venel, N. 2004. *Musulmans et citoyens.* Paris: PUF/Le Monde. Coll. Partage du savoir.

Vermeren, P. 2012. *La France en terre d'islam. Empire colonial et religions XIXe-XXe siècles.* Paris: Belin.

Pew Research Center, The Future of the Gobal Muslim Population, 2011.

Zarka, Y.-C. 2004. L'islam en France : vers la construction d'une minorité tyrannique?, *Cités,* Hors-série, L'islam en France, PUF (p. 1–4).

Webography

Michael Lipka, «La population musulmane d'Europe continuera de croître mais son ampleur dépend de la migration», décembre 2017, La population musulmane d'Europe continuera de croître | Centre de recherche Pew (pewresearch.org). Accessed: 22. Dec. 2022.

Franck Frégosi is CNRS Senior Research Fellow, member of the laboratory UMR 8582 "Groupe, Sociétés, Religions et Laïcités" (PSL Campus Condorcet) and director of the Certificate "Pluralité religieuse, Droit, Laïcité et Sociétés" (training approved by the Central Office of Cults of the Ministry of the Interior) at Sciences Po Aix, where he is lecturer on sociology of religion. His research focuses on the governance of Islam in French contemporary society. His latest publications focus on the analysis of religious public policies towards Islam in the secularized French State. Selected publications: *La Formation des cadres religieux musulmans en France. Approches socio-juridiques* (dir.), L'Harmattan, 1998; *Le Religieux dans la commune. Les régulations locales du pluralisme religieux en France* (with J.-P.Willaime), Geneva, Labor et Fides, 2001; *Lectures contemporaines du droit islamique. Europe et Monde arabe* (dir.), Strasbourg, PUS, 2004; *Bruno Etienne, le fait religieux comme fait politique,* La Tour d'Aigues, l'Aube, 2009; *L'islam dans laïcité, Paris,* Fayard, Pluriel, 2011; with Julien O'Miel and Julien Talpin, *L'islam et la cité. Engagements musulmans dans les quartiers populaires,* Lille, Presses Universitaires du Septentrion, 2017.

Muslims in Belgium: From Immigrant Guestworkers to a Polymorphic and Contested Minority

2

Corinne Torrekens

Abstract

The vast majority of the Belgian Muslim population is tied in one way or another to an appeal made to immigrant guest workers by the Belgian public authorities in the 1960s. Despite the lack of previous colonial relations and thanks to strong economic ties and significant coordination efforts by Belgian diplomats and representatives there, Morocco and Turkey became the main countries of origin. A large fraction of Moroccan and Turkish migrants were granted Belgian nationality in the 1970s. Consequently, Islam became increasingly visible in the public space and former immigrants were increasingly labelled as Muslims. One of the first research agendas related to the insertion of Islam in Belgium focused on its institutionalization into the Belgian state and church system. If the study of the various forms of belonging to Islam has been the topic of much research, the study of minority groups within Islam is scarce. And if some very interesting research exists on mobilizations seeking the political representation of Muslims, the analysis of Islamist movements is complexified by the hysterical nature of the public debate related to Islam and Muslims in the aftermath of terrorist attacks. Finally, regarding future challenges, despite the enormous account on institutionalization of Islam, few research have described the trajectories of Imams and even less how religious content produced by woman and/or on social media influences the construction of religious authority.

C. Torrekens (✉)
ULB, Université libre de Bruxelles, Brussels, Belgium
e-mail: corinne.torrekens@ulb.be

© The Author(s), under exclusive license to Springer Fachmedien Wiesbaden GmbH, part of Springer Nature 2024
R. Ceylan and M. Mücke (eds.), *Muslims in Europe*, Islam in der Gesellschaft, https://doi.org/10.1007/978-3-658-43044-3_2

Keywords

Immigration • Institutionalization • Political representation • Heterodoxy • Individualization • Imams • Religious authority • Gender

1 The Historical Development of Islam and Muslim Populations

Despite the presence of several Muslim families in Belgium as early as the nineteenth century (Renaerts and Manço 2000; Djelloul and Maréchal 2018), the vast majority of the Belgian Muslim population is tied in one way or another to an appeal made to immigrant guest workers by the Belgian public authorities in the 1960s. After World War II, the need for reconstruction and the will to be and remain competitive during the "Coal War" implied recruiting foreign workers. An agreement was signed with Italy in 1946 and a decade later with Spain. However, the dramatic incident in a coal mine in Marcinelle, a small town in Wallonia, in 1956, in which 262 workers died, among them 136 Italian nationals, put an end to the agreement with Italy (Rea 2006). Belgium signed other bilateral agreements with Greece (1957), Morocco and Turkey (1964), Tunisia (1969) and Algeria and Yugoslavia (1970). Despite the lack of previous colonial relations and thanks to strong economic ties and significant coordination efforts by Belgian diplomats and representatives there (Frennet-De Keyser 2003; Manço and Manço 1992), Morocco and Turkey became the main countries of origin. Indeed, in the 1960s, while Algeria was seeking to limit emigration since the departure of thousands of French families after the 1958–1962 war of independence, Morocco and Turkey sought to facilitate emigration because of high unemployment rates. More precisely, the Moroccan authorities were focusing on departures from specific regions as remittances were expected to reduce poverty, unemployment, and discontent, and thus function as a political safety valve (Berriane 2015). Moreover, Belgian authorities considered the Moroccan population to be more religious and consequently more docile than the Algerian one (Frennet-De Keyser 2003). In the case of Turkey, the country liberalized its economy in the 1950s: in rural areas, the means of productions were mechanized which created very high unemployment rates and significant rural exodus (Manço and Manço 1992). Emigration was thus a means to reabsorb this surplus workforce on the domestic market. Nowadays, even if precise demographic data are lacking (we will come back to this issue later), scholars continue to consider that the vast majority of the Muslim population in Belgium to be of Moroccan and Turkish descent (Torrekens 2020).

Besides obvious economic reasons, Belgium was also interested in international immigration because of demographic issues: its population was ageing, and the birth rate was in decline (Manço 2000). Stabilizing the population of guestworkers thus became a public leitmotiv. Consequently, family reunification was introduced as a right of the worker in the bilateral agreements and was conceived as a first step towards integration. And this despite the fact that concrete integration public policies only began being implemented in the late 1980s. The economic crisis and oil shocks of the 1970s put an end to the bilateral agreements. However, despite the official stop put to immigration, the migrant population continued to grow due to natural birth cycles, family reunification processes, refugees, and some channels of undocumented stay.[1] At the time, Belgium's nationality Code was one of the most liberal in Europe and recognized *jus soli*. Consequently, a large fraction of Moroccan and Turkish migrants were granted Belgian nationality. This new period in the history of the immigration to Belgium of the Muslim population opened two trends: the increasing visibilization of Islam in the public space through habits, practices, and symbols on the one hand, and the ethnic and religious diversification of the Muslim population itself on the other hand. Indeed, family reunification and the birth of children in Belgium highlighted the need for cultural and religious transmission in a context where Islam was in a minority position and even in fact quite unknown. Many Muslims (mostly men at the beginning) invested energy and time in creating and organizing the first Muslim associations and places of worship which have functioned as places of information gathering and support for diverse administrative undertakings. Those efforts cannot be totally separated from the revival of Islamist reformist movements in some Muslim countries (like Egypt for example). Indeed, some militants were pushed into exile by state repression and were involved in this first wave of Islamic activism in Europe during the 1970 (Meijer and Bakker 2012). Islam became increasingly visible in the public space and former immigrants were increasingly labelled as Muslims (and self-identified as such) leading to the first controversies and public debates in the 1980s. The issue of young women wearing headscarves in public schools was in Belgium, as it was in other European countries, certainly the first public debate illustrating this

---

[1] Persons from non-EU countries can for example get, under strict conditions, a temporary visa to study or to work. At the end of this period, if they decide to stay in Belgium, their permit is no longer valid and they thus enter in a phase of "illegal" stay on the territory.

move from discussions centred around the socio-economic integration of immigrants (unemployment, ethnic discrimination in housing, language abilities, etc.) towards fierce disputes over the compatibility of a new religion and its visible signs with Belgian "values", "traditions", and "way of life". However, with the arrival of new migration waves stemming from several international conflicts and coming from Iran, Kosovo, Bosnia, Pakistan, Afghanistan, Iraq, Somalia, and more recently Syria, it is increasingly difficult to speak of a homogenous Muslim "community" even if the vast majority of Belgian Muslims still belong to Sunnism. Consequently, there is a kind of paradox here: Belgian public opinion tends to consider Islam as a monolithic whole whereas Islamic populations are increasingly diverse in terms of ethnicities, periods of arrival in Belgium, religious currents and habits, gender, generations, socio-economic status, etc.

Accurate estimations of the Muslim population are an issue of intellectual dispute between scholars involving methodological and ethical considerations. We have already underlined the fact that scholars still connect the vast majority of the Muslim population to the immigration of guestworkers coming mostly from Morocco and Turkey. We have also already highlighted the presence of many other ethnic groups. And any attempt to count and survey the Muslim population raises the question of how to take converts into account since Belgium forbids registering the religious and philosophical affiliation of the population during the census. Consequently, scholars must make do with estimations that have various (severe) limitations. Very detailed estimates are regularly produced by independent researcher (formerly University of Gent) Jan Hertogen (Husson 2020). His latest estimates (for 2019) were of 936,674 Muslims out of 11,405,130 residents, or 8.2% of the population (Husson 2020). Hertogen's numbers are based both on countries of origin and on countries where Islam is the primary religion. By doing this, Jan Hertogen tends to consider that any person whose parents and grandparents come from a country where Islam is dominant is therefore before and above all Muslim. This is forgetting the many Catholic and Jewish minorities that were living in Morocco, Turkey, Tunisia, etc. This also obliterates the relationship that certain groups have with Sunni Islam: some Alevi groups for example will deny any connection with Islam. Moreover, this also challenges the fundamental right to religious freedom: some persons, for numerous reasons, have a distant relationship with their cultural and religious background, do not believe in God, and do not maintain any kind of religious practice. Consequently, they just do not define themselves as Muslims and would not appreciate being considered as such and maintained in a group they do not desire to belong to by a sort of postcolonial gesture of white people giving themselves the right to fix the identity boundaries of minority groups. To address these criticisms, Hertogen uses data (without providing any reference) of a survey study from 2008 on a sample of 5000 persons in Germany and measuring the secularization process of different ethnic groups.[2] This comparison is tricky because of the obvious differences between both countries in terms of immigration history, integration models and laws and public debate. In 2016, Hertogen's tally was accompanied in the French-speaking press by a map of Muslims in all municipalities, highlighting statistical aberrations such as 0,9% of Muslims in the locality of Gerpinnes.[3] Those numbers are closely link to fears of invasion as there is a tendency towards a general overestimation in Belgian public opinion: in 2015, an Ipsos survey showed that the number of Muslims in Belgium was estimated by respondents to be 29% of the population, 23 points higher than the (most generous) range of statistical estimates at the time (Husson 2020). As we see, counting Muslims is not simply a methodological quarrel between scholars but, on the contrary, raises highly sensitive ethical considerations.

2 Current Issues and the State of Academic Research on Muslims and Islam

Several elements explain the fact that scholars have taken time to address the issue of Islam in Belgium. Firstly, because of their training, experts on immigration were not interested in the religious dimension of the installation of migrants, convinced that it was a residual and insignificant phenomenon doomed to disappear in the process of assimilation (Dassetto 2007). And scholars in the field of religion were confined to the expertise of both traditional catholic movements' secularization processes and new religious developments such as New Age (Dassetto 2007). Finally, the tradition of Islamology in Belgium was weak in contrast to neighbouring countries such as France and the Netherlands. This is due to the lack of contact with Muslim countries during the colonial period

---

[2] See his blog http://www.npdata.be/BuG/448-Moslims/ (accessed the 18th of November 2022).

[3] 781.887 musulmans vivent en Belgique: découvrez la carte, commune par commune, Sudinfo.Be, 25th of Mai 2016, https://www.sudinfo.be/art/1580627/article/2016-05-24/781 887-musulmans-vivent-en-belgique-decouvrez-la-carte-commune-par-commune (accessed the 18th of November 2022). It was possible to click on each locality to access the precise percentage of Muslims. This option is no longer available, maybe because of the controversy the publication of this map has raised, see for example: Stigmatisation ou sociologie ? Une carte des musulmans belges fait polémique, FranceInfo, https://www.francetvinfo.fr/monde/europe/stigmatisation-ou-sociologie-une-carte-des-musulmans-belges-fait-polemique_146 7419.html, (26th of May 2016 accessed the 18th of November 2022).

(Dassetto 2007). One of the first research agendas related to the insertion of Islam in Belgium focused on its institutionalization into the Belgian state and church system. Regarding the relations between church and state, Belgium is a "separatist country" which follows a principle of reciprocal non-interference and neutrality of the State. However, Belgium officially recognizes religious groups and non-confessional beliefs (such as Buddhism for example). These recognition agreements tend to roughly follow the pre-existing arrangements with the Catholic church which remains in a privileged position within the system. This process grants recognized religious groups opportunities to collaborate with the state, a level of autonomy of organization, and a certain presence in the public sphere. For example, religious classes are organized in public schools during school hours and religious schools can be (under strict conditions) financially supported by the state on the same level as public schools. Moreover, the salaries of the teachers of the different recognized faiths and of religious staff are also paid by the public authorities. This is to say that issues related to the recognition of a religious or non-confessional community are important. However, this system requires that public authorities identify a principal representative of the religious or non-confessional community in question. When Islam was recognized in 1974, much research was dedicated to the issues and obstacles this process raised for Muslims: how to create a "representative" of Belgian Islam? With what role and functions? And how to include Islamic minority groups in this process? (Loobuyck, Debeer, and Meier 2013; Sägesser and Torrekens 2008; Panafit 1999). After years of conflict between parallel institutions and a series of public debates on how to organize this representation, a compromise was found in 1998 which led to elections (mainly in mosques) to set up the first Muslim Executive. A second electoral process took place in 2005. Recently, new elections were postponed due to the Covid19 pandemic. However, to this day, multiple concerns over the functioning of the Muslim Executive are regularly raised. An important part of these concerns is related to structural links with the institutional forces of non-EU countries who have their own political agenda regarding Islam and the role played by religion in the public space. For years, this proximity with non-EU countries of the main Belgian Muslim organizations involved in the process of institutionalizing Islam was not really considered to be a problem but was seen rather as a way to ensure a "moderate" representation of Muslims. However, things have gradually changed and escalated as the interference of non-EU countries has come to be perceived as threatening Belgian sovereignty. For example, in December 2020, the Belgian Minister of Justice, Vincent Van Quickenborne, sparked controversy by declaring that some of the prominent members of the Muslim Executive were agents of foreign interference (Husson 2021). In this context, the Muslim Executive's 639000 euros public subsidy was suspended.[4] Normally, religious communities do not receive public funds for their internal organization. In the case of Islam, this particular subsidy was negotiated considering the long and difficult process of institutionalization which led to a certain form of institutional discrimination of Muslims[5] compared to other religious communities and the fact that the Muslim Executive did not have the means (human resources, real estate, etc.) to create its own organization (Sägesser 2020). Suspending the subsidy had already been used in the past by public authorities to push the Muslim Executive to reform and/or find solutions to long-lasting internal crises. A couple of months later, the Minister of Justice announced he was rescinding the recognition of the Muslim Executive, thus throwing the institution into a new period of uncertainty.[6]

Of course, the study of the various forms of belonging to Islam has been the topic of much research. The book *L'islam transplanté* (Bastenier and Dassetto 1984) was one of the first to offer a sociographic analysis of mosques and Islamic organizations in Belgium. This work was enriched a decade later by the book *Les facettes de l'islam belge* (Dassetto 1997). Another seminal book discussed the link between femininity, minority, and Islam around the issue of the hijab (Brion 2004). Several other studies have analyzed the ethical self-making of Muslim subjects by focusing on questions of piety and embodiment (Fadil 2013, 2009; Smits, Ruiter and Van Tubergen 2010) or of professional values (Kolly 2018). This axis of research has been impacted by the revival of interest and the anxieties regarding the development of radical trends within Muslim minorities since 9/11 (Zemni 2011). However, it is important to stress that this is not a new trend in the research agenda regarding Islam in Belgium as it had already emerged in the late 1970s due to the activism of Algerian Islamist movements (Grignard 2003). Today, the current scientific literature seems to be traversed by a certain tension: it shows that a growing number of second-generation youths are opting for a more secular way of life, while an equally increasing group is choosing Islamist ideologies or at least a more conscious form of Islam (Timmerman,

---

[4] Pas de subsides pour l'Exécutif des Musulmans de Belgique en 2022. (2021, December 16). Le Vif. https://www.levif.be/belgique/pas-de-subsides-pour-lexecutif-des-musulmans-de-bel gique-en-2022/. (accessed the 21th of September 2022).

[5] While Islam was recognized in 1974, the first recognitions of mosques (and thus of imams) for example only occurred in 2004 in Flanders.

[6] Vincent Van Quickenborne a procédé au retrait de la reconnaissance de l'Exécutif des Musulmans de Belgique. (2022, September 15). RTBF.Be. https://www.rtbf.be/article/vin cent-van-quickenborne-a-procede-au-retrait-de-la-reconnaissance-de-lexecutif-des-musulm ans-de-belgique-11067134 (accessed the 21th of September 2022).

Vanderwaeren and Crul 2003). Nowadays, on the one hand, we find researchers who emphasize the growing processes of secularization, reflexivity, and "bricolage" among the young generations of Muslims (Torrekens et al. 2021) while others stress their radicalization, orthopraxy, and intolerance (Koopmans 2015; Kotek and Tournemenne 2020). If prominent researchers have tried to understand what brings young people to be attracted to the so-called Islamic State (Coolsaet 2016), others have sought to describe counter-radicalization public policies and their impact on the targeted groups of Muslims (Fadil et al. 2019).

Another research agenda is at least partially related to the previous one and focuses on the "turn to politics" of immigrants with a Muslim background, defined as a growing number of mobilizations seeking the political representation 'of Muslims' (or the opposition thereof) but also as the emergence of discourses critical of the political system, especially via social media (Nielsen, 2013). A certain number of studies have focused on the political participation of Belgian Muslims, most often centred around their presence on candidate lists and the election of 'Muslim' candidates based on their family name or background (Sandri and De Decker 2008; Rea, Jacobs, Teney and Delwit 2010; Zibouh 2012). Indeed, since the mid-1990s, numerous candidates of Muslim origin—presenting as or perceived to be Muslim—have held mandates both locally (town council member, county magistrate, mayor, etc.) and regionally, as well as at the federal level, both within the Executive Branch and within Parliament. Yet there are other types of Muslim collective political mobilizations that are not restricted to the electoral period, for example, those centred on the infra-political level, those organized as a type of lobby dedicated to the activation of political consciousness among both Muslim and non-Muslim public opinion or those who criticize the participation of Muslims in the democratic system. Among the latter groups, Sharia4Belgium, organized around the personality of Fouad Belkacem, and the group Resto du Tawhid structured around the convert Jean-Louis Le Soumis were engaged in *street dawa* performances to pursue "spectacle activism", meaning a "disruptive, confrontational and mobilising repertoire in the public sphere attracting increased media attention" (de Koning, Becker and Roex, 2020: 5). For those groups, participating in the electoral system equated committing the sin of *taghout* (idolatry). Another group attracted tremendous media and political attention from 2012 to 2018: the ISLAM political party. This movement, which was at first structured around 4 people, emerged a few weeks before the 2012 local elections. They mainly distributed their leaflets in the areas of Brussels with a strong concentration of Muslim populations and campaigned on three pragmatic topics: the authorization of the veil in public schools, the organization of a halal menu in

2 Muslims in Belgium: From Immigrant …

school restaurants, and the inclusion of public holidays respecting the main Muslim festivities in the calendar. They succeeded in attracting a little over 5000 votes and gained seats on the local counsel in two Brussels localities (Molenbeek and Anderlecht). After the elections, they opened their press conference by reciting the *Shahada* and expressing their will to establish *sharia* in Belgium. It seems that participating in the elections was a first step for them to establish an Islamic State, even if they had enormous difficulties in defining with any precision what *sharia* meant for them. In the regional elections of 2014 and, despite receiving more votes than in 2012, they did not gain any seats. In 2018, one member of the political party sparked tremendous controversy by refusing to shake the hand of a woman on a television set and by expressing his will to end gender diversity in public transportation. But the party was only able to present two lists and received less than 2000 votes. The movement disappeared from the political scene. However, there is no doubt that Islamist groups and movements are still active in Belgium via political Salafi groups or networks affiliated with the Muslim Brotherhood. But the analysis is complexified by both the plasticity of those movements and the hysterical nature of the public debate related to Islam and Muslims in the aftermath of terrorist attacks. Allegations of proximity with Islamists are regularly made (most often on very vague basis) about several Muslim personalities and organizations leading to harmful situations (a lack of trust and of financial support from public authorities, issues in their professional life, threats to their reputation, etc.).

3 Future Challenges

When religion emerged as an important—if not major—feature of the integration of Muslim populations in Western Europe under the triple effect of the colonial relations some European countries had with Muslim nations, labour immigration agreements, and flows of population under refugee status, most researchers focused their attention on 'majority', namely Sunni, Islam (Sunier 2014). Heterodox groups have therefore been largely understudied, and within Sunnism the minority groups that have been most highlighted are the radical (Meijer 2013; Adraoui 2015) and fundamentalist ones (Dassetto 1998). There are of course notable exceptions to this. One of the first to study minority Islam in Europe was Duran (1991), whose work explored conversions to Sufism in Germany. On the Anglo-Saxon side, Spellman (2004) illustrated the constructional process in which Sufi individuals engage when confronting the tensions between different definitions of belonging and differentiation, especially when they are estranged from both the versions of Islam being promoted by Muslim countries and the national debates surrounding Muslim integration in British society. Nabti (2007) highlighted the ways in which a contemporary North African brotherhood and its mystical doctrine gain a foothold in France. The work of Hamid (2016) also included Sufis in the main Islamic trends competing for the attention of those second- and third-generation Muslims who were raised in the UK; and Ritter (2016) investigated several ethical and normative practices of Sufis in Denmark. However, as followers of Sufism may be at the intersection of religious schism and ethnic and racial divisions, very little work has been done on the processes of racialization occurring within Muslim communities that are themselves subject to expressions of subordination, racism, and decolonial demands (King 2021). Indeed, racialization is often applied to white converts to Islam experiencing the process of subordination (Galionnier 2015). And concern is raised in Arabic countries about the expression of racism towards African citizens (Al-Khamri 2019). However, to our best knowledge, no research in Belgium has tried to explore the intersection of racialisation and belonging to heterodox Islamic trends (such as Sufism) for Black Muslims as it is the case of some research in neighbouring countries (Larisse 2019).

Regarding European Shia Muslims, Scharbrodt (2020) studied the creation of a diasporic public sphere in Britain including its positioning towards Iran and its aspiration to be the political leader of global Shiism. In Sweden, Olsson (2017) analyzed the 'othering' of Shia in the publications of a Swedish Sunni website and what effects this might have if put into practice, especially in day-to-day situations. Based on an ethnographic analysis of the Muharram rituals of Iraqi Shi'is in London, Degli Esposti (2018) took religious rites as a starting point from which to elaborate a performative theory of identity change to highlight the role of ritual and performance in shaping changing notions of identity at both the individual and collective level. Exploring the British and Dutch cases, van den Bos (2012) investigated cross-border and cross-ethnic organization among Shiites. In the French-speaking world, Sèze (2015) has shown how, in a society hit hard by Islamist terrorism, Ahmadiyya communities—considered to be heretics by both Sunni and Shia (Schäfer 2015)—attempt to embody an acceptable form of Islam in the French public space. With regard to the Alevis, Gokalp (1984) paved the way for research on this ethnic and religious subgroup. Akgönül (2005) has focused on the networks of Turkish Islam transplanted in Europe taking Alevis into consideration. Furthermore, Massicard's (2005) work on this religious and ethnic minority in France, Germany, and Turkey is authoritative.

However, with regard to Belgium especially, there has been extremely little research on those groups. One can cite the work of Lechkar (2017a) on the conversion of Sunnis to Shi'ism and on the role of emotions in the process of socialisation of Moroccan Belgians into Shia faith (2017b). El Asri (2009) also dedicated part of his doctoral research to the musical practices of European Muslims in groups that fall within the Sufi and Shia dynamics. Regarding the Alevis, mention can be made of Lebrecht's (1997) dissertation-based work and, more recently, of Servantie's (2015) article describing the various Alevi organisations in the particular context of the institutionalisation of Islam in Belgium and the creation of the Muslim Executive. However, no research has focused on the racialization processes within the Muslim community and Sufi and Ahmadiyya dynamics, for example, are poorly explored (if at all). This brief state of the art shows that there is a need to gather and update data on minorities within the Belgian Muslim population from both a sociological and political perspective. Among those minorities, we must not forget converts: despite the fact that different public initiatives and NGOs exist, few researches deal with how converts navigate between norms and ethnic belonging.

Moreover, if the institutionalization process of Islam, as we have seen, has attracted some attention, there has been almost no research on Imams. This is striking if we take into consideration the number of public debates around their role and possible impact in (de)radicalization. Indeed, since the bombings in Madrid (2004) and London (2005) and the murder of the Dutch filmmaker Theo van Gogh in 2004, the securitizing public policies of several European governments have sponsored or endorsed programs to train "Euro-friendly" Imams (Haddad and Balz 2008). Imams are thus an important contemporary target of secular governmentality (Ahmad and El-Yousfi 2021). From the exploratory study of Loobuyck and Meier (2014) of the case of Flanders, we learn that a significant part of the Belgian Imams surveyed was born abroad and find it difficult to express themselves in the different national languages. Some of them officially came as Imams for a limited time but then stayed and applied for citizenship, others became Imams almost "by accident," replacing an absent Imam or filling a long-standing vacancy (Loobuyck and Meier 2014). Moreover, if the essential meaning of Imam is "leader of the prayer," the responsibilities and functions of the Imam in an immigrant context are much broader including spiritual, social, and familial support (Loobuyck and Meier 2014). Finally, we also learn that the surveyed Imams see any training funded by the government with some reluctance. This hesitation can be partially explained by their insufficient ability to speak French and/or Dutch but also by some fear of being instrumentalized, of being involved in a game in which the state seeks interlocutors to produce and legitimize the "good" interpretation of Islam (Groeninck 2021). As in neighboring countries, we can certainly add some lack of confidence in the expertise of the non-Muslim academics teaching the programs and a refusal by some institutions linked to the country of origins such as the Turkish Presidency of Religious Affairs (Diyanet) to cooperate with universities to set-up the programs (Sözeri, Altinyelken and Volman 2019). However, regarding this research agenda, very few studies have integrated how gender, individualization processes, and the development of the Internet have challenged the way authority and leadership are constructed among the different Muslim communities. For example, if it is clear that the relation between religious authority and "ordinary" Muslims is under pressure in the sense that older, established configurations of authority are destabilized and increasingly challenged by rival voices and practices (Sunier 2018), research could focus on the impact of religious content produced on social media (Carvalho 2018), and especially on how female religious leaders trouble the male monopoly of religious knowledge and authority (Kramer and Schmitdkte 2006) or instead play the game of religious nationalism (Borrillo 2018).

References

Adraoui, M.-A. 2015. Le salafisme en France—Socialisation, Politisation, Mondialisation. *Confluences Méditerranée* 95: 69–80.
Ahmad, Z., and A. El-Yousfi. 2021. Muslim ethical self-making and secular governmentality in Europe: An introduction. *Religion, State and Society* 49(4–5):289–296.
Akgönül, Samim. 2005. Islam turc, islams de Turquie: Acteurs et réseaux en Europe. *Politique Étrangère* 1:35–47.
Al-Khamri, Hana. 2019. Un racisme anti-noir outrancier inonde les télévisions arabes en période de Ramadan. Les Cahiers de l'Islam. https://www.lescahiersdelislam.fr/Un-rac isme-anti-noir-outrancier-inonde-les-televisions-arabes-en-periode-de-Ramadan_a1839. html. Accessed: 09 Jan. 2023.
Bastenier, Albert, and Felice Dassetto. 1984. *L'Islam transplanté: Vie et organisation des minorités musulmanes de Belgique*. Brussels: EPO.
Berriane, M., H. de Haas, and K. Natter. 2015. Introduction: Revisiting Moroccan migrations. *The Journal of North African Studies* 20(4):503–521.
Borillo, Sara. Islamic female religious authority between agency and governmentality. From the Moroccan model to 'multicultural' Europe. In *Imams in Western Europe: Developments, transformations, and institutional challenges*, Ed. M. Hashas, J. J. de Ruiter, and N. Valdemar Vinding, 205–228. Amsterdam: Amsterdam University Press.
Brion, Fabienne. 2004. *Féminité, minorité, islamité. Questions à propos du hijâb*, Louvain-La-Neuve: Academia-Bruylant.
Carvalho, Claudia. i-Imams studying female Islamic authority online. In *Imams in Western Europe: Developments, Transformations, and Institutional Challenges*, Ed. M. Hashas, J. J. de Ruiter, and N. Valdemar Vinding, 185–204. Amsterdam: Amsterdam University Press.

2 Muslims in Belgium: From Immigrant ...

35

Coolsaet, Rik. 2016. Facing the fourth foreign fighters wave. What drives Europeans to Syria, and to Islamic State? Insights from the Belgian case. Egmont-Royal Institute of International Relations. https://rikcoolsaet.be/fr/book/facing-the-fourth-foreign-fighters-wave-what-drives-europeans-to-syria-and-to-islamic-state-insights-from-the-belgian-case/. Accessed: 05. Dec. 2022.

Dassetto, Felice. 2007. De l'islam transplanté à l'islam multiple : état des recherches. In Immigration et intégration en Belgique francophone, Eds. M. Marco, A. Rea and F. Dassetto, 401–421. Louvain-La-Neuve: Academia-Bruylant.

Dassetto, Felice. 1998. Le Tabligh en Belgique. Diffuser l'islam sur les traces du Prophète. Louvain-La-Neuve: Academia.

Dassetto, Felice. 1997. Facettes de l'islam belge, Louvain-La-Neuve: Academia-Bruylant.

Esposti, Degli, and Emanuelle. 2018. The aesthetics of ritual—contested identities and conflicting performances in the Iraqi Shi'a diaspora: Ritual, performance and identity change. Politics 38(1):68–83.

De Koning, M., C. Becker, and I. Roex, Eds. 2020. Islamic Militant Activism in Belgium. The Netherlands and Germany: Palgrave Macmillan.

Djelloul, G., and B. Maréchal. 2018. L'islam et les musulmans en Belgique: Quelques repères historiques, démographiques et organisationnels. Dossier documentaire du CIS-MODOC. http://hdl.handle.net/2078.1/197410. Accessed: 05 December 2022.

Duran, Khalid. 1991. Muslim Diaspora: The Sufis in Western Europe. Islamic Studies 30(4):463–483.

El Asri, Farid. 2009. L'expression musicale de musulmans européens. Création de sonorités et normativité religieuse. Revue européenne des migrations internationales 25(2):35–50.

Fadil, N., F. Ragazzi, and M. de Koning, Eds. 2019. Radicalization in Belgium and The Netherlands: Critical perspectives on violence and security. Bloomsbury Publishing.

Fadil, Nadia. 2013. Performing the Salat [Islamic Prayers] at Work: Secular and Pious Muslims Negotiating the Contours of the Public in Belgium. Ethnicities 13(6):729–750.

Fadil, Nadia. 2009. Managing affects and sensibilities: The case of not-handshaking and not-fasting. Social Anthropology 17(4):439–454.

Fadil, Nadia. 2004. Individualizing Faith, Individualizing Identity: Islam and Young Muslim Women in Belgium. In European Muslims and the Secular State, Ed. J. Cesari and S. McLoughlin, 143–154. Farnham: Ashgate.

Frennet-, Keyser, and Anne. 2003. La convention belgo-marocaine du 17 février 1964 relative à l'occupation de travailleurs marocains en Belgique. Courrier Hebdomadaire Du CRISP 1803(18):5–46.

Galionnier, Juliette. 2015. The racialization of Muslims in France and the United States: Some insights from white converts to Islam. Social Compass 62(4):70–583.

Grignard, Alain. 2003. L'islam radical et sa présence en Belgique. In Islam et musulmans dans l'espace européen, Ed. Ch. and Cheref-Khan, 45–70. Brussels: Espace de Libertés.

Groeninck, Mieke. 2021. Difference and negotiation from the borders: Islamic religious actors providing theological counternarratives for deradicalisation in Belgium. Religion, State and Society 49(4–5):331–349.

Gokalp, Altan. 1984. La Turquie et l'émigration turque. Paris: ADRI.

Haddad, Y.Y., and M.J. Balz. 2008. Taming the Imams: European Governments and Islamic Preachers since 9/11. Islam and Christian-Muslim Relations 19(2):215–235.

Hamid, Sadek. 2016. *Sufis, Salafis and Islamists: The Contested Ground of British Islamic Activism*. London: I.B. Tauris.

Husson, Jean-François. 2021. Belgium. In *Yearbook of Muslims in Europe*, Eds. E. Račius, S. Müssig, S. Akgönül, A. Alibašić, J. Nielsen and O. Scharbrodt. vol 13. Brill.

Husson, Jean-François. 2020. Belgium. In *Yearbook of Muslims in Europe*, Eds. E. Račius, S. Müssig, S. Akgönül, A. Alibašić, J. Nielsen, and O. Scharbrodt. vol 12. Brill.

King, Stephen J. 2021. Black Arabs and African migrants: Between slavery and racism in North Africa. *The Journal of North African Studies* 26(1):8–50.

Kolly, Maryam. 2018. Professional identity and religious identity. Inter-minority solidarity among future social workers. *Brussels Studies* 122.

Koopmans, Ruud. 2015. Religious fundamentalism and hostility against out-groups: A comparison of Muslims and Christians in Western Europe. *Journal of Ethnic and Migration Studies* 41(1):33–57.

Kotek, J., and J. Tournemenne. 2020. Libéralisme culturel, conservatisme et antisémitisme : en immersion chez la jeunesse belge. Fondation Jean Jaurès. https://www.jean-jaures.org/publication/liberalisme-culturel-conservatisme-et-antisemitisme-en-immersion-chez-la-jeunesse-belge/?post_id=16645&export_pdf=1. Accessed: 05 Dec. 2022.

Kramer, G., and S. Schmitdkte, Eds. 2006. *Speaking for Islam: Religious authorities in Muslim societies*. Leiden: Brill.

Larisse, Agathe. 2019. Affiliation volontaire à l'islam et assignation raciale: Français et Britanniques d'ascendance caribéenne convertis à l'islam face à la «question noire». *Archives De Sciences Sociales Des Religions* 186: 93–116.

Lebrecht, Michaël. 1997. *Alévis de Belgique. Approche générale et étude de cas*. Louvain-la-Neuve: Academia Bruylant/Sybidi.

Lechkar, Iman. 2017a. The power of affective encounters and events: why Moroccan Belgian Sunnis become Shia. In *Moroccan Migration in Belgium. More than 50 Years of Settlement*, Eds. C. Timmerman, N. Fadil, I. Goddeeris, N. Clycq, and K. Ettourki, 367–380. CeMIS Migration and Intercultural Studies: Leuven University Press.

Lechkar, Iman. 2017b. Being a "True" Shi'ite: The poetics of emotions among Belgian-Moroccan Shiites. *Journal of Muslims in Europe* 6:241–259.

Loobuyck, P., and P. Meier. 2014. Imams in Flanders: A research note. *Islam and Christian-Muslim Relations* 25(4):471–487.

Loobuyck, P., J. Debeer, and P. Meier. 2013. Church-state regimes and their impact on the institutionalization of islamic organizations in Western Europe: A comparative analysis. *Journal of Muslim Minority Affairs* 33(1):61–76.

Manço, Ural. 2000. *Voix et voies musulmanes de Belgique*. Brussels: Publications des Facultés universitaires Saint-Louis.

Manço, A., and U. Manço. 1992. *Turcs de Belgique. Identités et trajectoires d'une minorité*. Brussels: Info-Türk.

Massicard, Élise. 2005. *L'Autre Turquie. Le mouvement aléviste et ses territoires*. Paris: Presses universitaires de France.

Meijer, Roel, Ed. 2013. *Global Salafism. Islam's new religious movement*. Oxford: Oxford University Press.

Meijer, R., and E. Bakker, Eds. 2012. *The Muslim brotherhood in Europe*. London: Hurst & Company.

2 Muslims in Belgium: From Immigrant …

Nabti, Mehdi. 2007. Des soufis en banlieue parisienne. Mise en scène d'une spiritualité musulmane. *Archives de sciences sociales des religions* 4(140):49–68.

Nielsen, Jórgen., Ed. 2013. *Muslim political participation in Europe*. Edinburgh: Edinburgh University Press.

Olsson, Susanne. 2017. Shia as internal others: A Salafi rejection of the 'Rejecters.' *Islam and Christian-Muslim Relations* 28(4):409–430.

Panafit, Lionel. 1999. *Quand le droit écrit l'islam: L'intégration juridique de l'islam en Belgique*. Louvain-La-Neuve: Bruylant Academia.

Rea, A., D. Jacobs, C. Teney, and P. Delwit. 2010. Les comportements électoraux des minorités ethniques à Bruxelles. *Revue Française De Science Politique* 60(4):691–717.

Rea, Andrea. 2006. Les politiques d'immigration: Des migrations ordonnées aux migrations débridées. In *Penser l'immigration et l'intégration autrement*, Ed. B. Khader, 184–192. Brussels: Bruylant.

Renaerts, M., and U. Manço. 2000. Lente institutionnalisation de l'islam et persistance d'inégalités face aux autres cultes reconnus. In *Voix et voies musulmanes de Belgique*, Ed. U. Manço, 83–106. Brussels: Facultés universitaires Saint-Louis.

Rytter, Mikkel. 2016. By the beard of the Prophet: Imitation, reflection and world transformation among Sufis in Denmark. *Ethnography* 17(2):229–249.

Sägesser, Caroline. 2020. L'organisation et le financement public du culte islamique. Belgique et perspectives européennes. *Courrier Hebdomadaire Du CRISP* 2459–2460:5–72.

Sandri, G., and N. De Decker. 2008. Le vote des musulmans le 10 juin 2007. In *Le vote des Belges. Le comportement électoral des Bruxellois et des Wallons aux élections du 10 juin 2007*, Ed. P. Delwit and E. Van Haute, 39–53. Brussels: Editions de l'Université de Bruxelles.

Schäfer, Saskia. 2015. Renegotiating Indonesian secularism through debates on Ahmadiyya and Shia. *Philosophy & Social Criticism* 41(4–5):497–508.

Scharbrodt, Oliver. 2020. Creating a diasporic public sphere in Britain: Twelver Shia networks in London. *Islam and Christian-Muslim Relations* 31(1):23–40.

Servantie, Alain. 2015. Les Alévis en Belgique. En quête d'une reconnaissance au-delà de l'islam. *Anatoli* 6:191–211.

Sèze, Romain. 2015. L'Ahmadiyya en France. Une minorité musulmane en quête de reconnaissance. *Archives de sciences sociales des religions* 3(171):247–263.

Smits, F., S. Ruiter, and F. Van Tubergen. 2010. Religious practices among Islamic immigrants: Moroccan and Turkish men in Belgium. *Journal for the Scientific Study of Religion* 49(2):247–263.

Sözeri, S., H. K. Altinyelken, and M. Volman. 2019. Training imams in the Netherlands: The failure of a post-secular endeavour. *British Journal of Religious Education* 41(4):435–445.

Spellman, K. 2004. A national Sufi order with transnational dimensions: The Maktab Tarighat Oveyssi Shahmaghsoudi Sufi order in London. *Journal of Ethnic and Migration Studies* 30(5):945–960.

Sunier, T., and K. Hajji. 2018. The making of Islamic authority in Europe. In *Imams in Western Europe: Developments, Transformations, and Institutional Challenges*, Ed. M. Hashas, J. J. de Ruiter, and N. Valdemar Vinding, 51–68. Amsterdam: Amsterdam University Press.

Sunier, T. 2014. Domesticating Islam: Exploring academic knowledge production on Islam and Muslims in European societies. *Ethnic and Racial Studies* 37(6):1138–1155.

Timmerman, C., E. Vanderwaeren, and M. Crul. 2003. The second generation in Belgium. *International Migration Review* 37(4):1065–1090.

Torrekens, C., N. Bensaïd, and K. Dimokritos. 2021. Young Belgian Muslims: Between religious reactivity and individualization. *Ethnic and Racial Studies* 45(11):2049–2068.

Torrekens, Corinne. 2020. *Islams de Belgique*, 2020. Bruxelles: Presses de l'Université de Bruxelles.

Den Bos, Van, and Matthijs. 2012. European Shiism? Counterpoints from Shiites' organization in Britain and the Netherlands. *Ethnicities* 12(5):556–580.

Zemni, Sami. 2011. The shaping of Islam and Islamophobia in Belgium. *Race & Class* 53(1):28–44.

Zibouh, Fatima. 2012. La participation politique des musulmans en Belgique : La mobilisation des réseaux sociaux. In *Islam belge au pluriel*, Ed. B. Maréchal and F. El Asri, 273–289. Louvain-la-Neuve: Presses Universitaires de Louvain.

Corinne Torrekens is Professor of political science at the Université libre de Bruxelles and director of the of the Group for research on Ethnic Relations, Migration and Equality (GERME). Her last book *Islams de Belgique* (2020, Presses de l'Université de Bruxelles) provides an insight on both the historicity of the installation of Muslim families in Belgium and on the current challenges facing the rooting of Islam in a post-attack society.

Islam in the Netherlands: Denominational Pillar or 'Fifth Column'?

3

Thijl Sunier

Abstract

Religion has always been a constitutive factor of national politics in the Netherlands, despite the relatively rapid post-war deconfessionalisation, the break-down of the pillar system, the strong commitment to the separation of religion and state, and not least the Dutch self-image of being a secular and above all libertarian country. The arrival of labour migrants and their families with a Muslim background from the 1960s onwards, has thrown this self-image into stark relief and determined to a large extent how Dutch policies towards Islam and Muslims evolved over the years. In the development of Islam as a policy category in the Netherlands, I distinguish three stages with concomitants public discourses and images, modes of governance, and characteristics of the Islamic landscape. These stages should not be taken as contexts unto itself, but as subsequent steps in a long-term unfolding process.

Keywords

Muslim migrants · Domestication of religion · Islamisation of migrants · Integration · Securitisation

---

T. Sunier (✉)
Vrije UniversiteitNetherlands, Amsterdam, Netherlands
e-mail: j.t.sunier@vu.nl

© The Author(s), under exclusive license to Springer Fachmedien Wiesbaden GmbH, part of Springer Nature 2024
R. Ceylan and M. Mücke (eds.), *Muslims in Europe*, Islam in der Gesellschaft, https://doi.org/10.1007/978-3-658-43044-3_3

1 Introduction

There are almost one million people with an Islamic background in the Netherlands, 6% of the total population. The overwhelming majority of Muslims in the Netherlands have a background of labour migration. Immigrants from Turkey constitute the largest immigrant population (404.000), followed by Moroccans (397.000), Indonesians (360.000), Surinamese (350.000), Syrians (90.000), Iraqis (61.000), Afghans (47.000), Iranians (42.000), Somalis (39.000), and Pakistanis (23.000) (Butter and Van Oordt 2017).[1] In most cases Muslims comprise over 90% of these foreign nationals; in other cases, less than 50% (Surinamese 10%, Iranians 35%, Iraqis 60%, Syrians 70%, and Indonesians 3%). Migrants from Syria, Iraq, Afghanistan, and Somalia are predominantly refugees. About 14.000 Muslims in the Netherlands are converts, 70% of whom are women (Van Nieuwkerk 2006; Vroon-Najem 2014).

A majority is born in the Netherlands or has Dutch nationality, whose parents or grandparents may have arrived as labour migrants. Exact figures do not exist because they are statistically 'invisible', which can lead to unfounded assumptions about their position, outlook, and attitude towards society.

The Ahmadiyya Mobarak Mosque in The Hague was the first mosque in the Netherlands opened in 1955 (Ryad 2013). A mosque for the Moluccan community opened in the late 1950s in the village of Balk. More than a decade later, the first makeshift mosques appeared for labour migrants. Today there are an estimated 450 to 500 mosques in the Netherlands. The overall number of mosques did not change significantly over the last decades, but the number of newly built mosques has risen to approximately 160.[2]

Most mosque associations are still organised along ethnic lines (244 mosques are Turkish, 178 Moroccan, and 53 Surinamese and Pakistani). The number of Dutch and multi-ethnic mosques is increasing. Most mosque associations belong to supra-local umbrella organisations. Among Muslims with a Turkish background, the largest is the Dutch Islamic Foundation (ISN) with 143 local mosque associations. ISN is the Dutch branch of Diyanet (Turkish Presidency of Religious Affairs). In the 1980s, Diyanet made agreements with several European governments to send imams, paid by the Turkish government (Sunier and Landman 2011). The remaining Turkish mosques are part of various religious movements (Sunier and Landman 2015; Sunier 2021).

---

[1] https://www.cbs.nl/nl-nl/zoeken?q=islam. Accessed November 2022.

[2] www.maroc.nl/forums/forum.php; https://moskeewijzer.nl/. accessed November 2022.

3 Islam in the Netherlands: Denominational Pillar or 'Fifth Column'?

About 50% of the Moroccan mosques in the Netherlands are member of the Union of Moroccan Muslim Organisations in the Netherlands (UMMON). The Dutch Council of Moroccan Mosques (RMMN) represents a number of local networks of Moroccan mosques. A relatively high number of Moroccan mosques is independent, some of which are commonly depicted as Salafi.

About 70.000 Muslims in the Netherlands have a Shi'a background. Most of them came as refugees from Iraq and Afghanistan. About 50.000 people of Turkish origin are Alevis. They have founded some 23 local organizations. About 50% of these organizations are part of the Dutch national umbrella organisation HAK-DER (Neijenhuis 2008; Sunier and Landman 2015; Butter and Van Oordt 2017).

Currently the Council Muslims and Government (CMO) is the biggest and most influential supra-ethnic national representative body for Muslim organisations. Today they represent only Sunni Muslim organisations. In practice mainstream Sunni organisations are most powerful and dominate contacts with the government.

One of the oldest Muslim organisations in the Netherlands is al Nisa, an organisation for Muslim women founded in 1982. Al Nisa started as a network for women to improve mutual contact. In almost four decades, they developed into an influential platform of Muslim women who explicitly define themselves as Dutch and who take issue with many thorny and sensitive topics, such as homosexuality, domestic violence, and apostasy. On many occasions, they have questioned the male-dominated Islam in the Netherlands.

The first Islamic primary schools were established in the 1980s, a time when the institutionalisation of Islam via mosques advanced rapidly (Landman 1992). After these first successful initiatives, the number of Islamic primary schools grew slowly but steadily to up to 61 schools at the moment. Even though this is a relatively small portion of the overall number of schools with approximately 15.000 pupils (one percent of the total number of pupils and 1.7% of the estimated number of Muslims), the steady development of Islamic state funded education was and remains highly contested (Merry and Driessen 2016; Driessen 2021).[3]

Many overviews about Islam and Muslims in various countries, either in Europe or elsewhere, commonly start with facts and figures in the way I did. This is supposed to be self-evident objectified information, that is crucial to understand the position of Islam and Muslims in the country. Such data are especially used

---

[3] For a broad and instructive overview (in Dutch) of the Islamic landscape in the Netherlands, see Butter and Van Oordt (2017). See Poorthuis and Salemink (2011) for a historical overview of the imaging of Islam and Muslims in the Netherlands from the mid-nineteenth century till today.

in statistical overviews and policy reports. However, before I start to unfold my argument, I want to add some warnings to these figures, particularly the number of Muslims. Numbers are always 'up for grabs', for politicians, journalists, and collective actors alike. Administrative authorities use figures for policy development, politicians use them to take issue for or against the presence of Muslims, and Muslim activists use them to engage with societal problems, to visualise modes of discrimination and to ask for equal rights, even if they themselves have differing views about what it means to be Muslim.

Facts about the Islamic infrastructure, the number of mosques, the educational arrangements, representative bodies, and legal arrangements tell us something about the bureaucratic encapsulation of Islam in the country (Sunier 2022). But it would be wrong to assume that these characteristics provide us with an adequate picture of Islam and Muslims presence in the country.

Even though facts and figures may be considered as a side issue, or plain background information according to many academics, they continue to be applied unreflectively. As religious affiliation is not a category that is applied in citizenship registration in the Netherlands, figures about the number of Muslims are based on statistical data about the number of immigrants from certain countries, which is absolutely misleading when it concerns religious affiliation, or even background. Researchers have therefore developed criteria to 'count' Muslims. These criteria include the observance of religious duties, dress codes, attitudes towards non-Muslims, etc. (see e.g., SCP 2012). Although these criteria are highly debatable and ambiguous, they continue to be applied by influential think tanks and advisory institutes for the government. In general, an estimated 50 per cent of people statistically classified as Muslims are actually practicing religion, but even those figures tell us little about what is actually meant by 'practicing Muslim'. As Rogers Brubaker argues: "[…] what does it mean to study 'Muslims' in European countries of immigration? Who -and what- are we talking about when we talk about 'Muslims'? The answer is by no means self-evident." (Brubaker 2013, p. 2; see also Grillo 2004; Spielhaus 2010).

Following Brubaker's line of argumentation, the subsequent parts of this chapter unfold as the ways in which 'Muslim' and 'Islam' became policy categories. I shall do that by providing a historical account of the presence of Muslims and the development of the Islamic infrastructure in the Netherlands against the background of the specific relation between state and religion, and the evolving policies of integration of migrants and of the bureaucratic encapsulation of Islam into society. I furthermore address the ways in which collective actors act upon and engage with these policy categories, with administrative authorities, politics, and society, and how this impacts on the Islamic landscape in the Netherlands.

3 Islam in the Netherlands: Denominational Pillar or 'Fifth Column'?

For individual Muslims the question what it means to be Muslims has transformed in the course of years as well. This transformation concerns the making of Muslim-selves in the first place (Bracke 2008; Moors 2009; Abaaziz 2021). As this falls outside the scope of this chapter, I mainly focus on the political dimension.

The main focus is on the post-World War immigration as this was decisive for the development of Islam and Muslims as policy categories. I conclude the chapter by discussing the social climate with regard to the presence of Muslims and provide some reflections on the future of Islam.

2 Domestication of Religion and the 'Making of Islam' in the Netherlands

Despite the widespread secularisation after World War II and the building of secular liberal nation-states, religion, and culture, in different modalities and disguises, have always been part and parcel of nation-building discourses and imaginations. The main aim of nation-building projects in this regard is to develop particular modes of governance to 'nationalise' religion and bring the organisation of religious activity in line with national formats. I have used the term 'domestication' to analyse that process with regard to Islam in Europe (Sunier 2014). This implies actively creating governable categories for administrative authorities and policymakers with regard to Islam and Muslims for that national project. Thus, the "[…] translation of Islam into a language of bureaucracy. […] into the codes, procedures, and symbols, or language, of bureaucracy and, simultaneously, produces its own meanings that are unique to specific discursive arenas" Müller (2018, p. 214).

But domestication is more than applying bureaucratic statecraft. It involves the state's intervention and regulation of many aspects of socioreligious life, and to prioritise 'appropriate' forms of Islam, and to delegitimise other forms. As Mahmood has argued, secularism is not a political formation in which religion has simply been removed or relegated to the private sphere. For secularity as political program a particular definition of the religious domain is a prerequisite. Thus:

> "On the one hand, the liberal state claims to maintain a separation between church and state by relegating religion to the private sphere, that sacrosanct domain of religious belief and individual liberty. On the other hand, modern governmentality involves the state's intervention and regulation of many aspects of socioreligious life, dissolving

the distinction between public and private and thereby contravening its first claim" (Mahmood 2016, p. 4).

Also, in the Netherlands religion has always been a constitutive factor of national politics despite the relatively rapid post-war deconfessionalization, the break-down of the pillar system, the strong commitment to the separation of religion and state, and not least the Dutch self-image of being a secular libertarian country. The arrival of labour migrants and their families with a Muslim background from the 1960s onwards, has rendered domestication a more explicit and more urgent character.

In the first half of the twentieth century a relatively small number of Muslims from the Dutch colonies (Indonesia and Surinam) lived in the Netherlands, most of them arrived as students. In addition, there were followers of the Indian mystic Inayat Khan who founded the Sufi movement in Geneva in 1923. Also, the Ahmadiyyah movement founded a branch in the Netherlands (Landman 1992; Ryad 2013). After WW II a small proportion of the Moluccan families that were deported from Indonesia to the Netherlands in 1951 were Muslims.

At the time when these communities settled in the Netherlands, the country was in the heydays of the pillarisation era. Pillarisation refers to the Dutch political and societal structure roughly between the 1920s and the 1960s when Dutch society was organised along confessional lines. As the pillarized political culture and history is relevant for the place of Islam in Dutch society, I shall dwell on this history a bit. From the 1920s onwards Dutch society gradually became divided along vertically organised communities, the so-called 'pillars', corporate religious communities, or blocs. Pillars were made up of a wide array of organisations and associations ranging from local sports clubs to political parties, trade unions, schools, and broadcasting companies, all associated with the denominational identity of the pillar, and with a strong internal sense of belonging. There were two religious pillars, a Catholic and a Protestant one.

Churches were at the heart of these pillars, and the lives of the members of each pillar would be completely embedded in the pillar. Welfare, relief, social and economic support were administered by private organisations attached to the pillar. Jews were to a certain extent also organised as a pillar, but their position in the interbellum was in no way comparable to that of the other religious communities, let alone 'exotic' fringes such as Islam or Hinduism. More importantly, they did in no way belong to the political elite. The two confessional pillars comprised more than 50% of the Dutch population and ran through all social classes. They dominated the political scene, even in the 1980s and the 1990s (Sunier 2004).

3 Islam in the Netherlands: Denominational Pillar or 'Fifth Column'?

An important characteristic of the system was the strong emphasis on sovereignty of the pillars. Especially the two confessional pillars demanded no state interference whatsoever in matters related to the daily life of their communities, and in moral issues. The generally accepted (often rigid) stability, characteristic of the pillar structure, rendered the system its seemingly 'natural' character. These politico-confessional blocks not only determined to a large extent the political relations in the Netherlands; they also shaped the ideational dividing lines within the Dutch population. Solidarity within each pillar was supposed to overrule class, political and other dividing lines, as all members of a pillar would have the same interest. The pillars were principally considered equal and balanced vis-à-vis one another. Social conflicts were pacified and neutralized by closely cooperating ruling elites at the top of the pillars. Due to the rigidity of the system political developments were extremely inert in the Netherlands between the 1920s and 1960s.

The pillars have structured the political landscape to large extent for almost half a century. There was also a socialist movement and a so-called liberal sphere. They were part of the political structure and functioned as a pillar, and in the course of years developed into the same corporate blocs as the confessional ones (Stuurman 1983).

In the course of the 1960s the system gradually lost its function and in most sections of civil society a breakdown of the pillar structure took place. Today the societal forces that sustained the pillarisation process have almost completely been replaced by the centralizing mechanisms of the modern welfare state, but the juridical remnants of the system do still play a role in some crucial areas. In addition, the system continued to shape political relations for a considerable period of time, even in the 1970s and 1980s. The main reason for that was the strong position of the Christian Democrats, who support the pillarized school system, in political decision-making in post-war Netherlands. It should be noted that the communitarian approach to society as they were developed by Etzioni (1968), have always been rather central in Christian democrat thinking and they are being revived and refurbished in the neo-liberal age (see Schinkel and Van Houdt 2011; Van Houdt and Schinkel 2014).

The educational system in the Netherlands is the most prominent and visible remnant of the pillarisation era. According to article 23 of the Constitution, confessional communities have the right to set up their own schools. When they fully comply with the general requirements that apply to all schools, they are subsidised equally to state schools (Sunier 2004; Driessen 2021). Also, the broadcasting companies and trade unions are still organised along confessional lines, but religious boundaries are very quickly fading away.

3 Islam and Pillarisation

The relevance of the pillarisation era for the position of Islam and Muslims in the Netherlands is complex. As I have argued before, Muslims who arrived in the first half of the twentieth century, but also Muslims from former colonies who arrived in the 1950s, had in no way bearing on the pillar structure. They simply did not constitute a part of it.

In the years prior to the labour migration, two important processes evolved in Dutch society: the break-down of the pillar system and a relatively rapid deconfessionalisation among the population. These developments were not necessarily related to one another, but they occurred simultaneously and thus a particular narrative gradually took shape in the media and in the public opinion: 'we have dismantled the pillar system and banished religion as an organizing principle of society because we realised that religion is a private matter.' This oversimplified account of the course of events, became the basis of subsequent policy rhetoric in the Netherlands in the 1980s and 1990s (Rath and Sunier 1994; Sunier 1996; Rath et al. 2001). Migrants brought with them their cultural and religious background, but it was assumed that they would follow the same course as the Dutch in the aftermath of the break-down of the pillar system and the rapid deconfessionalisation in the 1960s. They would also soon 'do away' with religion because it would not have any function anymore in society.

In the development of Islam as a policy category in the Netherlands, I distinguish three stages with concomitants public discourses and images, modes of domestication, and characteristics of the Islamic landscape. An important aspect of the domestication of religion are the conceptions about proper national citizenship. Nationalist discourses and rhetoric are not just framed as a religious-secular opposition; they are also made up of narratives and self-images of a historically grown Dutch individualised Christian identity and how this contributed to 'our' present privatised religious attitude. In these discourses the Dutch pillarisation legacy and the post-war rapid marginalization of religious reasoning, is a crucial frame of reference to demonstrate what (integration) trajectories Muslim inhabitants should follow. These stages should not be taken as contexts unto itself, but as subsequent steps in a long-term unfolding process.

4 The Genealogy of Islam as a Policy Category, First Stage: The Islamisation of Migrants

The first stage started roughly at the beginning of the 1980s. As I showed above, the vast majority of Muslims in the Netherlands have a migrant background, or rather they are descendants of former labour migrants. In the 1970s, the religious background of migrants did not play any significant role in debates about their position in society. This was very reminiscent of the position of Muslim communities that arrived earlier. Migrants were primarily seen as members of a temporary labour force who would return to their countries of origin soon. The acknowledgment in the early 1980s that most migrants would stay permanently resulted in a stronger emphasis on the cultural background of these new settlers.

In the early 1960s secular parties successfully amended legislation that had initially been designed exclusively for Christian denominations to include 'Mohammedans', by invoking the equality principle (Hampsink and Roosblad 1992; Rath et al. 2001; Brand 2005; Van Sasse van Ysselt 2013). This formal equality made it possible for Muslims to benefit from a financial program for the reconstruction of houses of worship after WW II. This resulted in the first post-war purpose-built mosque in 1974. But the legal changes, however, did not affect the privileged position of the Protestant Church, a remnant of the Dutch Republic.

In 1983 a fundamental change in the Constitution was effectuated which implied the abolition of the formal ties between church and state that remained, and consequently of the final remnants of the dominant position of the Protestant Church. Formally, all financial relations between the state and the church were broken off (Hampsink and Roosblad 1992, p. 9). Combined with an increasing cultural de-pillarisation (Bracke 2013), this meant that Muslims now lacked the resources the churches had had in the past, and they slowly but gradually stood out as 'still' being religious in a society that was increasingly defined as secular (De Koning and Sunier 2021).

But the constitutional changes also provided Muslims with opportunities to participate in society as Muslims. From then on, all religions were considered equal in law (including 'new' religions such as Islam and Hinduism). The Dutch Constitution provides a legal basis for a specific mode of religious equality, including no registration of individual religious affiliation, no definition of religious denominations and communities in legal terms, equality of all religions. This can be understood as the 'non-recognition' principle: since religious denominations are not mentioned in the Constitution explicitly, there is no legal ground for recognition. Consequently, all religious denominations are equal on those grounds (Szumigalska 2015).

In practice, however, religious equality Dutch style is malleable and applied situation by situation by administrative authorities, ranging from non-intervention (citing the separation of religion and state) to exclusion (on the grounds that Muslim communities do not exist in legal terms). This has had a variety of effects on the position of religious communities, depending on political preferences and temporal and situational conditions. The place of Islam in Dutch society depends to a large extent on political decision-making, and the bargaining position of Muslim actors. (De Koning and Sunier 2021).

In the public and political opinion, the rapid growth of the Islamic institutional landscape in the 1980s was basically perceived as 'delayed pillarization'. Especially the Christian parties considered the development of an Islamic pillar a viable emancipation trajectory for Muslims and an obvious route to integration. Indeed, Muslim founded schools based on the educational system inherited from the pillar era. Although there were heated debates about this 'pillarized emancipation' model, there was a general consensus and an optimism that Muslims would eventually be absorbed into Dutch society, with or without their own pillar.

With regard to research and academic output, the presence of Muslims and the place of Islam in the Netherlands became a topic for research from roughly from the mid-1980s onwards.[4] This was the time when the Dutch government acknowledged that labour migrants would stay here permanently. Initially, and apart from publications written from a theological comparative perspective to explore differences and similarities between various religious communities and worldviews, Islam was not a very prominent research topic. Most research dealt with the arrival, settling and subsequent integration of large groups of labour migrants and their families mainly from Turkey and Morocco. The main focus was housing, labour market and education as the primary routes to integration (see e.g., Penninx 1988; Rath et al. 2001).

To the extent that cultural or religious background was addressed in this body of literature, it was predominantly informed by a culturalist perspective, that is to attribute explanatory power to cultural background and to consider migrant groups as bounded entities and bearers of a specific culture (Sunier 1996; Lentin 2014; Chemla and Keller 2017). This culturalist approach would become even

---

[4] In the literature on migrants published in the 1970s and early 1980s religion, notably Islam, was not addressed except in a few cases (see e.g., Joemman and Lokhorst 1977; Theunis 1979; Cappelle 1979).

3 Islam in the Netherlands: Denominational Pillar or 'Fifth Column'? 49

stronger with respect to the explanatory power of Islam in the course of the 1980s, especially in the development of integration policies.

The policies of integration took shape at a time when dramatic events, such as the revolution in Iran and the assassination of the Egyptian president Sadat, were taking place in the Islamic world. These events caused a tremendous increase in the number of publications about Islam and its adherents. Suddenly migrants from countries such as Turkey and Morocco were 'discovered' as Muslims.[5] A new cultural category emerged: 'Muslim migrant'. People with completely different backgrounds were lumped together under the heading of 'Muslim culture'. Since predominantly Muslims were facing problems of deprivation with respect to housing, labour, and education, 'Muslim culture' rendered specific meaning.

Islam increasingly became the explanatory factor, not only for specific (collective) behaviour of Muslims, but also for all kinds of societal problems they faced. The 'Islamisation of migrants', narrowed down perceptions on people's acting and thinking: 'when one wants to know what goes on in the head of a Muslim then one should study Islam'. All other possible explanations were in fact reduced to 'the' Islam (Rath and Sunier 1994, p. 57; Sunier 2020).[6]

The Islamisation of migrants also had an unexpected beneficial effect for Muslims who were negotiating religious accommodation. By emphasising their disadvantageous position as migrants, they were eligible for state subsidies. From the side of the government, the aim was to let the integration process evolve smoothly; subsidising various organisations of (Muslim) migrants would facilitate this process. This resulted in a relatively quick growth of the number of local mosques in the 1980s. Many of these mosques had a tea house and rooms for activities. In this way these mosque associations were physical 'proofs' of the conflation of Islam and migration (Sunier 1996).

5 The Genealogy of Islam as a Policy Category, Second Stage: Islam and the Dutch Nation

The awareness that the majority of Muslims were 'here to stay', together with the fact that the Islamic landscape was more persistent than was expected, invigorated a debate, in the course of the 1980s about the place of Islam in Dutch

---

[5] The 'discovery' of Islam in a country that has ruled over the most populous Muslim region of the world, Indonesia, is at least remarkable.

[6] See e.g., De Graaf (1983; 1985); Van den Berg (1986); Custers (1987); Dassetto and Nonneman (1996).

society. The crucial question emerged whether or not a permanent presence of Muslims would negatively affect the envisioned secular-liberal and tolerant character of the Dutch nation-state. The Rushdie affair in 1989 counted as catalytic in emphasizing this line of political thinking. Liberals worried about the 'liberal roots' of the Dutch nation being jeopardized. Where Christians would emphasize the similarities between Islam and Christianity as people of faith in the 1970s and 1980s, they increasingly started to point at the cultural and religious 'gap' between Islam and the proclaimed Christian (Protestant) roots of the nation.

Many intellectuals argued for a deepening and dissemination of national awareness and protection of Dutch national identity, both in relation to the presence of ethnic minorities and European unification. Their plea for more attention to national roots fitted within a general change in the political climate that took place in the course of the 1990s. The main idea is that the Dutch seem to be at a loss when they have to define precisely what the Dutch nation is. What is Dutch about Dutch national culture? What does it consist of? This may pose a dilemma for ethnic minorities: if they are willing to integrate into the nation, what is required of them? The uncertainty about what the Dutch nation stands for was pitted against the strong moral standards that were considered inherently connected to 'Islamic culture' (Sunier and Van Ginkel 2006).

The 1990s also marked the rise of Islam-critics such as Pim Fortuyn, Ayaan Hirsi Ali and Theo van Gogh, and later on, Geert Wilders. Their views on Islam and Dutch national culture were completely in line with those of mainstream politicians. Especially the publications of the public intellectual Fortuyn reflected the Dutch self-image of a libertarian country. In 1997, he published *Tegen de islamisering van onze cultuur* (Against the Islamisation of our Culture). In this much-read pamphlet, he warned that culture relativism was still dominating Dutch politics. 'Islamic cultures' are not equal to 'our liberal culture', he stated. Fortuyn emphasised the libertarian attitude, which he regarded as characteristic of Dutch society and discussed a number of issues where this would become critical. One was sexual morals. Fortuyn was gay and stated in the book and in numerous public speeches that his sexual identity would come under threat if Islam would gain influence. It would undermine the very foundations and accomplishments of the 'Judaeo-Christian Humanist' bedrock of 'our' society. Fortuyn's call to society to take these achievements seriously, resonated widely. In the nationalist agenda taking shape in the late 1980s and 1990s, propounded by mainstream politicians, many of the ideas articulated by Islam-critics could be found in official documents. They were phrased in a more moderate tone, but the message was principally similar (Silverstein 2005; Lentin and Titley 2012; De Koning and Sunier 2021).

3 Islam in the Netherlands: Denominational Pillar or 'Fifth Column'? 51

In the 1990s the academic focus shifted from the exploration of how migrants with an Islamic background would be absorbed to the question whether or not Islam would fit in the secular liberal nation-states in Europe (see e.g., Lewis and Schnapper 1994; Koopmans and Statham 2003; Statham et al. 2005).

6 The Genealogy of Islam as a Policy Category, Third Stage: Coercion and Securitisation

At the end of the 1990s a shift occurred in the thinking about the relation between Islam and national identity. The attack on the Twin Towers in September 2001 would enhance this transition in a compelling way, and it is tempting to adduce the terrorist attack as a watershed, a breach with the past and a turning point in the Dutch integration agenda, and as legitimisation for fundamental policy changes. However, this argumentation has two major interrelated flaws. The first is the persistent assumption that multiculturalism was at the heart of the Dutch integration policies in the 1980s and well into the 1990s. In a seminal opinion article in the daily *NRC* by publicist Paul Scheffer, titled 'The Multicultural Drama' (2000), the author, in a worrying and alarming tone, referred to the successful integration of poor Dutch people in the mid-twentieth century and similar programs in earlier years. The author also referred to the "successful Dutch past in dealing with the integration of strangers".[7]

His moral call for a more assertive Dutch national identity went hand in hand with further dismantling of policy tools that recognized religious diversity and multiculturalism. Multiculturalist politics according to Scheffer had caused a governmental mess because of its alleged opposing requirements. The depiction of the integration policies of the 1980s and 1990s as 'multicultural neglect' took root not only in the Netherlands; across Europe there was a widespread multicultural backlash (Vertovec and Wessendorf 2010).

However, integration policies in the Netherlands were in no way based on multicultural ideas of equality of cultures. Historically the idea of a multiplicity of identities under one national umbrella sustained by a tolerant political climate was a strong constituent element of the Dutch Republic in the seventeenth century. At least it was part of the republican myth and continued to shape the narrative a Dutch national identity. Only in recent decades this narrative changed (Nell and Rath 2010). In the 1980s there was a general trust that religious differences would dissolve when migrants would be integrated and absorbed by society and

---

[7] https://www.nrc.nl/handelsblad/2000/01/29/#105 accessed 15 November 2022.

its 'superior liberal civil culture and value system'. When this did not occur, the trust was replaced by the general assumption is that cultural diversity jeopardises social cohesion and that social equality cannot be accomplished without strict and coercive assimilationist policies. Today's adage is: 'if they are not convinced themselves, we have to force them', in other words a shift from 'assimilation by conviction' to 'assimilation by coercion'. The apparent policy shift in the Netherlands had to do with 'shattered trust' in the eroding effect of 'our own culture' and certainly not with a re-evaluation of cultural differences (Sunier 2010).

In that respect, and that is the other flaw, the attack on the Twin Towers, and subsequent terrorist attacks in Europe, did not constitute a watershed, but a catalyst. It reinvigorated and reemphasised the countries self-image and heightened the urge to assimilate Muslims. Even de assassination of Pim Fortuyn in 2002 by an animal-rights activist was incorporated in an anti-Islam discourse. The urgency according to a growing number of people to confront newcomers, especially those of 'non-western' origin with a dominant civil culture has only become stronger in subsequent years. A nation-wide consensus emerged about the importance of a so-called dominant 'Leitkultur'. Even leftist parties who were hitherto very hesitant to refer to national culture, were hammering on the importance of shared cultural values. When the Dutch queen Maxima (Argentinian by origin) stated in 2007 that she did not yet have met 'The' Dutch and that there is not just one Dutch identity, she was sharply criticized for her statement.

In the Netherlands, probably more than in other European countries, this assimilationist urgency is predominantly framed in an integration idiom. Even the rapidly increasing securitisation of Muslims and Islam and the prevention measures against the radicalisation of young Muslims, is often cast in pedagogical integration rhetoric. The benign trust in the eroding effect of the 'superior' Western culture, characteristic of the 1980s, has been replaced by suspicion about the intentions of Muslims.

In the second half of the 2000s, as in other European countries, security issues have become an essential part of the Dutch policies on Islam and Muslims. Controlling mechanisms have been scaled up as a result of the deteriorating political climate, the obsession with security and the constant problematisation and racialisation of Muslims. Schirin Amir-Moazami (2022) refers to this obsession as 'Interrogating Muslims' and argues that academics have contributed to this situation by systematically construing a binary between Muslims and the rest of society as a lens through which Islam in Europe is perceived. This perspective reduces the analysis to a simplified juxtaposition that ignores the complexity of

3 Islam in the Netherlands: Denominational Pillar or 'Fifth Column'?

the field (see also Schinkel 2017). Nadia Fadil (2019) has analysed this development and states that scholarship on Islam in Europe currently finds itself in a double epistemological impasse. On the one hand, Muslims in Europe are assessed primarily as 'Europe's Other' while, on the other, religious claim-making by Muslims causes unease and discomfort among those scholars who implicitly or explicitly assess Muslim activity through the lens of secularism, and from the beginning of the current century also through the lens of security (De Koning and Sunier 2021).

The combination of securitisation and integration discourses makes it often difficult for Muslims to do what they are legally entitled to. Even though Muslims have the constitutional right for example to set up their own schools, the conditions that initiators face are more challenging than for other religious denominations because these schools would isolate Muslim children. In their argumentation politicians combine concerns about safety ('schools as possible hotbeds for radical ideas') with concerns about integration ('schools isolate Muslim children from the rest of society') (Ahajjaj et al. forthcoming).

Securitisation in combination with suspicion have sometimes led to very bizarre and malign measures. In 2021 journalists discovered that municipalities across the country commissioned a private research institute to conduct undercover research in at least ten Dutch mosques.[8] This research took place while at the same time mosque organisations were in constant negotiation with local administrations. The case caused an enormous breach of trust among Muslim communities.

7 Future Prospects

Two crucial developments will to a large extent shape the future prospects of the Dutch Islamic landscape. The first and most fundamental development is the relatively rapid upward socio-economic mobility of young Muslims. Compared to earlier generations their position and their level of education has increased considerably, and today they work in every sector of the labour market. Most of them have been born and raised in the Netherlands and consider themselves Dutch citizens. They are not in the least isolated from society, as politicians would suggest. They know society, they are vocal and demand a place not as guests, but

---

[8] https://www.nrc.nl/nieuws/2021/10/15/undercover-naar-de-moskee-hoe-gemeenten-al-jaren-een-bedrijf-inhuren-om-heimelijk-islamitische-organisaties-te-onderzoeken-a4061964 accessed October 2022.

as equal citizens and on their own terms. Some of them turn away from society, but the vast majority consider themselves to be European citizens (Bouras 2012; Dessing et al. 2016).

Some young Muslims are actively involved in developing an Islam that is grafted on the Netherlands, built by Dutch citizens, by Dutch Muslims. This is the other crucial development. Although the Islamic landscape is still dominated by the established organisations and elites, there are indications that the parameters of the Islamic landscape are gradually shifting. Muslim women play an increasingly crucial role in this development. Due to their experience as Muslim and as woman, they unmask and disentangle the complex mechanisms of power, exclusion, and oppression (see Abu-Lughod 2002; Jouili and Amir-Moazami 2006, 2008; Bano and Kalmbach 2012).

As of now, scholarly attention to these developments is still limited. The often-heard argument is that the established organisational and institutional status quo is still firmly in place. Although this is true, not least because administrative authorities have a keen interest in keeping this status quo intact, it is the task of researchers to take novel developments and initiatives seriously.

References

Abaâziz, Btissam. 2021. *'Ze waren onwetend.' Een onderzoek naar de religieuze beleving van de eerste en tweede 'generatie' Marokkaanse Nederlanders.* (dissertation) Rotterdam: Erasmus University.

Abu-Lughod, Lila. 2002. Do Muslim Women really need saving? Anthropological reflections on cultural relativism and its others. *American Anthropologist* 104(3):783–790.

Ahajjaj, Jamal, Martijn De Koning, and Thijl Sunier. Forthcoming. Teaching Muslims: Active citizenship in Dutch Islamic schools. In *Doing difference and sameness in European schools—perspectives from European Anthropology of Education*, Eds. L. Gilliam and C. Markom. London: Berghahn Publ.

Amir-Moazami, Schirin. 2022. *Interrogating Muslims: The liberal-secular matrix of integration.* London: Bloomsbury.

Brand, Charlotte. 2005. Moorse minaretten op kosten van de staat? Overheidssubsidie voor moskeeën (1960–1990) *Jaarboek Parlementaire Geschiedenis 2005*, 76–88. Nijmegen: Centrum voor Parlementaire Geschiedenis.

Bano, Masooda, and Hilary Kalmbach. 2012. *Women, leadership and mosques: Changes in contemporary Islamic authority.* Leiden: Brill.

Bouras, Nadia. 2012. *Het land van herkomst: perspectieven op verbondenheid met Marokko, 1960–2010.* Hilversum: Verloren BV.

Brubaker, Rogers. 2013. Categories of analyses and categories of practice: A note on the study of Muslims in European countries of immigration. *Ethnic and Racial Studies.* 36(1):1–8.

3 Islam in the Netherlands: Denominational Pillar or 'Fifth Column'? 55

Bracke, Sarah. 2008. Conjugating the modern-religious, conceptualizing female religious agency: Contours of a 'Post-secular' conjuncture. *Theory, Culture and Society.* 25(6):51–68.

Butter, Ewoud and Roemer van Oordt. 2017. *Zuilen in de Polder?* Den Haag: Ministerie van Sociale Zaken en Werkgelegenheid.

Capelle, M. C. 1979. *Hij is als u zelf. Achtergrondinformatie over de wereld van moslimwerknemers en hun kinderen.* Kampen: Kok.

Chemla, Karine, and Evelyn Fox Keller, Eds. 2017. *Cultures without culturalism. The making of scientific knowledge.* Durham: Duke University Press.

Custers, Marcel. 1987. Moslims in Nederland: nieuwkomers in een gevestigde maatschappij. In *Islam in Nederland. Islam op School,* Ed. K. Wagtendonk, 13–31. Muiderberg: Coutinho.

Dassetto, Felice and Nonneman, Gerd. 1996. Islam in Belgium and the Netherlands: toward a typology of transplanted islam. In *Muslim communities in the New Europe London,* Eds. G. Nonneman, T. Niblock, and B. Szajkowski, 187–2018. Reading: Ithaca Press.

De Graaf, Hein. 1983. *Functies eigen organisaties buitenlanders.* Den Haag: NIMAWO.

De Graaf, Hein. 1985. *Plaatselijke organisaties van Turken en Marokkanen.* Den Haag: NIMAWO.

De., Koning, and Martijn and Thijl Sunier. 2021. Page after page I thought, that's the way it is': Academic Knowledge and the Making of the 'Islam Debate' in the Netherlands. *Journal of Muslims in Europe.* 10(1):85–112.

Dessing, Nathal, Jorgen Nielsen, Nadia Jeldtoft, and Linda Woodhead, Eds. 2016. *Everyday lived Islam in Europe.* London: Routledge.

Driessen, Geert. 2021. Islamic primary schools in The Netherlands: The founding, the debate, and the outcomes. *Nazhruna: Jurnal Pendidikan Islam* 4(1):18–31.

Etzioni, Amitai. 1968. *The active society.* New York: The Free Press.

Fadil, Nadia. 2019. The anthropology of Islam in Europe: A double epistemological impasse. *Annual Review of Anthropology* 48:117–132.

Grillo, Ralph. 2004. Islam and transnationalism. *Journal of Ethnic and Migration Studies* 30(5):861–878.

Hammer, Juliane, and Riem Spielhaus. 2013. Muslim women and the challenge of authority. *The Muslim World.* 103(3):287–431.

Hampsink, Rene and Judith Roosblad. 1992. *Nederland en de islam. Steunverlening aan islamitische gebedsruimten. Een rechtssociologisch onderzoek.* Nijmegen: Katholieke Universiteit Nijmegen.

Joemman, M.A.K., and S.L.G. Lokhorst. 1977. *Onderzoek naar het godsdienstig gedrag van in Utrecht wonende Marokkaanse en Turkse gastarbeiders (Research about the Religious Behaviour of Moroccan and Turkish Guestworkers in Utrecht).* Utrecht: NCB.

Jouili, Jeanette, and Schirin Amir-Moazami. 2006. Knowledge, empowerment and religious authority among pious Muslim women in France and Germany. *Muslim World.* 96:617–642.

Jouili, Jeanette, and Schirin Amir-Moazami. 2008. Knowledge, empowerment and religious authority among pious Muslim women in France and Germany. In *Islamic Feminism: Current Perspectives,* Ed. A. Kynsilehto, 57–90. Tampere: Peace Research Institute.

Koopmans, Ruud, and Paul Statham. 2003. How national citizenship shapes transnationalism: A comparative analysis of migrant claims-making in Germany, Great Britain, and the Netherlands. In *Toward Assimilation and Citizenship. Immigrants in Liberal Nation-States*, Eds. Joppke, Christian and Ewa Morowska, 195–238. New York: Palgrave Macmillan.

Landman, Nico. 1992. *Van mat tot minaret; de institutionalisering van de islam in Nederland.* Amsterdam: VU-Uitgeverij.

Lentin, Alana. 2014. Post-race, post politics: The paradoxical rise of culture after multiculturalism. *Ethnic and Racial Studies.* 37(8):1268–1285.

Lentin, Alana, and Gavan Titley. 2012. The crisis of 'multiculturalism' in Europe: Mediated minarets, intolerable subjects. *European Journal of Cultural Studies.* 15(2):123–138.

Lewis, Bernard, and Dominique Schnapper, Eds. 1994. *Muslims in Europe.* London: Pinter Publishers.

Mahmood, Sabah. 2016. *Religious difference in a secular Age. A minority report.* Princeton: Princeton University Press.

Moors, Annelies. 2009. 'Islamic fashion' in Europe: Religious conviction, aesthetic style, and creative consumption. *Encounters* 1(1):175–201.

Merry, Michael, and Geert Driessen. 2016. On the right track? Islamic schools in the Netherlands after an era of turmoil. *Race Ethnicity and Education.* 19(4):856–879.

Müller, Dominik. 2018. Bureaucratic Islam compared: Classificatory power and State-ified religious meaning-making in Brunei and Singapore. *Journal of Law and Religion.* 33(2):212–247.

Nell, Liza, and Jan Rath, Eds. 2010. *Ethnic Amsterdam.* Amsterdam: AUP.

Neijenhuis, Karin. 2008. *Sjiiten in Nederland (master thesis).* Utrecht: University of Utrecht.

Penninx, Rinus. 1988. *Minderheidsvorming en Emancipatie.* Alphen a/d Rijn: Samsom.

Poorthuis, Marcel, and Theo Salemink. 2011. *Van Harem tot Fitna: Beeldvorming over de islam in Nederland 1848–2010.* (From Harem to Fitna: Representation of Islam in the Netherlands 1848–2010). Nijmegen: Valkenhof Pers.

Rath, Jan, and Thijl Sunier. 1994. Angst voor de islam in Nederland? In *Kritiek: Jaarboek voor socialistische discussie en analyse 93–94*, Eds. W. Bot, M. van der Linden, and R. Went, 53–63. Utrecht: Stichting Toestanden.

Rath, Jan, Rinus Penninx, Kees Groenendijk, and Astrid Meyer. 2001. *Western Europe and its Islam.* Leiden: Brill.

Ryad, Amr. 2013. Te gast in Den Haag – discussies moskeebouw in Nederland vóór de Tweede Wereldoorlog *Tijdschrift voor Religie. Recht En Beleid.* 4(2):59–78.

Spielhaus, Riem. 2010. Media making Muslims: The construction of a Muslim community in Germany through media debate. *Contemporary Islam* 4(1):11–27.

Statham, Paul, Ruud Koopmans, Marco Giugni, and Florence Passy. 2005. Resilient or adaptable Islam? Multiculturalism, religion, and migrants' claims-making for group demands in Britain, the Netherlands and France. *Ethnicities* 5(4):427–459.

Szumigalska, Agnieszka. 2015. *Annotated legal documents on Islam in Europe: The Netherlands.* Leiden: Brill.

Sunier, Thijl. 1996. *Islam in Beweging. Turkse Jongeren en islamitische Organisaties.* Amsterdam: Het Spinhuis.

Sunier, Thijl. 2004. Naar een nieuwe schoolstrijd? *BMGN—Low Countries Historical Review.* 119(4):552–576.

3 Islam in the Netherlands: Denominational Pillar or 'Fifth Column'? 57

Sunier, Thijl, and Rob van Ginkel. 2006. At your Service! In *Reflections on the rise of neo-nationalism in the Netherlands In neo-nationalism in Europe and beyond*, Ed. A. Gingrich and M. Banks, 107–125. Oxford: Berghahn.

Sunier, Thijl. 2010. Assimilation by conviction or by coercion? Integration policies in the Netherlands. In *European Multiculturalism Revisited*, Ed. A. Silj, A., 214–235. London: Zed Press.

Sunier, Thijl. 2020. The religious legacy: Dutch nationalism redefined. In *Religion and Neo-Nationalism in Europe*, Eds. T. Meireis, M. Pally, and F. Hoehne, 163–177. Baden-Baden: Nomos Publ.

Sunier, Thijl. 2014. Domesticating Islam: Exploring academic knowledge production on Islam and Muslims in European societies *Ethnic and Racial Studies*. 37(6):1138–1155.

Sunier, Thijl. 2021. Islam and Muslims in the Netherlands. *Encyclopaedia of Islam, THREE*, Eds. K. Fleet, G. Krämer, D. Matringe, J. Nawas, and E. Rowson. Leiden: Brill.

Sunier, Thijl. 2022. *The Janus-face of bureaucratic incorporation of Islam in Europe. Tales from the field* (valedictory lecture). Amsterdam: Vrije Universiteit.

Sunier, Thijl, Nico Landman, Heleen van der Linden, Nazli Bilgili, and Alper Bilgili. 2011. *Diyanet. The Turkish directorate for religious affairs in a changing environment*. Amsterdam: VUA/ Utrecht University.

Sunier, Thijl, and Nico Landman. 2015. *Transnational Turkish Islam. Shifting geographies of religious activism and community building in Turkey and Europe*. Basingstoke: Palgrave Macmillan.

SCP (Sociaal en Cultureel Planbureau). 2012. *Dichter bij elkaar? De sociaal-culturele positie van niet-westerse migranten in Nederland*. Den Haag: SCP.

Silverstein, Paul. 2005. Immigrant racialization and the new savage slot: Race, migration, and immigration in the New Europe. *Annual Review of Anthropology*. 34:363–384.

Schinkel, Willem. 2017. *Imagined societies. A critique of immigrant integration in Western Europe*. Cambridge: Cambridge University Press.

Schinkel, Willem, and Friso Van Houdt. 2010. The double helix of cultural assimilationism and neo-liberalism: Citizenship in contemporary governmentality. *The British Journal of Sociology*. 61(4):696–715.

Stuurman, Siep. 1983. *Verzuiling, kapitalisme en patriarchaat: Aspecten van de ontwikkeling van de moderne staat in Nederland*. Nijmegen: SUN.

Theunis, Sjef. 1979. *Ze zien liever mijn handen dan mijn gezicht: Buitenlandse Arbeiders in ons Land* (They Prefer to See My Hands Rather Than My Face. Foreign Workers in our Country). Baarn: Wereldvenster.

Houdt, Van, and Friso, and Willem Schinkel. 2014. Crime, citizenship and community: Neoliberal communitarian images of governmentality. *The Sociological Review*. 62(1):47–67.

Nieuwkerk, Van, and Karin, Eds. 2006. *Women embracing Islam. Gender and conversion in the West*. Austin: University of Texas.

Sasse, Van, and Paul van Ysselt. 2013. Financiële verhoudingen tussen overheid, kerk en religieuze organisaties *Tijdschrift voor Religie. Recht En Beleid*. 4(1):65–86.

Van den Berg-Eldering, Lotty. Ed. 1986. *Van gastarbeider tot immigrant. Marokkanen en Turken in Nederland. 1965–1985*, 15–47. Alphen aan den Rijn: Samson.

Vertovec, Steven, and Susanne Wessendorf. 2010. *The Multiculturalism Backlash: European Discourses, Policies and Practices*. London: Routledge.

Vroon-Najem, Vanessa. 2014. *Sisters in Islam. Women's Conversion and the Politics of Belonging: A Dutch Case Study.* (dissertation). Amsterdam: University of Amsterdam.

Thijl Sunier Thijl Sunier is professor (em.) of cultural anthropology of religion at the Vrije Universiteit Amsterdam, chair 'Islam in European Societies'. He has conducted research on Islamic authority, religious critique, religious organisation, leadership, and knowledge production in Europe, and on Islam and digitisation. His latest academic publication: Making Islam Work. Islamic Authority among Muslims in Western Europe (2023 Leiden: Brill). He is chairman of the board of the Netherlands Inter-University School for Islamic Studies (NISIS) and executive editor of the Journal of Muslims in Europe (JOME/Brill).

The Academization of Islam in Germany—Structural Integration and Competitive Struggles Over Interpretive Authority in the Religious Field

4

Rauf Ceylan

Abstract

Since the beginning of labor migration from Islamic countries, integration policy in Germany has pursued a paradoxical program. On the one hand, migrants were supposed to return to their home countries after a temporary stay without incurring social follow-up costs. On the other hand, it was assumed that the integration of Muslim migrants willing to stay will take place automatically, without targeted concepts. Both strategies have failed. Another peculiarity of this integration policy was that the importance of religion for the integration process was completely ignored. Due to global and national developments, a so-called delayed integration policy began in Germany in the 2000s. Muslims should participate equally in all dimensions (economic, cultural, social, educational). This also includes the policy goal of creating a German-Muslim scientific community to promote an enlightened theology in the European context. Against this background, the academization of Islam has been promoted by the state at a rapid pace, making Germany a pioneer compared to other Western societies with a Muslim minority. This paper will discuss the origins, development, and challenges of the structural integration of Islam. The impact

---

R. Ceylan (✉)
University of Osnabrück, Osnabrück, Deutschland
e-mail: rauf.ceylan@uniosnabrueck.de

© The Author(s), under exclusive license to Springer Fachmedien Wiesbaden GmbH, part of Springer Nature 2024
R. Ceylan and M. Mücke (eds.), *Muslims in Europe*, Islam in der Gesellschaft,
https://doi.org/10.1007/978-3-658-43044-3_4

of this academization on the dynamics in the Islamic religious field will also be considered.

Keywords

Islamic Theology • Muslims in Germany • Muslims and Integration • Imams • Islamic Organisations • German Islam Conference

1 Introduction

Since the beginning of labor migration from Islamic countries, integration policy in Germany has pursued a paradoxical program. On the one hand, migrants were supposed to return to their home countries after a temporary stay without incurring social follow-up costs. On the other hand, it was assumed that the integration of Muslim migrants willing to stay will take place automatically, without targeted concepts. Both strategies have failed. Another peculiarity of this integration policy was that the importance of religion for the integration process was completely ignored. Due to global and national developments, a so-called delayed integration policy began in Germany in the 2000s. Muslims should participate equally in all dimensions (economic, cultural, social, educational). This also includes the policy goal of creating a German-Muslim scientific community to promote an enlightened theology in the European context. Against this background, the academization of Islam has been promoted by the state at a rapid pace, making Germany a pioneer compared to other Western societies with a Muslim minority. This paper will discuss the origins, development, and challenges of the structural integration of Islam. The impact of this academization on the dynamics in the Islamic religious field will also be considered.

2 The German Islam Conference—A Step Towards the Recognition and Structural Integration of Islam

Since the immigration of the so-called "guest workers" from Islamic countries, politics and the public have been concerned with the integration of this population group. At the latest since the 1970s, when it became increasingly apparent that migrants would settle permanently, integration has been a political issue right up

4 The Academization of Islam in Germany—Structural ...

to the present day. All dimensions of integration, such as the German language, naturalization, job opportunities, the housing market, security policy and health, were increasingly specified until the early 2000s, and studies regularly used these indicators to empirically measure the success of migrants' integration. Against this background, the German government presented an indicator-based study on the state of integration for the first time in 2009 (Institut für Sozialforschung und Gesellschaftspolitik/Wissenschaftszentrum Berlin für Sozialforschung 2009). To this day, the problem with the quantification of integration includes not only the controversial definition of terminology and its often one-sided demand for integration from migrants without raising the readiness of the majority society to integrate. But likewise, the functional role of religion for migrants played only a minor role in both public debates as well as in empirical studies. Yet numerous mosque congregations emerged in the 1970s with the reunification of families, and they have developed into important institutions as sociocultural centers (Ceylan 2006). At a higher level of aggregation, numerous Islamic umbrella organizations with different political and denominational orientations were founded, which not only accept the local mosque congregations as members, but also claim to act as religious and political representatives of the interests of Muslims in Germany. Some of the Muslim children and young people have also been enjoying a religious education in the mosque communities for a good fifty years, whose numbers have now grown to over 2300. This has ensured for over fifty years that new members are socialized for the congregations. Despite this relevant development in the establishment of a Muslim infrastructure, German integration policy has hardly taken the dimension of religion into account for decades.

It was not until September 11, 2001, that the integration debate was broadened. Although the debate was primarily focused on security policy aspects, there were nevertheless increasing calls to promote a "German Islam". If one evaluates the debates at the beginning of the decade, the following aspects stand out in particular:

- The problematization of the import of Imams from Islamic-influenced countries, especially Turkey, who work in the mosques. The following points have been criticized to date: the Imams are not German-speaking, do not know German culture and are mediators of a traditional theology that is incompatible with the reality of life for Muslim youth in Germany.

- the question of introducing Islamic religious instruction in state schools, equivalent to Christian religious instruction. This is intended to provide Muslim students with protected spaces at school for critical reflection on Islam and to educate them to religious maturity.

- the question of an enlightened Islam offered at German universities. The background to this postulate is the demographic increase of Muslims, the expansion of mosque congregations and the influence on Muslims of foreign theologians and organizations. In addition, it is intended to prevent young Muslims from Germany from going abroad to study Islam (Egypt, Saudi Arabia, etc.).

- the question of the legal equality of the Islamic umbrella organizations with the Christian churches. This is intended to bring the numerous Islamic organizations together, establish church-analogous structures and serve as a central point of contact for the state.

The last point remains a controversial political and legal issue to this day. Without going into detail, the dispute can be summarized as follows: the state lacks a central point of contact, as there are nearly nine large Islamic umbrella organizations with different ethnic, political, and religious orientations. In addition, many smaller umbrella organizations have been founded in the meantime. Furthermore, the close political ties of these organizations to their country of origin are sometimes problematized by German politics. A popular example is the Turkish-Islamic umbrella organization DITIB, which has close structural and personnel ties to the state religious authority in Turkey. Every year, the Turkish state sends Imams—who are officials of the religious authority—to Turkish-German mosques on a rotational basis (Yasar 2012). Under the AKP government of Recep Tayyip Erdogan, the political instrumentalization of the umbrella organization DITIB in Germany has also increased. One example is the organization of election campaigns inside DITIB mosques for the parliamentary elections in Turkey planned for May 2023.

So, while the issue of legal equality for the Islamic umbrella organizations has still not been resolved, great successes have been achieved in the other issues listed above. The main reason for these successes can be traced back to the German Islam Conference (DIK), which was initiated for the first time in 2006 by the then Federal Minister of the Interior, Wolfgang Schäuble. State representatives, members of the Islamic umbrella organizations (DITIB, Central Council of Muslims, Islamic Council for the Federal Republic of Germany, Association of Islamic Cultural Centers as well as the Alevi Community in Germany) and Muslim public figures as representatives of non-organized Muslims were invited. This was the first time that discussions were held with the Islamic umbrella organizations at the level of top German politics, which until then had either been completely ignored or judged in the public discourse as an obstacle to integration for Muslims in Germany (Ceylan 2017). With their participation in this conference, the Muslim umbrella organizations have experienced a political upgrading and recognition. They have been recognized in their role as Muslim interest groups as well as in their role as bridges. At the same time, with the participation of non-organized Muslims, the conference has demonstrated the plurality and the interpretive struggles on Islamic issues among Muslims in Germany. Thematically, the conference focused on Islamic theology in Germany at state universities, Imam training, pastoral care, Muslim welfare, and anti-Muslim hostility. In addition, the conference commissioned several empirical studies on Islam and Muslims in Germany. As a result of these studies, important research gaps on data and facts about Muslims have been filled (Deutsche Islam Konferenz 2023).

Already at the beginning of the conference, the question of the participants, both among the Muslim participants and in the public, was a controversy. On the part of non-organized Muslims, criticism was heard that the federal government was granting a platform to orthodox organizations and thus strengthening their influence. On the Islamic Umbrella Organization side, on the other hand, there was criticism that non-organized Muslims could not claim representation for the Muslim base. The controversy over the Muslim participants runs like a thread through to the present day and characterizes the competitive battles over interpretive sovereignty on Islam.

Overall, the DIK achieved major milestones, which not only led to the recognition of the Islamic umbrella organizations and, at the same time, non-organized Muslims as interlocutors for top-level politics, but also identified central integration issues and worked together with the participants on their solution until the present. One of the main successes of this conference is the academic implementation of Islam, which will be discussed next.

3 The Recommendations of the German Council of Science on the Establishment of Centers for Islamic Theology at German Universities.

The German Council of Science (Wissenschaftsrat) is the most important body in Germany advising policymakers on the organization and management of science and on the funding of research institutions. The body is organizationally divided into a scientific commission and an administrative commission. The scientific commission includes scientists and representatives of public life who formulate far-reaching recommendations that are usually implemented by German policymakers. Against this background, the year 2009 is historic, when this institution formulated its "Recommendations for the Further Development of Theologies and

Sciences Concerned with Religions at German Universities." Due to Germany's development into a multi-religious society, the importance of religion in everyday life and in science is pointed out. Due to the quantitative increase of Muslims in Germany, the recommendations postulate the establishment of centers for Islamic theology. These institutes, which are to be founded at two to three locations, are to pursue the following goals:

- The training of Muslim teachers for Islamic religious education in state schools.
- The training of theologians for community work in mosques.
- The qualification of young scientists for the Muslim scientific community.
- The establishment of courses of study for Muslim social work (Wissenschaftsrat 2010, p. 82).

The background for the first goal is formed by the at least 600,000 Muslim (Engelhardt et al. 2020, p. 2) students at German schools, who generally only have an opportunity for religious education in their families and at weekends or school vacations in mosques. Since the 1970s, mosques and their staff have offered Islamic instruction with the goal of long-term community bonding (Ceylan 2014). While Christian religious education is also offered for Christian students in state schools, there were no alternatives for Muslim students. Thus, due to the equal rights requirement, the training of Muslim religious education teachers should compensate for this deficit in schools. At the same time, one would like to build up a counterweight to mosque instruction so that Muslim children and young people can experience protected spaces for reflecting on their own religion. The basis for the second goal is the many Imams and preachers (over 2000) who are often recruited from abroad to the German mosques. At DITIB, the professionals are always hired on a rotation basis in the local mosques. That means they work in the community for about four years and then must return to Turkey. For the communities, this rotation means that an Imam can hardly integrate into society and the community. The first year is used for their own orientation. The last year is used to prepare for their return to Turkey. As a net time, the Imam is left with two productive years in the community. Further problems arise from the fact that these theologians do not know the German language. This means that conflicts are bound to arise in communication with the younger members of the congregation, who do not have a good command of the Turkish language (Ceylan 2021).

The discussion about a European-influenced, enlightened theology forms the background for the third goal. In the medium term, a German-Muslim scientific community is to be formed through the qualification of doctoral and post-doctoral students, who are to contribute to an enlightened theology.

Finally, the offer of a Muslim social work is recommended. The background of this recommendation is the increasing social challenges for institutions such as hospitals, old people's homes, or prisons. In recent years, different welfare organizations have tried to respond to religious diversity by opening up interculturally (Caspar-Seeger 2022). In the context of Muslims, responding to the multi-religious society means an urgent institutional opening to Muslim clients. Second, hiring from the Muslim staff. However, this attempt is only a small solution. For neither are the institutions sufficiently conceptually prepared (e.g., for prison chaplaincy) for these opening processes, nor are the hired Muslim professionals qualified for their role as social workers or chaplains. The postulation of Muslim social work as a course of study at the Institutes of Islamic Theology should solve this problem.

4 Foundation of the Institutes for Islamic Theology and Heterogeneous Profiling.

- The recommendations of the German Council of Science and Humanities were promptly implemented by German policymakers as of 2011. The first universities to establish an Institute for Islamic Theology were Tübingen and, as cooperating universities, Frankfurt-Gießen, Erlangen-Nuremberg and Münster-Osnabrück. These institutions were funded by the Federal Ministry of Education and Research. Central challenges for all locations were the following aspects:

- Recruitment of professors
- Recruitment of scientific staff
- Design of curricula
- Cooperation structures with the Islamic umbrella organizations
- International cooperation with institutes from Islamic countries
- Confidence-building measures with the Muslim base to achieve acceptance of Islamic theology.
- Public relations work, primarily in the direction of politics and the media, to convince the public of the "Islamic Theology" project.

- Profile building: Due to the numerous locations and different currents, the institutes were challenged to develop corresponding theological profiles.[1]

In the following, the development of the locations will be briefly outlined based on the first founded institutions. The focus is primarily on the universities of Münster, Osnabrück and Frankfurt, since they are more visible in public discourse and, moreover, their theological profiles reflect the different research directions for current developments in Germany:

- University of Münster: The University of Münster had already appointed the lawyer and Islamic scholar Sven Kalisch as professor in 2004. However, he had to resign his professorship in 2010 and switch to philology. This was preceded by a controversy, according to which Sven Kalisch doubted the historicity of the Prophet Muhammad. The criticism is based on the early Islamic origin story, which for him is a pure construction (Kalisch 2021). Due to protests from Muslim organizations, Kalisch's teaching authority for Islamic theology was withdrawn. He was succeeded by sociologist Mouhanad Khorchide, who holds the professorship to this day and pushed for the establishment of the Institute of Islamic Theology with staff beginning in 2012. Relatively early controversies in Münster have repeated themselves after Khorchide published his popular book "Islam is Mercy" (Khorchide 2012), which is conceptually strongly oriented to Christian theology. Within the book he calls for a humanistic Islam, rejecting a punitive God and thus all punishments in the afterlife. The premise of a humanistic religion had been theologically corrupted at the latest with the Ummayads (from 661 AD), so that Islam had developed into a religion of submission (Khorchide 2020). Although there were protests again, he was able to retain his teaching authority due to his commitment to the premises (God, revelation, Prophet Muhammad). In the meantime, four more professorships have been appointed, but the profile of the institute in Münster is publicly shaped by Khrochide. In this way, he provides theological legitimacy above all to liberal, non-scientific currents.

- University of Osnabrück: In Osnabrück, the foundation for the establishment of an Islamic studies program was already laid in the early 2000s by the Professor of Intercultural Education, Peter Graf. The primary goal was not to establish an entire institute for Islamic theology, but to implement a course of study in Islamic religious education (Graf and Gibowski 2007). Against this background, Professor Bülent Ucar was appointed in 2007 for Islamic Religious Education

---

[1] This book provides an exemplary overview of the history of and challenges to the founding of the institutes: Martina Blasberg-Kuhnke/Ceylan, Rauf/Bülent Ucar (eds.).2019. Institut für Islamische Theologie. Entwicklung, Zwischenstand und Perspektiven, Peter Lang Verlag: Frankfurt a.M.

and in 2009 the author of this paper, Rauf Ceylan, as Professor for Contemporary Islamic Studies. The theological profile was shaped by Ucar, while Ceylan represented the sociology of religion in research and teaching. Both then eventually founded and expanded the institute in Osnabrück from the funding by the Federal Ministry of Education and Research in 2012. From the beginning, the goal was "innovation in tradition." No great leaps in theology by linking up with Christian or Jewish theology in Germany. But rather a successive development, through the reappraisal and reflection of the Islamic tradition as well as in exchange with non-Muslim theologies, to develop Osnabrück theology on a solid foundation. At the same time, this goal is intended to involve both the Islamic umbrella organizations and the Muslim base in Germany in this process and to take them along. Because of, among other things, this scientific path, the cooperation with the institute in Münster did not work out, so that after the first four years of funding by the Federal Ministry of Research, the cooperation was discontinued.

- The University of Frankfurt also has a longer history of laying the foundations for an Institute of Islamic Theology. As early as 2005, the University of Frankfurt signed a contract with the Turkish religious authority DIYANET for an endowed professorship and an endowed visiting professorship. The later appointment of the Koran exegete Ömer Özsoy, who introduced the historical-critical method of the so-called "Ankara School" as a research program, became formative for the profile. Unlike Khorchide, who interprets historical power politics as centuries of attempts to conceal the true message of Islam (humanism, mercy), Özsoy is concerned with the genesis and exegesis of the Koran and the question of the extent to which hermeneutics must be used to understand this text today. From the state funding of the institute in 2011 by the Federal Ministry of Education and Research, it was possible to expand Islamic theology in cooperation with the University of Giessen on the basis of six years of experience. In the meantime, four professors have been hired there.

All in all, 38 professors research and teach at the ten institutes of Islamic theology. In addition, individual professorships have been appointed at different locations and universities, so that the number of Muslim professors has risen to over 40. Thus, within ten years, a Muslim scholarly community has emerged with professors, research assistants, doctoral students, and postdoctoral fellows working on basic theological research in the German context. Numerous publications have appeared on this subject. In parallel, the network "German Society for Islamic Theological Studies" (DEGITS) has been founded, which forms a cooperation platform of all professors of Islamic theology (DEGITS 2023). This ensures a critical exchange between scholars. In addition, about 2400 Muslim students study Islamic theology or religious education (Dreier and Wagner 2020, p. 19). Parallel to theology, other structures have been implemented for Muslim academics that function as "elite factories". One of these is the Academy for Islam in Science and Society. The goal of this academy is not only to expand the interdisciplinary networking of Islamic theology in Germany, but also to fund research projects. Finally, another milestone has been reached with the founding of the Avicenna Studienwerk. This institution supports highly talented Muslim students as well as doctoral students in all disciplines. Admittedly, it does not primarily support students of Islamic theology. However, the promotion of highly talented Muslims, who in the future will occupy key positions in science, society, business, and politics, will have an impact on the discourse on Islam in the medium term. In particular, the previous perception that Muslims are primarily associated with the working class is undergoing a transformation.

5   Imams—Made in Germany

The structural integration of Islam outlined above has led to Germany taking a pioneering role throughout Europe in promoting a Muslim academic community. In particular, the expansion of Islamic theology has contributed significantly to the fact that the discourse on Islam is co-determined and co-shaped by Muslim theologians. However, this progress does not apply to the job market since the institutes of Islamic theology have not automatically developed career prospects for students. Only for students with the goal of working as teachers of Islamic religious education at state schools does the job market offer good opportunities. Islamic religious instruction is offered at about 900 schools. About 60,000 Muslim students participate in these classes. The total number of Muslim students is estimated to be at least 600000 (Ulfat et al. 2020; Mediendienst Integration 2020). This means that just 10% of the student body participates in religious education classes. These low participation numbers are due to two reasons: First, schools must be willing to offer religious instruction, and second, more teachers must be trained. This goal must be achieved in the next few years.

For Muslim theologians, on the other hand, who want to work in mosque communities, for example, as Imams, there are no job opportunities. This deplorable situation is due to various causes, which are listed as follows:

- First, there was a lack of training positions for Imams. This is because the Catholic and Protestant churches in Germany offer theology graduates two years of training so that they can be introduced to the practice of congregational work. This training is financed exclusively by the churches. Likewise, the content is

4 The Academization of Islam in Germany—Structural …

determined by the churches, so the state cannot intervene. This second phase of training was not considered at all when Islamic theology was founded. As a result, many students who completed their studies—with the goal of becoming Imams—did not have the opportunity to work in mosque communities.

- Second, the priests and pastors are hired and financed by churches after their training. Churches receive annual taxes from their members. In 2022, the tax revenue for the Catholic and Protestant was 13 billion euros (Hentze 2023, p. 1). The mosques are not familiar with the system of a mosque tax. Only small contributions are collected monthly from members in local congregations to keep the house of worship functioning. This money is often used to finance Imams from abroad. As a result, the salaries for these foreign Imams are often below average. Only the Turkish Imams of DITIB, who are financed by the Turkish state, receive adequate salaries.

- Third, women can also be ordained as pastors in the Protestant Church. In the more than 2300 mosque congregations, the hiring of women as Imams would be inconceivable. The predominantly Sunni and Shiite congregations belonged to Islamic orthodoxy. Although more women than men (60% to forty percent ratio) now study Islamic theology, there are currently no conceivable prospects for female graduates as Imams in the mosques.

- Fourth, in the Protestant church, homosexual men and women can also assume the office of pastor. For homosexual Muslims, the job market is absolutely limited. There are no job prospects in the majority orthodox Islamic communities.

- Fifth, most Christians are members of the Catholic or Protestant churches. This makes these two churches, with their more than 50,000 companies, the largest individual employers in Germany (WiWo 2011). The Islamic umbrella organizations cannot offer a corresponding range of jobs. Most Muslims work on a voluntary basis in the umbrella organizations or in local mosque congregations. A broadening of the professional perspective could only occur if Christian and secular welfare organizations were to open themselves interreligiously to Muslim workers. To be able to work in a church institution, potential applicants must have a confessional membership accordingly. However, exceptions are made when the employment of Muslims seems appropriate. This applies, for example, to Christian kindergartens that have a high number of Muslim children. This also applies to state institutions such as prisons or hospitals, which would hire Muslim chaplains for their Muslim clientele. As I said, these are exceptions rather than blanket regulations.

To address the structural deficit in Muslim social work, the University of Osnabrück has introduced a social work degree program at the Institute of Islamic Theology and appointed a professor for this purpose. To compensate for the deficit in the training of Imams and thus provide students with a professional perspective in mosque communities, the Institute for Islamic Theology at the University of Osnabrück has also started its training courses in the newly founded *Islamkolleg* in 2020 with the support of the Federal Ministry of the Interior as well as the Ministry of Science in Lower Saxony. This is a non-university, independent institution initiated by the members of the Institute of Islamic Theology. Two educational goals are being pursued: On the one hand, men and women are to be qualified for their community work. On the other hand, chaplains are being trained who, once qualified, can work in all areas of pastoral care (military, hospital, prisons, etc.) (Islamkolleg 2023).

Among the Islamic umbrella organizations, the founding of the *Islamkolleg* was met with a divided response. The *Islamkolleg* in Osnabrück was supported and co-founded by smaller organizations such as the Alliance of Malikite Communities in Germany (BMG), the Muslims in Lower Saxony (MiN), the Islamic Community of Bosniaks in Germany (IGBD) and the Central Council of Moroccans in Germany (ZRMD). Among the large umbrella organizations, only the Central Council of Muslims in Germany (ZMD) participates. All other large umbrella organizations, such as DITIB or Islamrat Deutschland, are critical of this initiative. They see state support as an encroachment on the religious community's right to self-determination and fear that a "state Islam" will be created. For this reason, these oppositional Islamic umbrella organizations have meanwhile founded their own training centers for imams to prepare young academics from their own communities for the profession in the mosque communities.

6   Conclusion

Based on the historical sketch of the structural integration of Islam and Muslims, it can be stated that a scholarly community, with the goal of creating a critically reflected theology in the European context, was founded at a rapid pace. It also became clear from the remarks that this development has not solved all problems. These include career prospects in Muslim communities for the hundreds of theologians who have already graduated in recent years. This also applies to the students currently enrolled in these institutes. In particular, the main goal of the policy, which was, after all, to stop the import of Imams from abroad with these theological institutes, has not been realized. It took almost eight years before a practical training center was even initiated as preparation for service in the mosques. Under religious law, this second phase of training is normally financed independently by the Christian religious communities. Due

4 The Academization of Islam in Germany—Structural ...

to their limited resources, the German state has funded a training position for those Islamic organizations that wish to train Imams in Germany. In response, the other major Islamic umbrella organizations, which do not wish to share their area of competence with the state, have created their own institutions to train Imams and chaplains. For these organizations, the interference of the German state represents a direct intervention in the Islamic religious field. In any case, these oppositional, orthodox Islamic umbrella organizations feel their interpretive sovereignty threatened by competition with the new Muslim associations and personalities who call themselves "liberal." Both orthodox and liberal currents use different means of distinction to distinguish themselves theologically. Orthodox Islam, which claims a religious monopoly, uses different means of distinction to exclude the liberal actors. Their teachings are labeled as "heresy." This is typical of "mainline churches," which label all groups outside church doctrine as "sects." In turn, the liberal groups likewise use means of distinction to attack the associations' position of power and portray them as backward. The representatives of this liberal current call for overcoming the dogmatic orientation of the Orthodox communities. This includes issues such as homosexuality, criticism of patriarchy, women as Imams and historical-critical interpretation of the Koran. At the same time, new academic actors are emerging in the religious field in the form of institutes for Islamic theology. Through the scientific-critical reflection of traditional sources as well as Imam training at the University of Osnabrück, new mechanisms of reproduction are being created, giving rise to new religious authorities for schools and mosques. As a result of this development, the religious field is very dynamic and subject to constant transformation processes. In sum, it can be said that the pluralization of Muslims in Germany has gained contours through the academization of Islam. As a result, not only controversial theological issues are being made public, but also the question of the political representation of Muslims is being controversially communicated. In this context, the power position of the orthodox organizations, which have been able to expand their leading role in the religious field since the 1970s, is being called into question. They are being pushed into a defensive position.

References

Caspar-Seeger, Ulrike. 2022. *Interkulturelle Öffnung als Herausforderung. Religiös-weltanschauliche Vielfalt bei Mitarbeitenden in der konfessionellen Wohlfahrt.* Stuttgart: Kohlhammer.

Blasberg-Kuhnke, Martina, Ceylan, Rauf, and Ucar, Bülent, Eds. 2019. *Institut für Islamische Theologie. Entwicklung, Zwischenstand und Perspektiven*. Peter Lang: Frankfurt a. M.

Ceylan, Rauf. 2006. Ethnische Kolonien. Entstehung, Entwicklung und Wandel am Beispiel türkischer Moscheen und Cafès. Wiesbaden: VS Verlag.

Ceylan, Rauf. 2014. Cultural-Time Lag. Moscheekatechese und islamischer Religionsunterricht im Kontext von Säkularisierung. Wiesbaden: Springer VS.

Ceylan, Rauf. 2017. Islamkonferenz. In *Integrationsland Deutschland. Begriffe—Fakten—Kontroversen*, aktualisierte 2. Aufl., Hrsg. Karl-Heinz Meier, Reinhold Weber-Braun, 204–207. Stuttgart: Kohlhammer.

Ceylan, Rauf. 2021. *Imame in Deutschland*. Freiburg: Herder Verlag.

Deutsche Gesellschaft für Islamisch-Theologische Studien (DEGITS). 2023. Islamische Theologie in Deutschland. https://www.degits.de/islamische-theologie.

Deutsche Islam Konferenz. Die DIK bisher. https://www.deutsche-islam-konferenz.de/DE/DIK/Die-DIK-bisher/die-dik-bisher_node.html.

Dreier, Lena, Constantin Wagner. 2020. *Wer studiert islamische Theologie?* Frankfurt a. M.: Akademie für Islam in Wissenschaft und Gesellschaft.

Graf, Peter, Gibowski, Wolfgang G., Eds. 2007. *Islamische Religionspädagogik—Etablierung eines neuen Faches. Bildungs- und kulturpolitische Initiativen des Landes Niedersachsen*. Göttingen: V&R Unipress.

Hentze, Tobias. 2023. Kirchensteuer: Austrittswelle hinterläßt immer größere Spuren. *IW-Kurzbericht. Nr.* 26(2023):1–3.

Islamkolleg Osnabrück. 2023. Das Islamkolleg stellt sich vor. https://www.islamkolleg.de/.

Kalisch, Sven. 2021. Islamische Theologie ohne historischen Muhammad—Anmerkungen zu den Herausforderungen der historisch-kritischen Methode für das islamische Denken. *Impramatur* 54:1. http://imprimatur-trier.de/2021/Imprimatur-2021-01_21.pdf.

Khorchide, Mouhanad. *Islam ist Barmherzigkeit. Grundzüge einer modernen Religion*. Freiburg: Herder.

Khorchide, Mouhanad. *Gottes falsche Anwälte. Der Verrat am Islam*. Freiburg: Herder.

Integration, Mediendienst. 2020. *Religion an Schulen: Islamischer Religionsunterricht in Deutschland*. Berlin: Mediendienst Integration.

Institut für Sozialforschung und Gesellschaftspolitik/Wissenschaftszentrum Berlin für Sozialforschung. 2009. *Integration in Deutschland. Erster Indikatorenbericht: Erprobung des Indikatorensets und Bericht zum bundesweiten Integrationsmonitoring*. Berlin: Beauftragte der Bundesregierung für Migration, Flüchtlinge und Integration.

Engelhardt, Felix, Ulfat, Fahimah, Yavuz, Esra. 2020. *Islamischer Religionsunterricht in Deutschland*. Frankfurt a. M.: Qualität, Rahmenbedingungen und Umsetzung. Akademie für Islam in Wissenschaft und Gesellschaft.

Wirtschaftswoche. 2011. Großkonzern Kirche. https://www.wiwo.de/unternehmen/dienstlei ster/finanz-riese-grosskonzern-kirche/5220262.html.

Wissenschaftsrat. 2010. Empfehlungen zur Weiterentwicklung von Theologien und religionsbezogenen Wissenschaften an deutschen Hochschulen. https://www.wissenschaft srat.de/download/archiv/9678-10.pdf?__blob=publicationFile&v=2.

Yasar, Aysun. 2012. *Die DITIB zwischen der Türkei und Deutschland. Untersuchungen zur Türkisch-Islamischen Union der Anstalt für Religion e. V.* Würzburg: Ergon.

Rauf Ceylan has been Professor at the University of Osnabrück/Institute of Islamic Theology (IIT) in Germany since 2009. He was a Visiting Professor in 2018 at the University of Zürich. His research focuses on the Sociology of Migration and Religion based on the study of the Turkish community in the Diaspora. He is a member of the Institute for Migration Research and Intercultural Studies (IMIS) and the Council for Migration (RfM eV).

Research on Conversion to Islam in Germany Between 1995 and 2022

5

Marvin Mücke and Sören Sponick

Abstract

In recent years, various parts of German society have become increasingly interested in the phenomenon of conversion to Islam. Despite this newfound attention, few scientific studies have addressed the phenomenon. In this literature review we bring together various strands of research on conversion to Islam in Germany in the period from 1995 to 2022, evaluate existing publications, and point out possible avenues for future research. We discuss the literature based on six topics: 1. methods and methodology 2. the status of conversion narratives 3. the conceptualization of conversion 4. Islam as the "Other" in conversion research 5. conversion and radicalization and 6. conversion and German-Muslim identity. While we have identified Monika Wohlrab-Sahr's (1999) approach as the starting point of a research tradition, many of the reviewed publications lack mutual references. The aim of this chapter is therefore to enable stronger mutual references and thus advance research on conversion to Islam in Germany.

Keywords

Conversion to Islam · Islam in Germany · Radicalization · Conversion theory · Conversion narratives · Conversion career · Conversion research

---

M. Mücke (✉) · S. Sponick
University of Osnabrück, Osnabrück, Germany
e-mail: marvin.muecke@uni-osnabrueck.de

S. Sponick
e-mail: soeren.sponick@uni-osnabrueck.de

© The Author(s), under exclusive license to Springer Fachmedien Wiesbaden GmbH, part of Springer Nature 2024
R. Ceylan and M. Mücke (eds.), *Muslims in Europe*, Islam in der Gesellschaft,
https://doi.org/10.1007/978-3-658-43044-3_5

1 Introduction

"The convert, the unknown being". This is the title German newspaper *Tagesspiegel* used for an article about converts to Islam in 2007 (Buntrock 2007). Therein the authors stated that not much was known about those – especially youth – who decided to abandon their former religion to embrace Islam. Neither was it known how many converts lived in Germany in total, nor how many people converted per year or what made converting to Islam appealing to them. This diagnosis has not changed much to this day. Scientific research on conversion to Islam in Germany still lacks verified knowledge on Muslim converts. In quantitative publications on Muslim life in Germany converts are frequently not considered either for methodological or statistical reasons, since their number is assumed to be too small (Haug et al. 2009, p. 58). Nevertheless, converts have increasingly come to the attention of the public, politicians, security authorities and PVE actors, following the arrest of the so-called *Sauerland terror cell*[1] in 2007 and multiple departures of converts to the territory of the so-called Islamic State from 2014 onwards (BKA 2016). This chapter undertakes a review of the scientific literature on conversion to Islam in Germany between 1995 and 2022. We intend to collect research on conversion to Islam in Germany, critically assess existing publications, and identify avenues for further research. We also follow Volkhard Krechs' (1995) review of the literature on conversion between 1983 and 1993. Due to the focus of this edited volume, we limit ourselves to scientific publications with a thematic focus on Germany and on religious conversion to Islam.[2] Research on conversion to other religions will not be considered. We also exclude journalistic publications on the subject (e.g. Filter 2008, Kaiser 2018) and autobiographies of converts such (e.g. Backer 2009, Schmitz 2016, Lau 2020).

Our contribution is structured as follows: (2.1) describes the development of methods and methodology in the field of empirical research on conversion to Islam in Germany in the past 27 years. This is followed by a discussion of five issues that we believe to emerge from the literature reviewed: (2.2) the status of conversion narratives, (2.3) the conceptualization of conversion, (2.4) the role of Islam as "the Other" in research on conversion, (2.5) the issue of conversion and

---

[1] The *Sauerland terror cell* was an Islamist terrorist group consisting of four young men, two of them converts, who were arrested by German authorities in 2007 for planning a terrorist attack on German territory. The name was given to them by German media after the central German region Sauerland where the group was arrested.

[2] Unfortunately, the current discourse on the status of conversion narratives in asylum processes cannot be addressed here, as most of them are Muslims who convert to Christianity. But see the publications by Karras (2019) and Stähler (2021).

radicalization and finally (2.6) conversion and its relevance for discussions about German and Muslim identity. We conclude with a summary where we point out possible avenues for future research.

2 The Starting Point: Research on Conversion to Islam in Germany Since 1995

The scientific study of conversions of non-Muslims to Islam in Germany does not have a long tradition. In our inquiry, the monographs by Gabriele Hofmann (1997) and Monika Wohlrab-Sahr (1999) as well as the study by Volkhard Krech and Matthias Schlegel (1998) can be seen as the beginning of a German research tradition on conversion to Islam. Wohlrab-Sahr's comparative study of "Conversion to Islam in Germany and the United States" (1999) laid the methodological foundation for nearly all subsequent research on conversion to Islam in Germany. Nina Käsehage (2016, p. 79) therefore describes Wohlrab-Sahr's study as well as Hofmann's as standard works of German conversion research on Islam.[3]

2.1 Methods and Methodology of Research on Conversion to Islam in Germany

We identified two dominant methodological approaches in empirical research on conversion to Islam in Germany between 1995 and 2022: a) a biography-theoretical approach and b) an ethnographic approach. Of all the works considered in this review, only Krech and Schlegel (1998) chose the focus-group method to analyse possible connections between conversion and religious identity. In their study, they compared religious interpretive patterns of adepts of the Neo-Sannyas movement[4] with those of members of a Sufi order. They define these patterns as "more or less fixed, socially regulated schemes" (ibid.:169) that specify how to perform one's religious identity as an authentic convert. Krech and Schlegel argue that the religious identities of members of both groups emerge from an interplay of social identity and ego identity. It is particularly in the process of communication about conversion that this religious identity can emerge (ibid.: 191). Due

---

[3] In our opinion, however, this assessment can only be made for the Wohlrab-Sahr study. Hofmann's text, on the other hand, is rarely referenced by subsequent studies.

[4] The Neo-Sannyas or Rajneesh movement is a spiritual group founded by the Indian mystic Chandra Mohan Jain in 1970.

to the dominance of the biography-theoretical and ethnographic approaches, we will discuss them in more detail in the following sections.

2.1.1 Biographical Approaches

This research strand focuses on the processes of how a convert transforms into a religious subject and the biographical functions conversion can fulfil. Questions arise concerning the temporal course of conversion, such as a) whether conversion takes place suddenly or over time, b) how radical this transformation must be for it to be considered a conversion, c) what factors underlie the change, and d) what the concrete object of change actually is (Krech 1995, p.134).

Wohlrab-Sahr's research interest refers to the "function that religious conversion fulfils within the framework of biographies" (Wohlrab-Sahr 1999, p. 20) as well as the identification of the reference problem [Bezugsproblem] of conversion by which she means the biographical problem for which conversion serves as a solution (ibid.). For this purpose, she conducted narrative interviews (Schütze 1976, 1983) with converts. For analysis she used Ulrich Oevermann's method of "objective hermeneutics" (Oevermann et al. 1979).

Since Wohlrab-Sahr's study in 1999, numerous authors have followed this methodological approach (Uhlmann 2021,[5] Käsehage 2016, Frank and Glaser 2018). The interweaving of research on processes and causes of conversion – already diagnosed by Krech in 1995 (p. 134) – became more dominant from the 2010s onwards. Questions about biographical problems receded, while conversion motives mentioned by converts themselves became more relevant (Uhlmann 2021, p. 1–2). Research in the 2010s also focussed more on the extent to which the reasons for conversion – especially of minors – can provide information about potentially anti-democratic attitudes (Uhlmann 2021, p. 1–2, Käsehage 2016, p. 7); a question, that was particularly relevant for security services. Anja Frank and Michaela Glaser (2018) also examined processes of minors turning to radical interpretations of Islam and asked how push-factors for radicalization make young people more susceptible to follow radical interpretations of Islam. The authors sought to understand how the appeal of Islamist groups relates to individual biographies (ibid.: p. 62). In doing so, they focused on the biographical function(s) of radical interpretations of Islam in adolescence (ibid.) and tried to draw conclusions for preventive measures against religiously based extremism. Amrei Sander's study on "Literalistically-Oriented female Christian and Muslim Converts in Comparison" (2019) combined causal and trajectory research. She

---

[5] Uhlmann's dissertation was submitted in 2014, but published only online in 2021. Empirical research was done between 2009–2011.

asked both about the "'why' of conversion as lasting change" (ibid.: p. 69) and "what functions conversion has developed for those concerned" (ibid.: p. 71).

Wohlrab-Sahr's methodical and methodological approach chosen more than 20 years ago continuous to have great influence on many of the studies on conversion to Islam in Germany to this day. Her approach still serves as a model for many current studies. However, we observed a tendency to refine Wohlrab-Sahr's approach conceptually. Sander (2019, 2021), for example, conceptualised conversion as a *multifunctional* problem-solving process in contrast to Wohlrab-Sahr who saw conversion as related to *one* biographical problem. Frank and Scholz (2022) did not follow Wohlrab-Sahr's approach. They instead used Goorens (2010) concept of "the conversion career" (ibid, p. 43) to examine the biographical trajectories and career paths of converts who turned to a radical interpretation of Islam.

2.1.2 Ethnographic Approaches

Ethnographic studies of Muslim converts in Germany focus on converts' everyday experiences in Germany against the backdrop of society's negotiation of Islam as a foreign religion. Thus, the focus lies not on the conversion motifs or on how conversion is narrated. Rather, these studies focus more on (subjective) strategies of action to deal with every-day experiences, techniques of milieu constitution, and performance as a Muslim religious subject. From the perspective of modernization and globalization theory, Jörg Hüttermann (2002) examined processes of religious self-transformation in a German branch of the Sufi Naqshbandīya order. He analysed the "technologies of the self" (Foucault 1993, p. 26), by which the members of the order, many of them converts, transform themselves into religious subjects through their own everyday religious practices. The study is based on one year of fieldwork, during which Hüttermann attended all the group's weekly meetings, especially the *dikhr*-meditation. In addition, he conducted in-depth individual interviews with some members of the order (Hüttermann 2002: p 5–6). He conceptualised those technologies of the self as a set of mutually enabling self- and milieu-centering practices and techniques with which the converts construct the Sufi milieu (ibid., p. 5).

Hüttermann highlights the "structural tension between the nominal uniqueness of reflexively assembled milieu symbols and the real diversity of biographical experience that refuses to be constrained by official symbols" (ibid., p. 38) within the Sufi order. This makes the 'made-up milieu' (ibid., p. 268) of Sufism in Western modernity fragile and precarious.

In her participant observation of converts in Berlin, Esra Özyürek (2009, 2015) investigated the everyday experiences of converts in the context of their social positioning as members of a minority religion perceived as foreign. She focused on individual experiences of discrimination and exclusion that result from the perspective of Islam as "the Other" (Özyürek 2015, p. 5). Her study is based on three field visits (2006/2007, 2009/2011, 2013). In the process, Özyürek accompanied converts not only during worship practices but also during leisure activities and gatherings in mosque communities. The participant observation is complemented by in-depth individual interviews with converts. In addition, Özyürek examined the converts' negotiation processes between their German and Muslim identities, which she claims, are perceived by majority society to be mutually exclusive (ibid., p. 5). In contrast, Özyürek found that German Muslim converts propagated a fit between Islam and the ideas of the European Enlightenment (liberalism, religious diversity, and curiosity for the "new" in general) (ibid., p. 29) and did not recognise a contradiction between the two identities.

Oleg Yarosh (2018) investigated the production of religious authority in two Sufi communities in Berlin and focused on the role of Muslim converts. Like Hüttermann (2002), he participated in religious events and used semi-structured interviews with religious personnel, (converted) members, and material from spontaneous conversations with members of both groups (Yarosh 2018, p. 180).

According to Yarosh, the question of which Muslim community converts join does not only depend on the "initial individual inclinations of its members and the authority of Sheikhs" (ibid., p. 180), but is also "determined by institutional patterns (i.e., hierarchy, communication) that constitute religious authority in these groups" (ibid.). With recourse to Max Weber's concept of charisma (2002, p. 212 ff.) Yarosh argued that, religious authority in Western Sufi milieus "represents a form of interaction between the charismatic leader, or sheikh, and his followers" (Yarosh 2018, p. 198). Religious authority shows itself as a "kind of exchange in which the leader satisfies religious and everyday life expectations of community members and receives their loyalty in return" (ibid.). "[A]wkward converts" (ibid., p. 185), who tend to have an eclectic understanding of Islam, are more likely to be found in communities that interpret the Islamic tradition more loosely, while others with a stricter understanding of religion prefer corresponding communities (ibid., p. 198).

Despite the various contributions ethnographic research has made to further our understanding of conversion to Islam in Germany, it remains debatable to what extend findings from each of the studies can be generalised. Most of the studies mentioned above refer to members of only *one* Sufi order or are locally limited. Özyürek and Yarosh for example only examined converts in Berlin. Studies that vary the context may help confirm, contradict, or refine the ethnographic findings and thus constitute a possible avenue for further research.

2.2 The Status of Conversion Narratives

In the early 1980s sociologists working on the phenomenon of religious conversion began to question whether it was possible to obtain reliable information on the causes of conversion based on what converts say when asked about it. Converts' stories were no longer assumed to be an accurate display of their past experiences but rather understood to be stories that are told from the post-conversion perspective in which present opinions and orientations of the converts may be found. The pre-conversion biography was assumed to be evaluated from the perspective of a conversion that had already happened. Based on this insight research on conversion began to question how converts *present* their experienced religious change. Conversion narratives became an object of study (Snow and Machalek 1984; Staples and Mauss 1987). For the German context it is particularly Ulmer's (1988) article on conversion narratives that stands for this development in conversion research. Ulmer identified the central communicative problem that every convert must solve when telling a conversion narrative. Converts need to "convincingly and plausibly present a personal religious experience as the cause for their own conversion" (Ulmer 1988, p. 31).

Most of the studies reviewed here emphasised the constructed nature of conversion narratives and referenced Ulmer (1988) (Wohlrab-Sahr 1999; Uhlmann 2021; Käsehage 2016). However, it appears that some studies beginning in the mid-2010s began to increasingly take what converts said in interviews at face value. Researchers for example accepted the alleged rationality of Islam and the criticism of the Christian notion of trinity as issues that converts have always – prior to conversion – been dealing with. To what extend these issues express genuine problems converts experienced prior to conversion and to what extend these narrations are part of a dogma of an Islamic conversion pattern that the converts adopted *after* conversion constitutes a question for further research (cf. Beckford 1978).

In the studies reviewed we found different degrees to which the nature of conversion narratives was reflected upon. Some approaches expect a "deeper" sense that manifests itself "behind" the text produced by converts. For example, Wohlrab-Sahr applies "objective hermeneutics" (Oevermann et al. 1979), an approach that seeks to identify latent structures of meaning. Wohlrab-Sahr hence does not take the conversion narrative at face value, a standpoint that becomes also apparent in the distinction she makes between the conversion history which refers to the totality of experiences that led to conversion and biographic story-telling which is what converts select and decide to tell [Konversionsgeschichte vs. biografische Erzählung] (1999, p. 95). Even though Wohlrab-Sahr's approach served as a blueprint for research on conversion to Islam in Germany (Sander 2019; Käsehage 2016; Frank and Glaser 2018) we can see that Sander (2019) in her analysis of biographical functions of conversion follows rather closely what converts *present* in their conversion narratives. This approach risks taking the reasons for conversion as presented by converts as the actual reasons for conversion. Käsehage (2016) also referenced Ulmer (1988) but did not explain how she reflected the nature of conversion narratives in her analysis. It is also in Uhlmann's (2021) study where a lack of the reflection of the status of conversion narratives becomes apparent. Uhlmann emphasised the importance of reflecting the nature of conversion narratives in the introduction (ibid., p. 87) but at a later point in her text assumed that the responses she received in her interviews with converts allow access to pre-conversion identities, opinions, and motifs of the converts (ibid., p. 232 ff.). Uhlmann also compares her results with Lofland and Stark's (1965) seminal work on conversion and finds differing results. For example, contrary to Lofland and Stark Uhlmann did not identify enduring tension among the converts she interviewed (ibid., p. 232). However, it would have been more precise to say that the converts did not *present* any personal tensions. We cannot tell whether they really experienced tensions, what we can say is that they did not *present* themselves as having had experienced tensions. Özyürek (2015) did not explicitly reflect the nature of conversion narratives with one exception (ibid., p. 73). Frank and Glaser (2018) also did not reflect the status of conversion narratives. For further research it would thus be useful to consistently reflect the fact that converts speak from a post-conversion perspective.

We identified several research gaps on Muslim conversion narratives. It is still necessary to ask how Muslim conversion narratives deviate from Ulmer's (1988) model (cf. Krech 1995, p. 149). Equally it needs to be asked how Muslim conversion narratives relate to the interpretative patterns of Muslim religious communities (cf. Beckford 1978). In this context it would be worthwhile to ask how conversion narratives differ between various Muslim religious communities such as Sunnis, Shias, Sufis, Ahmadiyya etc. In addition, Krech's (1995) observation that there might be several types of conversion narratives to the same religious community is still valid and may inspire further research on Muslim conversion narratives. Finally, it appears interesting to ask how different types of conversion narratives relate to different socio-structural milieus of converts (ibid., p. 149).

Hofmann's (1997) study was as a first attempt to find answers to these questions. She consistently reflected the status of conversion narratives and analysed recurring linguistic patterns in the conversion narratives of her interviewees. For example, Hofmann showed how Muslim converts create continuity with their pre-conversion life by emphasizing that they had always had problems with Christianity before they converted. It is not surprising that converts devalue their former religion. However, it is interesting that they present themselves as if they had *always* had a problem with it. Whether that is true, we do not know. What we do know is that they present themselves as such.

"Church was always kind of alien to me, I don't know. It might sound silly to an outsider, but it was always alien to me" (Monika) (ibid., p. 158).

Finally, there is another research gap in relation to Muslim conversion narratives. If we accept that conversion narratives can change according to the context in which they are produced, we may ask how conversion narratives to Islam in Germany have changed in the last decades. In Hofmann's study, which was conducted in the mid-1990s, we found that a contradiction between Western societies and Islam played an important role in the conversion narratives. It remains to be asked whether different aspects are pronounced today. For example, it may be that today converts emphasise more strongly positive effects of conversion to cope with the various challenges of daily life in a modern and individualistic society.

2.3   The Conceptualisation of Conversion

According to Krech (1995, p. 137) the question of conceptualising conversion is one of the most important topics in conversion research. This also holds true for the studies reviewed here. The debates "about passivity versus activity" (ibid.) of converts in the appropriation of their new religion and whether conversion should be understood as "process or event" (Uhlmann 2015, p. 1) continue to this day. Wohlrab-Sahr (1999) understands "conversion as a symbolic transformation of crisis experience" (ibid., p. 21) in biographies. In this constructivist perspective conversion to Islam functions as a solution for a convert's biographical problem. Conversion allows to process one's own experiences and re-interpret them within a new interpretive framework (Wohlrab-Sahr 2012, p. 28). The following question arises: For which biographical problem serves conversion as a solution? (Wohlrab-Sahr 2017, p. 46) Wohlrab-Sahr differentiates her conceptualisation from purely cognitive approaches to conversion. In this way "the entire process of articulating, dramatizing, and transforming crisis experience, through which problem processing and problem solving takes place, thus comes into view" (Wohlrab-Sahr 1999, p. 21).

Hüttermann (2002) also understands conversion as a process. He defines conversion as a self-technique with the help of which converts transform themselves into religious subjects and appropriate religion (ibid., p. 117 ff.). According to Uhlmann (2009, 2015, 2021), conversion to Islam should also be understood as a process that can take many years, extends far beyond the act of confession – the uttering of the Shahāda – and involves intensive self-reflection (2009, p. 27). Käsehage (2016, p. 15–16) follows Wohlrab-Sahr's understanding of conversion and adopts a functional perspective on conversion (ibid., p. 77). She focuses her study "on the reference problem of religious conversion and its character as problem solving or processing" (ibid.). Sander's (2019) study is also situated in the paradigm of active converts. She defines conversion as a "radical [...] transformation of a person's worldview [...], whereby this transformation refers to a specific canon associated with a [religious] worldview group in the sense of binding bodies of knowledge. In doing so, reference is made either to a competing worldview within the same religious system or else within another religious system" (ibid., p. 67). She further modifies Wohlrab-Sahr's approach in that conversion never solves only *one* biographical problem. Conversion, according to her, is always multifunctional. People only convert and maintain this decision if the conversion of faith solved several biographical problems (ibid., p. 311). This understanding is compatible with Frank's and Glaser's (2018) finding that turning to radical ideological interpretations of Islam is always conditioned by multiple intertwined biographical factors (ibid., p. 62, FNRP 2020).

Some of the studies reviewed here (Krech and Schlegel 1998, p. 170, Nieuwkerk 2006, p. 164) displayed a certain concern, whether the concept of conversion is applicable at all to describe a process of religious change that in the case of Islam can extend over a long period of time. This criticism was taken up by almost none of the studies considered here. According to van Nieuwkerk, the concept of conversion is unsuitable since it is not an emic concept, that is, a concept not used by the converts themselves to describe their own religious change (2006, p. 164). Uhlmann (2021, p. 49) mentioned van Nieuwkerk's rejection of the term but did so only to indicate that she agrees with van Nieuwkerk's view to retain the term for lack of a better one.

2.4   Islam as the "Other" in Conversion Research

It was Edward Said's seminal book Orientalism (2003) that has brought attention to the discursive production of the Orient and Islam in European societies. Since then, several studies have analysed how Islam is portrayed in European societies. These studies have in common that Islam is viewed as a religion that is foreign to Europe and that serves as Europe's Other. German educational science researcher

5 Research on Conversion to Islam in Germany Between 1995 and 2022

Paul Mecheril (2011) speaks of Islam in the German context as the "Religion of the Other". All studies reviewed relate in one way or another to this specific discursive production of Islam in German society. Particularly studies that expect conversion to fulfil certain biographical functions (Wohlrab-Sahr 1999, p. 291 ff.) rely on the position of Islam in German society to explain why conversion to Islam was chosen over other options. For example, one could start volunteering or join a sports club. However, compared to these functional equivalents Islam's position as a foreign and suspect religion allows conversion to Islam to fulfil specific functions such as rebellion against one's parents and criticism of society. Joining a sports club or converting from Catholicism to Protestantism may not fulfil these functions to the same extent. The discursive position of Islam in German society is thus the pre-condition for conversion to fulfil the function of demarcation. Hüttermann (2002, p. 125) in his study of a Sufi order also relies on the "Entirely Different" ["das Ganz-Andere"] as a factor that attracts converts to Islam. Similarly in Hofmann's (1997, p. 28–29) study on female Muslim converts the interviewees see in Islam an attractive alternative to Western values as well as a system of thought that contradicts Western conceptions of the role of women and family in society. The specific societal position of Islam in Germany is also relevant in the strand of research that focuses on the radicalization of converts. Conversion is seen as a means through which young people can distance themselves symbolically from their parents and majority society (Frank and Glaser 2018, p. 6). It may appear trivial to state that conversions always occur in a particular discursive context but a quick comparison with other religions in Germany would reveal the specificity of Islam and the specific functions conversion to Islam can fulfil. In this context it is interesting to ask what would happen if Islam became a "normal" part of German society and lost its position as a foreign religion. Based on the above mentioned it is conceivable that for some converts other forms of distancing would become more attractive as Islam could no longer offer this function as it used to. Özyürek (2015, p. 1 ff.) sought to understand what it means to convert to a minority religion that serves as a constitutive Other and is excluded from the national imagination in Germany. The anthropologist focused on the everyday experiences of German Muslims. Despite her study more research is needed on the questions of how the discursive production of Islam manifests itself in everyday experiences of German Muslims. This gap becomes particularly apparent when we compare the German state of the literature with English-language publications on the questions of everyday experiences of Muslim converts. For example, in the UK (Franks 2000; Moosavi 2015), the USA and France (Galonnier 2015, 2018), Denmark (Jensen 2008), Australia (Alam 2012) and the Netherlands (Sheva Hass 2020). These studies focused on the reactions of family members, the public, and fellow believers in mosque communities to conversions to Islam. Apart from Özyürek (2015), research on these questions in Germany is still missing (cf. Shooman 2014, p. 72).

2.5 Conversion and Radicalisation

Within the period from 1995 to 2022 we identified shifts in the thematic focuses of studies on conversion to Islam in Germany. Hofmann (1997), Wohlrab-Sahr (1999), and Hüttermann (2002) focused on conversion motifs of women, the biographic reference problem of conversion, and the techniques of self-transformation, respectively. Starting in 2008 a new thematic focus emerged that continues to this day: conversion and radicalization. The first study we identified in this strand is the journal article "European Converts to Terrorism" (2008) by political scientist Milena Uhlmann. The connection between conversion to Islam and extremism and violence can already be found in the title. Uhlmann wrote the article against the backdrop of a perceived increase in the number of converts who were involved in terrorism in the years prior to the publication and an increased interest by security agencies for converts. Uhlmann also positioned her article in relation to the increasing threat faced by so called homegrown terrorists who showed that the threat of Islamist extremism had shifted from an external to an internal threat, a development exemplified particularly well by converts involved in terrorism. Uhlmann discussed possible reasons for why converts may be particularly prone to radicalise. She mentioned factors such as new Muslims' zeal and a lack of religious knowledge that may leave them open to indoctrination by extremist groups. According to Uhlmann extremist groups valued European converts due to the ease with which they can travel and their knowledge of informal codes in European societies. European converts can move and act unsuspiciously in Europe.

We interpret the beginning of this new strand of research on conversion in 2008 as a reaction to the arrest of the so-called Sauerland terrorist cell in September 2007. The group included two converts and had planned to attack American targets in Germany. This strand of research continues to the present day (Uhlmann 2008, 2021; Özyürek 2009; Käsehage 2016; Frank and Glaser 2018). As a result, researchers like Uhlmann (2021) sought to understand "possible security and democracy-threatening aspects […] of conversions to Islam in Europe" (ibid., p. 5). She interviewed 27 converts in Berlin, London, and Paris between 2009 and 2011. Uhlmann developed two types of religious change a) conversion to reflexive Islam and b) alternation to a youth cultural version of Salafism. Based

5 Research on Conversion to Islam in Germany Between 1995 and 2022

on Giddens', Castells' and Goffman's identity theories Uhlmann showed that the first type is characterized by a long process in which the convert deals with Islam, the contents of belief, and the relevance of Islam for his or her own life. Identity change is slow, gradual but profound and occurs through conscious and continuous acts of self-reflection. In contrast, adopting a youth cultural Salafist approach to Islam is characterized by the superficial adoption of new roles in which a personal identity is completely absorbed by a collective identity as Muslim. Contrary to the first type no profound transformation of identity occurs and hence the author prefers to speak of alternation instead of conversion. In the case of alternation, Salafism satisfies needs for clarity, belonging and significance. Uhlmann's work makes an important contribution to recognizing the signs of radicalization among converts and helps objectify the discussion about conversion and radicalisation. At the same time, a dichotomy of possible conversion processes appears somewhat simplified. Do all conversions correspond to either the reflexive type or the alternation to Salafism? Are there not Salafists who have been dealing with ideology and Islamist beliefs? Uhlmann herself mentioned this possibility as a research desideratum (ibid., p. 256). It is also surprising that Uhlmann's findings are based only on interviews with converts who fall into the category of converts to reflective Islam. She drew on secondary data for her type b), the alternation to a youth cultural version of Salafism.

Käsehage's study (2016) serves as another example that makes a connection between conversion and radicalisation. In her monograph she aimed at addressing the issue of conversion to Islam in Germany with particular attention paid to constitutional questions (ibid., p. 7). Käsehage's research is based on 38 interviews with German converts which she conducted in 2011 in Germany. Main points of interest are conversion motifs and the questions how the new Muslims position themselves in relation to the Constitution of the Federal Republic of Germany. In Käsehage's words the question is about "a potential connection between conversion to Islam and the development or formation of opposing attitudes towards democracy" (ibid., p. 7). Again, a clear link is established between conversion and extremism. As a key finding the author presents four cases of converts whom she attributes to two types of conversions. The two types include the moderates (ibid., p. 80 ff.) and the Salafists (ibid., p. 101 ff.). However, it remains unclear how Käsehage arrived at these two types. The author's focus on possible constitutional issues that may arise from conversion to Islam is unprecedented in the literature reviewed. Despite this it is not clear why Käsehage analysed only four out of 38 interviews. In addition, the finding that only two types of converts exist (moderates and Salafists) appears too simple.

Frank and Glaser (2018) based their study more on reconstructive biographical research and tried to understand "why young people turn to radical forms of Islam and what it is that makes religious and non-religious extremist ideology attractive for them" (ibid., p. 62). By doing so they also focused on converts to Islam (ibid. p. 63). Biographical functions include "symbolic demarcation in the context of adolescent detachment and individuation" (ibid.: 69), the "methodisation of lifestyle and production of uniqueness" (ibid., p. 71), "Alternative educational paths and ways of life" (ibid., p. 72) and "Experience of self-efficacy and self-empowerment" (ibid., p. 73). Functions one and two resemble some of the functions that Wohlrab-Sahr (1999) presented roughly 20 years ago. The function "methodization of lifestyle" (ibid. 224) even has a similar name. Also, Wohlrab-Sahr's function "symbolic emigration and symbolic fight" (ibid., p. 143) is similar to Frank's and Glaser's function of symbolic demarcation. Finally, Wohlrab-Sahr (1999, pp. 145, 153, 183 and 234) also found that many converts started impressive careers in Islamic Institutions and Muslim civil society following their conversion.

Frank and Glaser (2018) were able to understand the attractiveness of radical forms of Islam from the perspective of young people (ibid., p. 77). According to the authors educators and PVE actors should take these subjective meanings seriously, try to find out what they are in each case, and pay particular attention to their individual appropriation (cf. ibid.). A case-by-case understanding is important as there is no one-size-fits-all approach to dealing with radicalised youth. The authors also point out that the "existence and also the nature of relationships with family members and other significant others are important both in the process of turning towards a radical form of Islam as well as for the process of regaining distance from radical forms of Islam" (ibid., p. 78). Unfortunately, Frank and Glaser do not discuss their results in relation to current conversion research. Frank and Glaser's work nevertheless establishes the clearest direct link to prevention work against religiously motivated extremism within the studies examined here.

Based on the entanglement of conversion research with questions of radicalisation and extremism, however, there is still a need to trace non-radical conversion processes. The strong civil society engagement of converts would be a particularly suitable field of study (cf. Vardar and Müssig 2011). There is also a danger of securitizing research on conversion to Islam.

2.6 Conversion and German-Muslim Identity

Another complex of issues that has become increasingly prominent since the beginning of the 2000s is the connection between conversion and a European-Muslim or, in the context of this article, a German-Muslim identity. This debate is still ongoing today (Güneş 2022). We observed a shift from an exclusivity of a German and a European identity to attempts of an amalgamation.[6] Hofmann (1997) found that her interviewees view Islam and the West as a pair of opposites. For these women Islam functions as a marker of demarcation from a Western society that is seen to be decadent and morally degenerate (ibid., p. 265). In contrast, according to Hüttermann (2002), it is above all converts, whom he describes as advocates of elitism, who see themselves as supporters of a multicultural World-Islam and at the same time as defenders of the cause of German Islam. They rejected mixing the pure, culturally neutral, universal Islam they upheld with the historically grown traditions of Islamic countries (ibid., p. 249). Despite this stance against connecting religion and culture, Hüttermann argues that Muslim converts' own culture, milieu and nation-state centricity is reflected in this argument (ibid.). While Hüttermann only touches on the connections between German and Muslim identity, these aspects are at the heart of Özyürek's (2009) study. She asked about the fit between these identities, which, according to her, are often perceived as incompatible by majority society (ibid., p. 3). According to Özyürek converts to Islam transcend the boundaries between Muslims and Germans and thus undermine the religious and cultural purity of the nation.

Käsehage (2016) distinguishes between two types of converts in her study: the moderates and those who name themselves Salafists. Moderate converts respect German law and place it above the Sharia. They also state that they would prefer living side by side with non-Muslims in Germany rather than living with fellow Muslims. For the Salafists (ibid., p. 79), on the other hand, the legal and social order, described in the Sharia, is above the Basic Law, even though they say they respect it. At the same time, they considered the transformation of German society into an (from their point of view) Islam-compliant society to be desirable (ibid., p. 118–119). Muslims who describe themselves as moderates often distanced themselves from Muslims of birth, because in their view the latter would mix culture and religion (ibid., p. 119 ff.). Yarosh (2018, p. 198) writes in this

---

[6] The cross-cultural comparative study on „European Islam " conducted by Nilüfer Göle shows that those processes of amalgamation are not restricted to Germany, but can be found in several European countries (Göle 2017, p.49ff., pp. 173–174).

regard: "Western converts often express their religious identity in modern forms as characterized by selective and individualist attitudes toward the Islamic tradition." A similar argument can be found in Özyürek (2015). "In its indigenous German Muslim context, an Islam free of culture means an Islam that has been purged of its often-stigmatized Arab and Turkish cultural practices. Once rectified like this, the reasoning goes, Islam will be more in line not only with its original spirit but also with European ideals of democracy, freedom, and tolerance" (ibid., p. 53, cf. Göle 2017, p. 199). In fact, Özyürek (2015) shows how German Muslim converts attempt to locate the history of Islam in Germany prior to the generally accepted starting point of a Muslim presence in Germany with the arrival of guest workers in the 1960s. Thereby converts try to establish an Islamic continuity in Germany (ibid., p. 39 ff.). "Migrant Muslims, defined by their traditional and thus automatically 'wrong' Islamic practices" (ibid.), are excluded in this process. According to Özyürek, a German or European Islam understood in this way opens up a space for German Muslims within the national body, but at the same time reinforces the distrust of majority society towards Muslims with a migration background who live according to their national or ethnic traditions (ibid.). According to Özyürek, Salafism, which presents itself as completely untouched by human interpretation and any tradition, therefore exhibits the greatest ability to accommodate new Muslims without a traditional orientation (ibid., p. 163). van Nieuwkerk attributes this ability to Sufism, "which has 'religious goods' to offer that contrast with those of modernist or Islamist versions of Islam" (van Nieuwkerk 2006, p. 5). She notes that converts therefore first identified themselves as members of Sufism and only later accepted Islam (ibid.).

The involvement of Muslim converts in Muslim communities and in German Muslim civil society is rarely considered in the discussion of German-Muslim identity. Nilden Vardar and Stephanie Müssig (2011, p. 28) show that converts often hold high status positions in these organizations and associations, a fact that is hardly perceived within the German public (ibid., p. 31). According to them, this commitment is currently not sufficiently taken into account either in research on Islam nor in civil society research (ibid.). According to Vardar and Müssig converts are familiar with the social, cultural, and religious codes of both the majority society and the Muslim immigrant community, which gives them the opportunity to act as mediators between the two spheres, which are perceived incompatible (ibid., p. 34). This social capital makes them attractive contact persons for the non-Muslim majority society (cf. Özyürek 2015, pp.:40–41). In the contributions mentioned above it remains open whether a) all converts attribute this social capital to themselves in the same manner and whether b) it is a self-attribution or an attribution by others, such as researchers.

3 Conclusion

This review of the scientific literature on conversion to Islam in Germany revealed only fragmentary mutual references. Most research contributions seem to be reactions to social events and problems. Foremost among these is the close interweaving of conversion research on Islam with questions of domestic security, which began in 2008. But also, the entanglement of conversion research with the field of PVE in adolescence has gained importance in recent years. Furthermore, different disciplines conduct research on conversion to Islam from their own perspectives and only partially refer to each other.

For future research on conversion to Islam in Germany, it would therefore be useful to pay attention to and build on the already existing research both nationally and internationally. A stronger linkage of the research contributions back to current research in the field of socialization and conversion theories also seems to be useful. A good example is the contribution by Anna Frank and Anna Felicitas Scholz (2022). Drawing on Henri Goorens conceptualisation of "conversion careers" (2010, p. 43), they frame "radicalization as a conversion process" (Frank and Scholz 2022, p. 244).

As a possible starting point for a joint research tradition on conversion to Islam in Germany we identified the study of Wohlrab-Sahr (1999). Even if her approach has so far been applied mostly affirmatively and modified only sporadically, her understanding of conversion as a transformation of crisis-ridden biographical experiences offers, in our view, a central point of reference for further research projects (e.g., Frank and Glaser 2017, p. 2, Sander 2019, p. 66, 2021, p. 133). It remains an open question whether all conversions must be based on a biographical crisis. It seems at least conceivable that conversions can also take place out of intellectual interest or enthusiasm for a new religion. It is also conceivable that a conversion can solve more than one biographical problem at once (Sander 2021, p. 133). Possible areas for further research include the specificity of Islamic conversion narratives, the civic engagement of Muslim converts (Vardar and Müssig 2011), and the everyday experiences of Muslim converts given the specific discursive production of Islam in Germany. The latter appears significant because most of the studies conceptualize Islam as a foreign religion in their analyses. We have shown that some studies (Wohlrab-Sahr 1999; Frank and Glaser 2018; Sander 2019) assume that conversion to Islam makes it possible to distance oneself from parents and society due to its specific societal position. It is also necessary to ask in the future to what extent conversion to Islam can continue to fulfil this function as Islam becomes a more natural part of German society.

References

Alam, Oishee. 2012. 'Islam is a blackfella religion, whatchya trying to prove?'. race in the lives of white Muslim converts in Australia. *La Trobe Journal* 89:124–139.

Backer, Kristiane. 2009. *Von MTV nach Mekka. Wie der Islam mein Leben veränderte.* Berlin: List.

Beckford, James A. 1978. Accounting for conversion. *The British Journal of Sociology* 29(2):249.

Bundeskriminalamt, Bundesamt für Verfassungsschutz und Hessisches Informations- und Kompetenzzentrum gegen Extremismus. 2016. Analyse der Radikalisierungshintergründe und -verläufe der Personen, die aus islamistischer Motivation aus Deutschland in Richtung Syrien oder Irak ausgereist sind. https://hke.hessen.de/sites/hke.hessen.de/files/2022-06/analyse_der_radikalisierungshintergruende_fortschreibung_2016.pdf. Zugegriffen: 18. December 2023.

Buntrock, Tanja, and Dernbach, Andrea. 2007. Politik: Der Konvertit, das unbekannte Wesen. In *Der Tagesspiegel*, 07.09.2007. https://www.tagesspiegel.de/politik/der-konvertit-das-unbekannte-wesen-1543273.html. Accessed: 11. Nov. 2022.

Filter, Cornelia. 2008. *Mein Gott ist jetzt Allah und ich befolge seine Gesetze gern. Eine Reportage über Konvertiten in Deutschland.* München: Piper.

Forschungsnetzwerk Radikalisierung und Prävention. 2020. Religion als Faktor der Radikalisierung? Eine praxisorientierte Handreichung aus dem ‚Forschungsnetzwerk Radikalisierung und Prävention' (FNRP). https://osnadocs.ub.uni-osnabrueck.de/handle/urn:nbn:de:gbv:700-202005183060. Accessed: 07.11.2023.

Foucault, Michel. 1993. *Überwachen und Strafen. Die Geburt des Gefängnisses.* Frankfurt am Main: Suhrkamp

Frank, Anja, and Michaela Glaser. 2017. „Ich hab' einen Standpunkt, das ist der Islam" Zur biografischen Bedeutung und Funktion radikaler, ideologisierter Islamauslegungen. In *Geschlossene Gesellschaften. Verhandlungen des 38. Kongresses der Deutschen Gesellschaft für Soziologie in Bamberg 2016*, Ed. Stephan Lessenich, 1–8. Deutsche Gesellschaft für Soziologie (DGS).

Frank, Anja, and Michaela Glaser. 2018. Biografische Perspektiven auf radikalen Islam im Jugendalter. In *Gewaltorientierter Islamismus im Jugendalter. Perspektiven aus Jugendforschung und Jugendhilfe*, Ed. Michaela Glaser, Anja Frank and Maruta Herding, 62–79. Weinheim: Beltz Juventa.

Frank, Anja, and Anna Felicitas Scholz. 2022. Wenn Jugendliche sich fremd machen – Islamistische Radikalisierung als Selbstbefremdung und Selbstausgrenzung. In *Islam in Europa. Institutionalisierung und Konflikt*, Ed. Monika Wohlrab-Sahr und Levent Tezcan, 241–269. Baden-Baden: Nomos.

Franks, Myfanwy. 2000. Crossing the borders of whiteness? White Muslim women who wear the hijab in Britain today. *Ethnic and Racial Studies* 23(5):917–929.

Galonnier, Juliette. 2015. The racialization of Muslims in France and the United States: Some insights from white converts to Islam. *Social Compass* 624:570–583.

Galonnier, Juliette. 2018. *Choosing faith and facing race. Converting to Islam in France and the United States.* Northernwest University: Ann Arbor, Paris.

5 Research on Conversion to Islam in Germany Between 1995 and 2022

Glaser, Michaela, Frank, Anja, and Herding, Maruta, Eds. 2018. *Gewaltorientierter Islamismus im Jugendalter*. Weinheim: Beltz Juventa.

Gooren, Henri Paul Pierre. 2010. *Religious conversion and disaffiliation. Tracing patterns of change in faith practices*. New York: Palgrave Macmillan.

Göle, Nilüfer. 2017. *The daily lives of Muslims. Islam in contemporary Europe. Islam and public confrontation in contemporary Europe*. London: Zed Books.

Gudrun Jensen, Tina. 2008. To be 'Danish', becoming 'Muslim': Contestations of national identity? *Journal of Ethnic and Migration Studies* 34(3):389–409.

Güneş, Merdan. 2022. Die Identitätsdebatte der Muslim:innen in Europa: ein Vergleich der Ansätze von Bassam Tibi und Tariq Ramadan zur Beheimatung des Islams und der Muslim:innen in Europa. In *Macht im interreligiösen Dialog. Interdisziplinäre Perspektiven*, Hrsg. Merdan Güneş, Andreas Kubik, und Georg Steins, 172–210. München: Verlag Herder.

Hass, Bat Sheva. 2020. Being a 'White Muslima' in the Netherlands ethnicity, Friendships and relationships—The Dutch conversion narrative. *Religions* 11(7):345.

Haug, Sonja, Stephanie Müssig, and Anja Stichs. 2009. *Muslimisches Leben in Deutschland*. Nürnberg: Federal Office for Migration and Refugees.

Hofmann, Gabriele. 1997. *Muslimin werden. Frauen in Deutschland konvertieren zum Islam*. Dissertation. Universität Frankfurt, Frankfurt am Main.

Hüttermann, Jörg. 2002. Islamische Mystik. Ein ‚gemachtes Milieu' im Kontext von Modernität und Globalität. Zugl.: Bielefeld, Univ., Diss., 1998 u.d.T.: Hüttermann, Jörg: Sufitum in Deutschland: eine Fallstudie zu Problemen artifizieller Milieuzentrierung am Beispiel einer interethnisch zusammengesetzten Gruppe des Naqshbandi-Ordens. Würzburg: Ergon-Verlag.

Kaiser, Susanne. 2018. *Die neuen Muslime. Warum junge Menschen zum Islam konvertieren*. Wien: Promedia.

Karras, Benjamin. 2019. Religiöse Konversionen im Asylprozess. Konrad Adenauer Stiftung. https://www.kas.de/de/analysen-und-argumente/detail/-/content/religioese-konversionen-im-asylprozess, Accessed: 25. Apr. 2022.

Käsehage, Nina. 2016. *Konversion zum Islam innerhalb Deutschlands. Unter besonderer Berücksichtigung verfassungsrechtlicher Fragen*. Hamburg: Verlag Dr. Kovač.

Krech, Volkhard. 1995. Was ist religiöse Bekehrung? Ein Streifzug durch zehn Jahre soziologischer Konversionsforschung. *Handlung Kultur Interpretation Bulletin für Psychologie und Nachbardisziplinen* 4(6):131–159.

Krech, Volkhard, and Matthias Schlegel. 1998. Auf der Suche nach dem ‚wahren Selbst': über den Zusammenhang von Konversion und der Konstitution religiöser Identität". In *Religiöse Konversion. Systematische und fallorientierte Studien in soziologischer Perspektive*, Eds. Volkhard Krech, Hubert Knoblauch und Monika Wohlrab-Sahr, 169–192. Konstanz: UVK.

Lau, Sven. 2020. *Wer ist Sven Lau?* Selbstverlag: Books on Demand.

Lofland, John, and Stark, Rodney. 1965. Becoming a world-saver: A theory of conversion to a deviant perspective. *American Sociological Review* 30(6):862.

Mecheril, Paul, and Oscar Thomas-Olalde. 2011. Die Religion der Anderen. In *Jugend, Migration und Religion: Interdisziplinäre Perspektiven*, Eds. Brigit Allenbach, Urmila Goel, Merle Hummrich, and Cordula Weissköppel, 33–66. Baden-Baden: Nomos Verlagsgesellschaft mbH & Co KG.

Moosavi, Leon. 2015. The racialization of Muslim converts in Britain and their experiences of Islamophobia. *Critical Sociology* 41(1):41–56.

Oevermann, Ulrich, Tilman Allert, Elisabeth Konau, and Jürgen Krambeck. 1979. Die Methodologie einer „objektiven Hermeneutik" und ihre allgemeine forschungslogische Bedeutung in den Sozialwissenschaften. In *Interpretative Verfahren in den Sozial- und Textwissenschaften*, Ed. Hans-Georg Soeffner, 352–434. Stuttgart: Metzler.

Özyürek, Esra. 2009. Convert alert: German Muslims and Turkish Christians as threats to security in the new Europe. *Comp Stud Soc Hist* 51(1):91–116.

Özyürek, Esra. 2015. *Being German, becoming Muslim. Race, religion, and conversion in the new Europe*. Princeton: Princeton University Press.

Roald, Anne Sofie. 2001. *Women in Islam. The Western experience*. London: Routledge.

Said, Edward W. 2003. *Orientalism. Reprinted with a new preface*. London: Penguin Books.

Sander, Amrei. 2019. *Literalsinnorientierte muslimische und christliche Konvertitinnen im interreligiösen Vergleich*. Göttingen: Vandenhoeck & Ruprecht.

Sander, Amrei. 2021. Konversion als multifunktionales Phänomen. In *Integration und Konversion. Taufen muslimischer Flüchtlinge als Herausforderung für Kirchen und Gesellschaft*, Ed. Henning Theißen and Knud Henrik Boysen, 131–142. Paderborn: Brill.

Schmitz, Dominic Musa. 2016. *Ich war ein Salafist. Meine Zeit in der islamistischen Parallelwelt*. Berlin: Econ.

Schütze, Fritz. 1976. Zur Hervorlockung und Analyse von Erzählungen thematisch relevanter Geschichten im Rahmen soziologischer Feldforschung: dargestellt an einem Projekt zur Erforschung von kommunalen Machtstrukturen. In *Kommunikative Sozialforschung. Alltagswissen und Alltagshandeln, Gemeindemachtforschung, Polizei, politische Erwachsenenbildung*, Ed. Ansgar Weymann, 159–160. München: Fink.

Schütze, Fritz. 1983. Biographieforschung und narratives Interview. *Neue Praxis* 13(3):283–293.

Shooman, Yasemin. 2014. „… weil ihre Kultur so ist". *Narrative des antimuslimischen Rassismus*. Bielefeld: transcript.

Snow, D. A., and Machalek, R. 1984. The sociology of conversion. *Annu. Rev. Sociol.* 10(1):167–190. 123.

Staples, Clifford L., and Mauss, Armand L. 1987. Conversion or commitment? A reassessment of the snow and Machalek approach to the study of conversion. *Journal for the Scientific Study of Religion* 26(2):133.

Strähler, Reinhold. 2021. *Einfach und komplex zugleich. Konversionsprozesse und ihre Beurteilung*. Leipzig: Evangelische Verlagsanstalt. https://ebookcentral.proquest.com/lib/kxp/detail.action?docID=6746965. Accessed: 21 December 2023.

Uhlmann, Milena. 2008. European converts to terrorism. *Middle East Quarterly* 15:31–37.

Uhlmann, Milena. 2009. Islam-Konversion – Warum Menschen übertreten. In *Islamistischer Extremismus, Konvertiten und Terrorismus. Bedrohungen im Wandel*, Ed. Ministerium des Innern des Landes Brandenburg, 21–33. No longer available online.

Uhlmann, Milena. 2015. Choosing Islam in West European societies - an investigation of different concepts of religious re-affiliation. Robert Schuman Centre for Advanced Studies. https://papers.ssrn.com/sol3/papers.cfm?abstract_id=2704399. Accessed: 21. December 2023.

Uhlmann, Milena. 2021. Konversionen zum Islam in westeuropäischen Gesellschaften. Eine explorative Studie der Konversion zum „reflexiven Islam" und der Alternation zu einer jugendkulturellen Ausprägung des Salafismus. https://edoc.hu-berlin.de/handle/18452/23743. Accessed 21.12.2023.

Ulmer, Bernd. 1988. Konversionserzählungen als rekonstruktive Gattung. *Zeitschrift für Soziologie* 17(1):19–33.

Vardar, Nilden, and Müssig, Stephanie. 2011. Zur Rolle von muslimischen Konvertierten im Gemeindeleben. In *Islam in Deutschland. Aus Politik und Zeitgeschichte*, Ed. Bundeszentrale für politische Bildung, 28–34 (13–14/2011). Bonn: Bundeszentrale für politische Bildung.

van Nieuwkerk, Karin, Ed. 2006. *Women embracing Islam. Gender and conversion in the West*. Austin: University of Texas Press.

Weber, Max, Ed. 2002. *Economy and society. An outline of interpretive sociology*. Berkeley, Calif.: Univ. of California Press.

Wohlrab-Sahr, Monika. 1999. *Konversion zum Islam in Deutschland und den USA*. Frankfurt: Campus.

Wohlrab-Sahr, Monika. 2012. Konforme Nonkonformisten. Soziologische Zugänge zum Thema Konversion. In *Treten Sie ein! Treten Sie aus! Warum Menschen Ihre Religion wechseln*, Ed. Kleeberg und Sulzenbacher, 20–30. Berlin: Parthas.

Wohlrab-Sahr, Monika. 2017. Von Konversion zu multiplen Säkularitäten. Wissenschaftsbiographische Anmerkungen und systematische Zusammenhänge. In *Religion soziologisch denken. Reflexionen auf aktuelle Entwicklungen in Theorie und Empirie*, Ed. Heidemarie Winkel und Kornelia Sammet, 45–68. Wiesbaden: Springer VS.

Yarosh, Oleg. 2018. Religious Authority and Conversions in Berlin's Sufi Communities. In *Moving In and Out of Islam*, Ed. Karin van Nieuwkerk, 179–203. Austin: University of Texas Press.

Marvin Mücke, M.A. is research assistant at the Institute for Islamic Theology at the University of Osnabrück and currently a Ph.D. candidate. His research interests lie in conversion to Islam, radicalization, and the prevention of radicalization. He holds a Master's degree in Arabic and Middle Eastern Studies from the University of Edinburgh.

Sören Sponick, M.A. is research assistant at the Institute for Islamic Theology at the University of Osnabrück and currently a Ph.D. candidate. His research interests lie in conversion to Islam, sociology of career, environmental sociology, and sociological theory. He holds a Master's degree in Sociology from the University of Bielefeld.

Islam and Muslims in Switzerland Through the Prism of Religious Visibility and Islamic Militancy

6

Mallory Schneuwly Purdie

Abstract

In this chapter on Islam and Muslims in Switzerland, Mallory Schneuwly Purdie firstly describes the historical development through which Islam has become the third largest religious denomination in Switzerland after Catholicism and Protestantism. Four confluent migration phases (economic, political, family reunification and humanitarian) explain the ethnic-linguistic diversity of Islam in Switzerland, where Muslims of Turkish, Bosnian, Albanian and North African origin predominate. Then, the author shows how Muslims have become both objects and subjects of media and political debates through the examples of religious visibility and Islamic militancy. She demonstrates that the 2008 popular initiative to ban the construction of new minarets in Switzerland and, in the mind of the initiators, to stop what they define as evidence of an "Islamisation" of Switzerland, has on the contrary contributed to the politicisation of Muslims in Switzerland. Moreover, it has fostered the emergence of an Islamic militancy that is no longer of foreign origin, but rooted in Switzerland.

Keywords

Religious visibility • Minaret ban • Islamic militancy • Arabic Transnational Links • Muslim Brothers • Muslim World League • Ahbash Network • Salafism • Politization of Muslims • Converts

---

M. Schneuwly Purdie (✉)
Swiss Center for Islam and Society, University of Fribourg, Fribourg, Switzerland
e-mail: mallory.schneuwlypurdie@unifr.ch

© The Author(s), under exclusive license to Springer Fachmedien Wiesbaden GmbH, part of Springer Nature 2024
R. Ceylan and M. Mücke (eds.), *Muslims in Europe*, Islam in der Gesellschaft,
https://doi.org/10.1007/978-3-658-43044-3_6

1 Historical Development

The Muslim presence in Switzerland is relatively recent and mostly due to international migration. Until the second half of the 20th, the number of people of Muslim culture or faith in Switzerland was only a few hundred (Stegmann et Schneuwly Purdie 2020). Since the 1960s, as a result of international migration, the Muslim presence has grown to represent today nearly 500'000 people (5.5% of the population) and become the second religion in Switzerland after Christianity. The Muslim population in Switzerland is ethnically, culturally, and socially very diverse. In 2021, 36% of Muslims in Switzerland had Swiss citizenship, but 97.2% of them are of foreign origin (Schneuwly Purdie et Tunger-Zanetti 2023). The majority come from the countries of the former Yugoslav republic, mainly Kosovo, Bosnia, Macedonia, and Montenegro. The second and third groups originate from Turkey, the Maghreb, and the Middle East respectively. A small minority of Muslims in Switzerland come from sub-Saharan Africa (Somalia, Senegal) or Asia (Afghanistan).

1.1 Four Phases of Immigration

Muslim migration to Switzerland has gone through four main phases. The first was in the 1960s. As the Swiss economy was booming, agreements were made with the Yugoslav Republic and Turkey. The workers, mainly men, were employed in industry or agriculture with a seasonal status. From the end of the 1960s until the 1980s, many students, union members and opponents of various military or dictatorial regimes went into exile. Switzerland hosted its first political refugees from North Africa, the Middle East and Turkey. It was also in the early 1980s that Muslim immigration diversified in terms of gender and generation. Indeed, from that time onwards, immigrant workers who had settled in Switzerland could apply for family reunification. Women and children thus joined Switzerland and contributed to the visibility of a presence that had remained very discreet until then, as it was until then essentially oriented towards a return to the countries of origin. The last phase in the 1990s marked a turning point and a significant increase in the Muslim population from Turkey and former Yugoslavia. On the one hand, the conflicts between the PKK and the Turkish army forced several thousand civilians to leave their regions; on the other hand, the war between 1992 and 1995 in Bosnia-Herzegovina also forced thousands of women and children to go into exile, soon followed by survivors of Srebrenica (Burri Sharani et al. 2010; Fibbi et al. 2014; Haab et al. 2010; Iseni et al. 2014).

Today, the Muslim population in Switzerland has stabilised at around 5.5% of the population. Muslim immigration is still very much present, as seen in particular in 2015 with the war in Syria and the 2021 takeover of Afghanistan by the Taliban regime. However, it is a mistake to reduce Muslim immigration to asylum. Today, it is work, but also the interplay of matrimonial alliances and transnational kinship networks that are mostly at the root of a migration project.

1.2 A Lack of Public Recognition

Despite a presence of some sixty years and a population of nearly 500,000 people, a third of whom are Swiss nationals, Islam is not yet legally recognised as a religion in Switzerland. Due to federalism, relations between the state and religious communities are the responsibility of the cantons (Monnot 2013; Schneuwly Purdie, Gianni, et Jenny 2009). Thus, each of the 26 Swiss cantons can adopt different ways of working with its religious communities (Cattacin et al. 2003). However, with the exception of Geneva and Neuchâtel, which are constitutionally secular, all the other cantons recognise a special status for the Roman Catholic Church and the Evangelical Reformed Church and do not grant any prerogatives to the other religious communities.[1] However, the presence of Muslims in all regions of Switzerland means that several cantons are now considering new forms of collaboration with their new religious communities.[2]

However, this lack of state legal recognition does not mean that Muslims have not organised themself collectively. From the 1970s onwards, Muslims have been legally constituted as associations under private law. Until recently, these associations were renting of their premises. Today, many have managed to become owners.

1.3 A Dynamic Associative Network

Over the last fifty years, the needs that Muslim associations have been called upon to meet have changed enormously. Indeed, the first associations were primarily

---

[1] Except for the Basel City canton which has recognized the Alevi community since 2012.

[2] For example, the canton of Vaud authorises in its Constitution of 2003 the recognition of public interest. A law and an application regulation set out the contours of the procedure. The Anglican and Christ-Catholic, Muslim and Free Evangelical communities have applied for recognition, and their applications are currently being evaluated.

concerned with the need for transmission. The uprootedness linked to migration made these associations privileged meeting places where to share a culture (food, music, folklore, sports), transmit a language and practice Islam. The first association committees were thus organised to provide suitable spaces for holding religious services, celebrating festivals (religious or national) and teaching the languages and culture of origin, with the result that the associative network became ethno-stratified. Albanian, Turkish, Bosnian, and Arabic have thus been the main languages of the activities of Muslim communities. Over the years, the associations have diversified their occupations. Today, in addition to worship and ritual activities, they are involved in youth and women's activities, social work (distribution of meals and food), collaboration with other local religious communities, inter-religious dialogue, organise visits of mosques for schools, offer family and professional counselling and mediation, and chaplaincy. There are currently some 260 mosque associations in Switzerland (Schneuwly Purdie et Tunger-Zanetti 2023). A special feature of this dense network of associations is that it is self-organised into an umbrella organisation at cantonal and federal level. This allows local associations to exist collectively at the cantonal or federal level and to be the interlocutor of the authorities and the media on matters that concern them. In addition to the regional network of associations, there are also three main ethnic-linguistic umbrella organisations (Albanian, Bosnian, and Turkish) which continue their national and transnational networking activities.

2 Religious Visibility and Conservative Positions: Issues and Challenges

Two main issues relating to Islam structure most public debates about Muslims in Switzerland: the religious visibility of Muslims and the resonance of conservative militant Islamic discourses.[3] At first glance, these two issues do not seem to be interconnected, but as we will see, they are closely linked. Although the Muslim presence in Switzerland became visible from the 1980s onwards, it is only since 2005 that the signs of the visibility of Islam become interpreted through the prism of militant Islam. Indeed, in the 1990s, Switzerland had already experienced a

---

[3] To define this militant Islam, I rely on the definition given by Samir Amghar, who refers to "groups based on a precise vision of the religious, affirming the recognition of Islamic precepts which they consider as supreme norms and values. In the name of a totalising Islam defining morality and ethics and governing life in society, and even political behaviour, they call for an Islamisation of the codes, practices and discourses of sociological Muslims" (Amghar, 2013, p. 15, own translation).

6 Islam and Muslims in Switzerland …   101

heated debate on the headscarf of a Geneva public school teacher and a Neuchâtel schoolgirl. Both cases, however, were the subject of a debate on the laicity of public schools and the confessional neutrality of the state. From 2004 and the vote on the facilitated naturalisation of second and third generation foreigners (Gianni 2009; Gianni, Giugni, et Michel 2015), the angle of the debates changed. Islam become more and more discussed through the prism of militant Islam and as a threat to the Swiss culture, its democratic principals, and its institutions.

2.1   The Minaret Ban: The Rise of Islam as a Political Object

A political uprising launched by members of right wing parties such as the Swiss People's Party (SVP) and the evangelical Federal Democratic Party against a so called Islamisation of Switzerland began and found its target in 2005 when a Muslim association submitted a permit to build a 5 to 6 m high minaret in the municipality of Wangen (canton of Solothurn). This minaret project sparked a national debate that led to a constitutional ban on the construction of new minarets in Switzerland in November 2009. Indeed, other minaret projects have been submitted in the cantons of Bern, Zurich and St. Gallen and are presented by right wing politicians as a tangible sign of the *"creeping Islamisation"* although Switzerland had only two minarets until 2005 (Geneva and Zurich).[4] In 2006, members of the SVP and FDP met in Egerkingen (the canton of Solothurn). They created the Egerkingen Committee and decided to launch the initiative to ban minarets. As Jean-François Mayer points out, the choice of the minaret is highly strategic: although it is characteristic of Islam, it is not compulsory for religious purposes, since not all mosques have one. This aspect prevents the initiative from being discredited as an obstruction to religious freedom. On the other hand, the initiators insisted that the minaret was an expression of a political power and that it had nothing to do with faith (Mayer 2018). In 2007, the Egerkingen Committee launched the signatures recollection in order to file a popular federal initiative. The initiative, duly accompanied by over 113,000 signatures, was submitted to the Federal Chancellery the 08.07.2008. At the press conference a National Councillor of the Swiss People's Party gave the initiative its militant colour by stating that *"Islam appears today as a model of simple, virile and combative identification of poor, prolific populations, set out to conquer wealth and consumer goods, in a*

---

[4] To date, Switzerland has four minarets. Apart from Geneva (1978) and Zurich (1963), Winterthur (2005) and Wangen (2009) managed to get their construction authorized and built before the ban (Tunger-Zanetti and Schneuwly Purdie 2015 p. 575).

desire for revenge for the humiliations suffered (…). The positive achievements of our culture, tolerance, equality of the sexes, respect and dialogue are thus destabilised by massive immigration, fed underhand by militants at war with modernity, whose weaknesses they despise" (quoted by Mayer, in Haenni and Lathion, 2009, p. 19). He goes on to call for the refusal of banners advocating an intolerant practice. The debate preceding the vote mixed the Madrid and London attacks, the riots over the Danish caricatures, requests for Muslim plots in cemeteries, veiled schoolgirls or university students, and exemptions from science and gym classes. The campaign posters associated minarets with niqab, compared minarets to missiles tearing apart the Swiss flag and its territory. The amalgamations of Islam, discrimination against women, political violence and terrorism surge and convince. Although the Swiss political authorities recommend rejecting the initiative, it was accepted in a popular vote on 29 November 2009 by 57,5% percent of the population. This vote thus constitutes a turning point on the place of Islam in Swiss society and raises the spectre of Islam as an external and internal threat. As a consequence, Gianni points that this expresses a *"shift from regulating Islam as a religion to securing Muslim practices and therefore Muslims"* (Gianni 2017). Since then, cases on the visibility of Islam and practices associated with Muslims have regularly made the headlines: handshakes with people of the opposite sex, burkini in municipal swimming pools, furtive prayers in the stairwells of a university, veiling of schoolgirls, university students or trainees, and of course the wearing of full-face veils in the public space.[5] These different manifestations of an islamity are seen as evidence of the infiltration of Islamic militantism into Swiss society and as precursors of communitarianism and parallel societies.

2.2 Islam and Muslims in the Media and Politics

Based on the analysis of a representative sample of articles published in 18 Swiss printed media between 2009 and 2017, Ettinger shows that when the press talks about Muslims, 80% of the cases refers to foreign Muslims. However, the author notes that Muslims in Switzerland are increasingly becoming the subject of articles (Ettinger 2018). He explains that the growth of their media presence is linked to two main factors: on the one hand, the attacks committed in neighbouring

---

[5] Indeed, after France, Belgium and Denmark, Switzerland also banned the niqab and its relatives in all public spacesin March 2021 (Schneuwly Purdie and Tunger-Zanetti 2023, p. 669), following an initiative launched by the same Egerkingen committee.

countries, and on the other hand, the political campaigns associated to popular initiatives. Ettinger highlights the impact of the anti-minaret campaign on the media treatment of Islam, which brought Muslims to the forefront as never before and never again. The content analysis of the articles confirms that religious visibility is an important social and political concern. It also points to an increased suggested association between the visibility of Islam and radicalisation. Indeed, 25% of the articles published during the observed period concern a subject related to visibility, in particular minarets and the veil (in all its forms). Next come articles related to radicalisation, including controversies about young people leaving for Syrian jihad territories, but also the governance of mosques, the preaching of imams, their theological positioning, and their education. Other themes include discrimination against Muslims (9%), the practice of religion (7%), threatened or perceived impossible integration (7%), Muslim organisations (7%), basic democratic rights (7%), successful integration (2%) and the daily life of Muslims (2%) (Ettinger, 2018, p. 13). The longitudinal analysis of the themes also shows that while visibility and radicalisation remain a "chestnut" of the written press, in 2015 the theme of radicalisation supplanted that of visibility. Thus, in 2017, more than one article out of two concerning Muslims in Switzerland had radicalisation and terrorism as an angle. This overrepresentation of topics related to visibility and radicalisation contributes to the belief that the more visible Islam is, the greater the risks to democracy and internal security. The study also points to a significant increase in articles that create distance between Muslims and the non-Muslim Swiss society: the percentage of articles producing distance has thus increased from 22% in 2009 to 69% in 2017, thus contributing to the fabrication of the category "Islam" and presenting it as incompatible with another constructed category "Switzerland". Moreover, as Ettinger points out, the voice given to Muslim actors in these debates is often that of clear-cut, divisive positions, unrepresentative of either the "silent majority" of Muslims in Switzerland (Gianni et al. 2008) or of official representatives of organised Islam.

The interest in the visibility of Islam and the risks of radicalisation is not limited to the media. It also reflects a growing concern of politicians for the same issues. Indeed, for the past ten years, Islam has also been a recurrent subject of parliamentary questions in the cantons and at the Confederation. A study by the Institute of Religious Law of the University of Fribourg in 15 Swiss cantons shows that some 140 parliamentary interpellations on religious issues were submitted between 2010 and 2018, of which 81 questioned a subject related to Islam (Ammann et Pahud de Mortanges 2019). One third of these interpellations on Islam were tabled by representatives of the Swiss Volk's Party (SVP), to which the majority of the Egerkingen committee members belong. These interpellations concern five main themes: legislative changes towards a public recognition, facial veiling and dress codes (hijab, burkini, sportswear), Islamic infrastructures (cemeteries, kindergartens, private schools, religious classes in public schools, chaplaincies, cultural centres, prayer rooms), value debates (handshake between opposite sexes, class dispensation, participation in camps and swimming lessons), radicalisation and terrorism (training of imams, control of "hate preachers", financing of Islamic associations, independence of Islamic organisations). At the level of the federal parliament, some 40 interpellations were registered between 2017 and 2022, the majority of which concerned issues related to internal security[6] such as the creation of a register of imams (often described as "hate preachers"), transnational relations in the governance of the mosques, financing of Islamic centres, banning of religious groups associated with Salafist movements and groups ideologically close to the doctrine of the Muslim Brotherhood, or the return of foreign fighters.

2.3   Militant Islam

If, as the respective studies by Ettinger (2017) and Amman and Pahud de Mortanges (2018) show, the media and political treatment of Islam as a social problem and risk for national security is essentially the domain of political parties and media close to the right, it would also be a methodological error to clear Muslim associations and some of their officials or religious leaders of any responsibility. Indeed, if the majority of Swiss Muslims, Islamic centres and their leaders are integrated and participate constructively to the social cohesion, there are also resistant and militant positions that call for non-participation in civil society and encourage Islamic discourses, positions and practices that are problematic in view of the Swiss legal order and subject to dissension with other Muslims and the Swiss population in general. In this contribution, even though there exist oppositional and political forms of militancy in some Turkish, Bosnian, or Albanian

---

[6] All parliamentary interpellations can be consulted on the internet site of the Swiss Parliament. https://www.parlament.ch/en, accessed 14 February 2023.

mosques, I only focus on Arabic-speaking transnational militant Islam.[7] Moreover, even though jihadism can be considered as a violent Islamic militancy, it will not be directly addressed in this article. However, it should be noted that individuals who left Switzerland to join groups linked to Al-Qaeda or Daesh mostly had contact with one or the other groups presented in this article.

2.4 First Generation Networks Linked to Transnational Movements

Firstly, individuals or groups inserted in transnational politico-religious networks are often attached to the modes of expression of Islam in their countries of origin and tend to import a political reading of religion. The former generally constitute associative structures such as mosques or prayer halls. Although these are often attended by a few (to several) hundred visitors, it is important to stress out that most of them do not share the politico-religious orientations of certain leaders. Those representatives are mostly authority figures in mosques founded by nationals from the Arab Middle East (Egypt, Saudi Arabia, Lebanon) or the Maghreb (Tunisia, Algeria, Morocco) who are connected not only with counterparts in their countries of origin, but also with fellow immigrants in neighbouring countries. In Switzerland, these are mainly affinities with politico-religious orientations close to the Muslim Brotherhood (Amghar 2009; Maréchal 2009; Schmid et al. 2022), the Wahhabi-Salafism of the Muslim World League (Amghar 2011; Schmid et al. 2022) and the Lebanese Ahbash doctrine (Amghar 2007; Schmid et al. 2022).[8] Thus, some Islamic centres or Muslim organisations (associations without a place of worship) are identified for their relations with these transnational movements. I will now look at these three networks.

The Muslims Swiss League Switzerland (SML), an association founded by the Franco-Tunisian Mohammed Karmous in 1992, is a known example of associative relations with MB fringes (Amghar 2009; Maréchal 2009; Rickenbacher 2020; Schmid et al. 2022). MSL has antennas in various cities in the French and German speaking parts of Switzerland (Neuchâtel, Geneva, Prilly an Bienne) as well as in

---

[7] The choice to focus on forms of militancy in Arabic-speaking Muslim communities is partly due to the current lack of research on militancy in Turkish, Bosnian or Albanian associations, but also to the fact that their militancy often mixes nationalism and religion. Furthermore, converts tend to attend Arabic-speaking mosques. As we shall see, converts play an important role in Islamic militancy.

[8] Note that the Tablighi are also present in Switzerland. However, they have so far only been studied in Swiss German-speaking part (Schmid et al. 2022).

Tessin (Lugano). However, since the majority of the Arab-speaking Muslims live in French-Speaking Switzerland, their activities are better known and attended in this region, as well as in the Tessin. MSL do not have its own premisses, but their leaders and some of their members are often active representatives of local mosques. The Islamic Centre of Geneva founded by Saïd Ramadan, son-in-law of the founder of the brotherhood Hassan al-Bannah and led to date by his son Hani Ramadan is such an example. MSL used to organise congresses during which French-speaking personalities ideologically close to the MB, such as Abdelfattah Moubrou, Hassan Iquouissen, or Hani and Tariq Ramadan were present. It would be wrong to describe the MB in Switzerland as a structured organisation. As Brigitte Maréchal (2009) points out, "the Muslim Brotherhood movement in Europe is primarily composed of various informal networks that are based on interpersonal ties and aim at long-term educational action" (p. 49). It is therefore difficult to label any of the associations as formally MB. It is more in the expression of family, marital or friendship ties, as well as in intellectual affinities with certain positions, particularly in education, the promotion of Islamic values, the protection of Muslim identity and the enhancement of religious practice, that a certain kinship may emerge.

Although the Saudi diaspora in Switzerland is not numerically large, the Muslim World League (MWL) nevertheless chose Geneva as the location for one of its most important centres of "religious diplomacy" in Europe in 1978 (Mouline 2020). Administered by a Saudi-represented board, the Islamic Foundation of Geneva has experienced several controversies over foreign interference, as well as turnover in its imams (most of whom were trained in Medina), some of whom may have held controversial positions in newspapers (Amghar 2011). In Switzerland, various mosques have been subject to Wahhabi-Salafi positions to the extent that one, An-Nur in Winterthur (canton of Zurich),[9] was closed by the authorities and Abu Ramadan, the imam of a Ar-Rahman Mosquee in Bienne was sentenced by the Federal Office of Justice for the discriminatory content of his statements and preaches (Saal 2020; Schneuwly et al. 2023, p. 670). A recent study by the University of Lucerne on Salafism in German-speaking Switzerland states that there is about one Salafist-oriented Mosque in the major cities of German-speaking Switzerland such as Zurich, Basel, Bern, Winterthur, Lucerne, St. Gallen, Biel, Thun, Fribourg and Schaffhausen (Endres et al. 2023).

A third example of this first form of a resistant and militant form of Islam is the Ahbash network Swiss Islam Council (SIC). Founded around the Islamic

---

[9] After the departure for Syria of some 15 young people, including minors, who had attended this mosque and the classes of its imam Abu Mohammed, the authorities ordered its closure.

Centre of Lausanne (CIL), it coordinates various centres in the cantons of Vaud, Neuchâtel, Geneva, Bern, and Zurich. Posing as a shield against violent extremism, the Ahbash condemn MB and Wahhabi discourses (Amghar 2007). However, their teachings also show a puritanical rigorism that brings them closer in many respects to those from whom they claim to distance themselves, especially in terms of dichotomising a world between 'Us' (good Muslims) and the 'Others'.

While these different groups and mosques were founded and are still run today by first generation Muslims, more research should be conducted to analyse how the second and third generation Muslims concretely envision the future governance of the local mosques.[10] The CIL, for example, makes a point of theologically training the next generation of teachers (male and female) and imams. It also takes great care to select its leaders and spokespersons from among the members closest to their imam Muwafak al-Rifaï.

2.5 Home Grown Resistant and Militant Movements

Secondly, groups founded in Switzerland by converts or third generation (or more) Muslims have emerged. These groups differ from the first ones in that they are not part of solidarity networks or premigratory political-religious affinities. On the contrary, these new kinds of groups oppose the Islam of their parents, which they consider to be distorted, full of un-Islamic beliefs and cultural practices. They advocate for an authentic and restored Islam and refuse the secularisation of public spaces. This second form of militant Islam is generally constituted as an informal group, more rarely as an association under private law. Although their members generally attend mosques, these groups share the particularity of having organised themselves on their margins. In doing so, the founders affirm a demarcation from the ethnocultural orientations that have characterised the Islamic associative milieu until now. Some of them have their own premises, others meet in mosques, and some meet in public spaces, such as sports halls, libraries, prayer rooms in public buildings or even in the house of one of them. Often at odds with the teachings given in most Islamic centres, they consume religious material online, on dedicated platforms, forums, channels, and social networks. In general, members adhere to and share conservative discourses, particularly in terms mixed spaces, modesty, sexuality, or gender equality before the law (inheritance, marriage, divorce, child custody). Their positions are dichotomised and politicised; and they call for communitarian-type arrangements. Some of them

---

[10] This is also true for the Albanian, Turkish and Bosnian centres.

are well established and organise preaching activities (da'wa); others remain in the background, concerned with preserving a mythologised Islamic purity from any contamination. This second group refers to a nebula of networks commonly grouped under the label of Salafism. In their studies of Salafi circles in German-speaking Switzerland, Endres et al. (2023) identify three clusters of Salafi groups: firstly, mosques with young preachers, often socialised in Europe, who have studied at the University of Medina and adopt Madkhali positions.[11] These circles are resolutely apolitical and oriented towards the acquisition of religious knowledge. Secondly, (supra)regional groups of women who meet online to develop their religious knowledge. According to the authors, this virtual format is appreciated because it allows them to reconcile their quest for Islamic knowledge with their family obligations. These women's groups are, however, linked to the Madkhali networks and to the third cluster represented by the Islamic Central Council Switzerland (ICCS). This association founded by converts is symptomatic of the tensions presented in this article between religious visibility and militant Islam.

2.6 The Islamic Central Council Switzerland, a Political Object or Subject?

While the Egerkingen Committee was pursuing the objective of slowing down the progress of the so called "Islamisation" and the visibility of Islam in Switzerland, 2009 was paradoxically also the year in which the Islam Central Council of Switzerland was born. It was in the midst of the campaign against the minaret initiative that a group of Swiss men and women who had converted to Islam founded an association whose "ostentatious Islamic habitus" (Leuenberger 2013) would reify the social representation of Islam as a risk to social cohesion. The members of the ICCS performs a militant and conservative Islam of Salafist type. As Leuenberger points out, the ICCS intends to encourage Islamic education projects in Switzerland and to contribute to the creation of an Islamic identity that transcends the ethnocultural differences that precisely characterise Islam and Muslims in Switzerland. The association aims to represent the moral interests and orthopraxis of Muslims and follows a clear political agenda. Their

---

[11] Madkhalism is a movement of Salafism that emerged in Saudi Arabia in the 1990s. It is named after its founder Rabi al-Makhdali, a former student of the University of Medina where he taught. Its masters include Salafist theologians such as Abd al-Aziz ibn Baz and Muhammad Nassirudinne al Albani. Madkhalism insists on the principle of obedience to the ruler as long as he does not commit religious infidelity, even if he makes illegitimate use of violence (Thomas 2020).

ideological positions are indeed at odds with the Swiss model of integration of religious minorities: defence of the niqab, plea for the creation of private Islamic kindergartens, schools, as well as a Swiss Fatwa Council. They also call for the practice of a so-called "authentic" Islam as practised by Muhammad and the "well-guided" caliphs. These new actors of Islam in Switzerland stand out in the Muslim associative milieu, which has been very discreet publicly and in the media until recently. For several years, the best-known members of the ICCS, Nicolas Blancho, Abdel Azziz Qaasim Illi, Nora Illi (who died in 2020) and Naïm Cherni, gave a series of interviews and participated in TV shows. They accused Switzerland of a growing Islamophobia and denounced violations of the religious freedom of Muslims. They organised public events: congresses, information stands, conferences, demonstrations (Schneuwly Purdie 2013). They performed a communicative and event-based activism which, contrary to what the Egerkingen committee had intended to, makes a section of Swiss Muslims not only visible but politicised. In 2017, Blancho, Illi and Cherni were charged with propaganda for Al Qaeda. This judicial procedure, which ended in 2021 (Schneuwly Purdie and Tünger-Zanetti 2019 and 2023), had consequences for the reputation of the association, which saw its financial resources from Qatar and Kuwait dry up. Since then, the association has become more discreet. It has not organised any major congress since 2014 and its members are less present in the written press and on television. On the other hand, the ICCS continues its activity online and on social networks. Its YouTube account, which is regularly updated with programmes such as Late Night Diwan, IZRS[12] News, and conferences on topics as diverse as anti-Muslim racism and wokism, is followed by nearly 20,000 people; its Facebook account has over 40,000 followers. The ICCS thus profiles itself as an association for the defence of Muslims in Switzerland and as a religious body capable of overcoming their cultural differences and uniting them around a common identity and an "authentic Islam". Through its program, the association intends to be an actor of Islam in Switzerland. However, its public image reflects the fears of a large section of the population that supported the initiatives against minarets and the niqab. It also contributes to make the ICCS both an *object* and a *subject* of domestic politics. The creation of the ICCS in the midst of the "anti-minaret" campaign is thus a sign of the by now common intertwining of controversies related to visibility and militant Islam. The militancy of its members, while unparalleled in any other Swiss Muslim association, reflects the present issues and challenges of tomorrow faced by Muslims in Switzerland, the authorities in the development of their religious policies and civil society.

---

[12] IZRS is the German acronym for ICCS.

References

Amghar, Samir. 2007. Les Ahbâch, ou le nouvel islam européen. *Politique Étrangère Automne* 3:605–615. https://doi.org/10.3917/pe.073.0605.

Amghar, Samir. 2009. L'Europe, terre d'influence des Frères musulmans. *Politique Étrangère Eté* 2:377–388. https://doi.org/10.3917/pe.092.0377.

Amghar, Samir. 2011. La Ligue islamique mondiale en Europe : Un instrument de défense des intérêts stratégiques saoudiens. *Critique Internationale* 51(2):113–127. https://doi.org/10.3917/crii.051.0113.

Amghar, Samir. 2013. *L'islam militant en Europe*. Gollion: Infolio.

Ammann, Max, et René Pahud de Mortanges. 2019. « Religion in der politischen Arena. Eine Auswertung parlamentarischer Vorstösse aud kantonaler Ebene ». Fribourg: Institut de droit des religions. https://www.unifr.ch/ius/religionsrecht/fr/assets/public/docume nts/Gutachten%20und%20Studien/Studie%20IRR%20-%20Religion%20in%20der% 20politischen%20Arena.pdf.

Burri Sharani, Barbara, Denise Efionayi, Stephan Hammer, Marco Pecoraro, Bernhard Soland, Astrit Tsaka, et Chantal Wyssmüller. 2010. «La population kosovare en Suisse». Confédération suisse – ODM – FMS – HES Lucerne.

Cattacin, Sandro, Cla Reto Famos, Michaël Duttwiler, et Hans Mahnig. 2003. «Etat et religions en Suisse. Luttes pour la reconnaissances, formes de la reconnaissance.» Berne: Commission fédérale contre le racisme.

Endres, Jürgen, Andreas Tunger-Zanetti, Silvia Martens, et Martin Baumann. 2023. «Salafiyya in der Deutschschweiz. Ergebnisse aus der Feldforschung». Lucerne: Zentrum für Religionsforschung.

Ettinger, Patrick. 2018. «La qualité de la couverture médiatique des musulmans en Suisse». Berne: Forschungsinstitut Öffentlichkeit und Gesellschaft, Univeristé de Zurich. https:// www.ekr.admin.ch/pdf/Studie_Qual_Berichterst_F.pdf.

Fibbi, Rosita, Bülent Kaya, Jehane Moussa, Marco Pecoraro, Yannick Rossy, et Ilka Steiner. 2014. «Les Marocains, les Tunisiens et les Algériens en Suisse». Confédération suisse – ODM – FMS.

Gianni, Matteo. 2009. «Introduction». In *Musulmans d'aujourd'hui. Identités plurielles en Suisse*, édité par Mallory Schneuwly Purdie, Matteo Gianni, et Jenny Magali, 13-22. Genève: Labor et Fides.

Gianni, Matteo. 2017. « Politisation de la question musulmane et dilemmes démocratiques ». *Hostilité envers les musulmans: Société, média, politique. Tangram* 40:83–86.

Gianni, Matteo, Marco Giugni, et Noémie Michel. 2015. *Les musulmans en Suisse. Profils et intégration*. Lausanne: Presses polytechniques et universitaires romandes.

Gianni, Matteo, Stéphane Lathion, Mallory Schneuwly Purdie, et Magali Jenny. 2008. «Vie musulmane en Suisse. Profils identitaires, demandes et perceptions des musulmans en Suisse». Rapport de recherche pour la Commission fédérale des étrangers. Berne: Commission Fédérale des Etrangers. https://www.ekm.admin.ch/dam/data/ekm/dokume ntation/materialien/mat_muslime_f.pdf.

Haab, Katharina, Claudio Bolzman, Andrea Kugler, et Özcan Yilmaz. 2010. « Diaspora et communautés de migrants de Turquie en Suisse ». Berne: Office fédéral des Migrations.

6 Islam and Muslims in Switzerland ...

Haenni, Patrick, et Stéphane Lathion. 2009. *Les minarets de la discorde*. Infolio. Gollion: Infolio.

Iseni, Bashkim, Didier Ruedin, Dina Bader, et Denise Efionayi-Mäder. 2014. *La population de Bosnie et Herzégovine en Suisse*. Office fédéral des migrations. Diaspora Studie. Berne.

Leuenberger, Susanne. 2013. «"I have become a stranger in my homeland": An analysis of the public performance of converts to islam in Switzerland.» In *Debating Islam. Negociating Religion, Europe and the Self*. Bielefeld: Transkript.

Maréchal, Brigitte. 2009. *Les Frères Musulmans en Europe. Racines et discours*. Proche-Orient. Paris: PUF.

Mayer, Jean-François. 2018. «Pas de minarets au paradis. Le vote suisse de 2009 et la "question islamique" en Europe». *Social Compass* 65(2):215-33.

Monnot, Christophe. 2013. *Croire ensemble. Analyse institutionnelle du paysage religieux en Suisse*. Zurich: Seismo.

Mouline, Nabil. 2020. «Arabie Saoudite : une nouvelle diplomatie religieuse?» *Politique étrangère* Printemps (1):43-55. https://doi.org/10.3917/pe.201.0043.

Rickenbacher, Daniel. 2020. The beginnings of political Islam in Switzerland: Said Ramadan's Muslim brotherhood mosque in Geneva and the Swiss authorities. *The Journal of the Middle East and Africa* 11(2):179–202. https://doi.org/10.1080/21520844.2020.1762152.

Saal, Johannes. 2020. *The dark social of religious radicals. Jihadi networks and mobilization in Germany, Austria and Switzerland, 1998–2018*. Wisbaden: Springer.

Schmid, Hansjörg, Noemi Trucco, et Federico Biasca. 2022. «Swiss Muslim Communitites in Transnational and Local Interactions. Public Perceptions, State of research, Case Studies». SZIG/CSIS-Studies 7. Fribourg: Centre Suisse Islam et Société. https://folia.unifr.ch/unifr/documents/313356.

Schneuwly Purdie, Mallory. 2013. «Performer l'islam, dessiner les contours de la "communauté musulmane" de Suisse. Le Conseil central islamique suisse comme performance d'un islam "authentique".» In *La Suisse des mosquées. Derrière le voile de l'unité musulmane*, édité par Christophe Monnot, 151–71. Genève: Labor et Fides.

Schneuwly Purdie, Mallory, Matteo Gianni, et Magali Jenny, éd. 2009. *Musulmans d'aujourd'hui. Identités plurielles en Suisse*. Genève: Labor et Fides.

Schneuwly Purdie, Mallory, et Andreas Tünger-Zanetti. 2019. «Switzerland. Country report 2018». In *Yearbook of Muslims in Europe*, édité par Oliver Scharbrodt, Samin Akgönül, Ahmet Alibasic, Jörgen Nielsen, et Edgunas Racius, Brill. Vol. 11. Leiden.

Schneuwly Purdie, Mallory, et Andreas Tunger-Zanetti. 2023. «Switzerland. Country report 2021». In *Yearbook of Muslims in Europe*, édité par Samim Akgönül, Jorgen Nielsen, Ahmet Alibasic, Stephanie Müssig, et Racius Egdunas, Brill, 14:667–83. Leiden.

Stegmann, Ricarda, et Mallory Schneuwly Purdie. 2020. «Qui sont les musulmans en Suisse? Histoire de la migration». *Islam&Society* (blog). https://islamandsociety.ch/fr/home-2/swiss/muslims/history/.

Thomas, Aude. 2020. *Madkhalisme en Libye : état des lieux et perspectives d'évolution des groupes madkhalistes*. Paris: Fondation pour la recherche stratégique.

Tunger-Zanetti, Andreas, et Mallory Schneuwly Purdie. 2015. «Switzerland. Country report 2014». In *Yearbook of Muslims in Europe*, édité par Oliver Scharbrodt, Samin Akgönül, Ahmet Alibasic, Jörgen Nielsen, et Edgunas Racius, Brill. Vol. 7. Leiden.

Mallory Schneuwly Purdie has a doctorate in the sociology of religion from the Ecole Pratique de Hautes Etudes (Sorbonne - Paris) and the University of Fribourg (Switzerland). She works as a researcher and lecturer at the Swiss Centre for Islam and Society at the University of Fribourg. In her research, she examines the role of the religious component in the construction of personal and collective identity. She also analyses the manifestations of Islam in the public space, from the perspective of discourses and practices. Her research questions have led her to study Islam and Muslims in prisons. In 2022, she co-authored a book and various articles on Islam in prison, for example: Schneuwly Purdie, M., Wilkinson, M., Quraishi, M., & Irfan, L. (2022). La prison comme expérience liminale du changement religieux: Une analyse des trajectoires religieuses de personnes détenues de confession musulmane. *Criminologie*, *55*(1), 139–165. Schneuwly Purdie, M., Irfan, L., Quraishi, M., & Wilkinson, M. (2021). Living Islam in Prison: How Gender Affects the Religious Experiences of Female and Male Offenders. *Religions*, *12*(5), 298–315.

Alevis and Turkish-Muslims in Austria: History and Current Developments

7

Hüseyin Çiçek

> **Abstract**
>
> Interest in Muslims and Islam has not only increased since 9/11. In Austria, Islam was for a long time associated only with Turkish immigration. Since the migration movements from various Muslim countries due to war and civil wars, for example, the multifaceted nature of Islam in Austria has increased. This article focuses on the development of the Islam Law and how individual Turkish-Muslim and Alevi communities have benefited from it.

> **Keywords**
>
> Islam Law · Islamgesetz · Turkish-Muslims · Islam-Alevis · AABF · Austria

1 Introduction

The history of Muslims in Austria and the Austro-Hungarian Monarchy began even before the implementation of the Islam Law (*Islamgesetz*) in 1912. In this context, it is important to consider the diplomatic links between the Ottoman Empire and the Austro-Hungarian Monarchy. Likewise, economic relations and cultural transfer before 1912 should not be overlooked. However, the implementation of the Islam Law in 1912 represents a special event and is fundamentally

---

H. Çiçek (✉)
Department of Religious Studies, University of Vienna, Vienna, Austria
e-mail: hueseyin.cicek@univie.ac.at

© The Author(s), under exclusive license to Springer Fachmedien Wiesbaden GmbH, part of Springer Nature 2024
R. Ceylan and M. Mücke (eds.), *Muslims in Europe*, Islam in der Gesellschaft,
https://doi.org/10.1007/978-3-658-43044-3_7

113

linked to the current developments of Islam in Austria. The Islam Law, or the legal recognition of Islam, enabled Muslims in Austria to benefit from Habsburg and later Austrian law. This enabled Muslims, at that time mainly from the region of Bosnia-Herzegovina, to organize themselves religiously within the territory of a majority Christian nation. Somewhat forgotten after World War 2, the Islam Law was "reactivated" in the context of the migration of Turkish guest workers beginning in 1964. Especially the increasing number of Muslims – among others from Turkey – led to the fact that in 1979 the Islamic religious community in Austria was officially founded and recognized as a religious community. The bases for this development were, among other things, the increasing religious needs of Muslims living in Austria, as evidenced, for example, by the need for religious education in schools. The *Islamgesetz* also promotes institutionalization and aims at ensuring that the Islamic faith community develops an Austrian identity with Muslim religiosity. For the Austrian state, it meant treating Muslims as part of Austrian law and subsequently integrating them into politics as well as society. This did not happen overnight, and by no means was it without challenges. It is hard to imagine the Austrian economy, social work, culture, and other important areas of everyday life without Muslims. The current Federal Minister of Justice of the Austrian Republic, Alma Zadic, whose parents come from Bosnia-Herzegovina, clearly shows that Muslims in Austria are part of the majority society. They are however not accepted as such by all Austrians.[1]

Coexistence between Muslims and the Austrian majority society is harmonious and many Muslims call themselves Austrian Muslims. The focus here is not on the everyday challenges of individuals, but rather on challenges regarding politics, the media, and Muslim organizations. The amendment to the Islam Act – will be discussed below– has made it clear that politicians are suspicious of Muslims and their organizations. This in turn has implications for the areas of integration and migration and, among other things, fuels the Islamophobia of a section of Austrian society. Justified criticism that Muslims in Austria, for example, should not be subject to influence from Turkey or other Muslim countries becomes entangled with populist alarmism that Muslims have no fundamental interest in integrating into the Austrian majority society.[2]

This article is about how Islam and Muslims have changed over time and how they are changing now in Austria. The figures, data, and facts presented in this

---

[1] The right-wing party FPÖ (Freedom Party Austria) and discussions by other right-wing groups about the federal minister show this very clearly.

[2] https://crippledsam.files.wordpress.com/2010/03/daham-statt-islam.jpg The FPÖ election poster, e.g. "Daham statt Islam". Accessed 03.03.2023.

7 Alevis and Turkish-Muslims in Austria: History and Current Developments 115

article are based, among others, on those of the Austrian Integration Fund (from here on IF) – Fund for the Integration of Refugees and Migrants.[3] Reference is also made to other research literature from recent years.

Before the historical developments are presented, it should first be pointed out how the Muslim community in Austria is currently organized structurally. The following numbering is for better orientation and is not meant as a form of evaluation.

The first group of Muslims in Austria is still formed by Muslim labor migrants from the 1960s. Not to be forgotten are also the non-Muslims born in Austria who converted to Islam, as well as their Muslim children, whose parents were neither born abroad nor Muslims by birth. In addition, there are Muslim refugees from various regions of the world. Muslims who hold citizenship in an EU member state and emigrate to Austria must also be added. Austria thus has a very heterogeneous Muslim population.

2 A Brief Overview of Historical Developments

Even before the rise of the Ottomans and their policy of expansion to the gates of Vienna, Christians and Muslims were not strangers to each other on European soil. Until the discovery of America by Columbus, for example, Muslims also ruled in Europe, including Spain. Likewise, the Crusades led to an increase in warlike entanglements between Muslims and Christians. A key aspect of these entanglements is that during the Middle Ages, conflicts between the two warring parties were primarily religiously dominated. The Crusades were triggered by a variety of circumstances, but among them were the destruction of the Church of the Holy Sepulcher in Jerusalem in 1009 by the then Caliph Al-Hakim and the prevention of Christian pilgrims from entering the Holy Land. These are only two circumstances that attest to the fact that religious causes were in the foreground as reasons for the conflictual actions between Christians and Muslims (Cf. Heine et al. 2012, p. 42).

As was mentioned in the introduction, there was a significant amount of conflict between Christians and Muslims before the Islamic Law of 1912. This was accompanied by various forms of cultural exchange between the two groups. Strictly speaking, the Habsburg and Ottoman empires bordered each other

---

[3] https://www.integrationsfonds.at/wien/?gclid=CjwKCAiA3pugBhAwEiwAWFzwdYR GGrpZLYyDK7oxYW1fLOHzbFQtJP7kRT4bDob36sNgXYnCMm3X-hoCxw0QAvD_ BwE Accessed 03.03.2023.

geographically. Somewhat more than other European powers of the time, the Habsburg monarchy had to respond to geopolitical realities. The proximity of the two empires made both confrontations and exchanges necessary. However, the interactions between the two powers were not exclusively determined by warlike confrontations. Through conquests, Muslims came under Christian rule or Christians came under Muslim rule. This also opened diplomatic channels because both powers were interested in winning over the respective Christian or Muslim populations for their own interests. This policy was intended to ensure that the respective subjects did not feel discriminated against and turned against the rulers or could be instrumentalized from outside. Similarly, the conquests led to the need to adapt the legal systems of the respective empires to the current realities. For example, the expansion of the Habsburg monarchy meant that the Catholic empire had to include non-Catholic Christians and Muslims in its existing legal system. Thus, a side effect of the expansion was a pluralization, albeit unintended, of the legal system. Of course, this was not only due to Christian charity but also, for example, because Orthodox Christians in the southeast were supposed to defend the borders of the Habsburg monarchy (Cf. Heine et al. 2012, p. 42).

The geopolitical entanglements of the two empires led to an increase in cultural transfer. Above all, the culinary influences of the Ottomans have been preserved in Vienna and Austria to this day. Coffee and coffee houses, as well as the Kipferl in the shape of the crescent moon, were adopted by the Habsburgs. Fashion in the Habsburg Empire was also influenced by the Ottomans. In addition, influences on the art trade, language, and music can be found. The opera "The Abduction from the Seraglio" by Mozart still bears witness to this today. Interest in the language of the Ottomans and their cultural and religious background also increased. The founding of the Imperial and Royal Academy for Oriental Languages in 1754 is a good testimony to this. The orientalist Joseph von Hammer-Purgstall (1774–1856) studied at this institution. Many graduates of the academy later served as diplomats.

Changing geopolitical realities, including war in the Balkans and parts of Eastern Europe, meant that the Muslim population had to repeatedly abandon their settlement areas and settle in new regions of the Balkans – or elsewhere in the Ottoman Empire. Muslims living in Slovenia had to leave their homeland with the army of the High Porte in 1680. Due to further loss of Ottoman control, Muslim citizens in other regions of the Balkans were forced to resettle as well. The Muslim population of Belgrade, for example, was forced to leave the city in 1686. With the reconquest of the city by the Ottomans in 1690 or 1691 part of the former population returned, only to emigrate again in 1739, when the region fell

7 Alevis and Turkish-Muslims in Austria: History and Current Developments

under Habsburg rule. Serbian uprisings in the nineteenth century, for their part, caused many Muslims to flee their hometowns or villages. Some of them emigrated permanently to the Ottoman Empire or settled in Bosnia and Herzegovina. As a result, the region became the last "bastion" of Muslims in the Balkans. In 1908, Bosnia and Herzegovina were occupied by the Habsburgs, and the Catholic rulers had to integrate a larger Muslim population into their domain.

It is at this point that the complexity of history once again became apparent. Even before the occupation, important events took place that paved the way for the Islamic Law of 1912. Important commanders of the Habsburg army in Bosnia and Herzegovina were urged as early as 1875 to treat the different nationalities and religions equally, with special attention to religious aspects. In 1875, a state bankruptcy of the Ottoman Empire occurred in Bosnia. This event offered the Habsburg monarchy an opportunity to claim the region for itself, in agreement with the geopolitical actors of the time. In order to ensure this in the best possible way politically and diplomatically, the Habsburgs had to realize the transfer of power as unspectacularly as possible and in a way that was "acceptable" to everyone. One way of doing this was to convince the various ethnic and religious groups that the new rulers would impose no or few restrictions on them in political, religious, or other matters. "[…] all sons of this country enjoy equal rights under the law; they are all protected in their lives, in their faith, and in their possessions." Emperor Franz Joseph announced on July 28, 1878 (Heine et al. 2012, p. 47).

Article II of the Treaty between the Habsburg Monarchy and the Ottoman Empire, which was signed on April 21, 1879, gave Muslims in Bosnia and Herzegovina the right to practice their religion freely. Likewise, the convention brought about a change in the organization of Islam at the level of the administration. Three years after it was signed, Bosnian Islam was hierarchized to make it more in line with Habsburg traditions. This meant that the Habsburg government and state could treat Muslims the same way they treated other religious groups: with the same demands and support. The Habsburgs also had to do this because they wanted to make the Muslims loyal citizens and stop discrimination and rebellion by making everyone equal before the law. On the other hand, this does not mean that the imperial and royal monarchies could correctly assess the situation in all matters concerning Muslims and act accordingly. For example, publications about the laws, norms, etc. of the Muslims were supposed to assist the administrative staff in their decisions (Cf. Heine et al. 2012, pp. 47–48).

Four years after the annexation of Bosnia and Herzegovina on July 12, 1912, the Islamic Law came into force. The Habsburgs used the experiences of the imperial and royal monarchies in Bosnia to formulate the content of the law.

In contrast to the Catholic community, the legislators understood that Muslims would need time to establish a religious community. Apart from that, the marriage law of the Muslims posed a challenge for the new rulers and could not simply be incorporated into the existing laws on monogamy. Other difficulties arising from the recognition of Islam were solved by Austrian lawmakers by limiting recognition to the Hanafi rite. It is very likely that the decision-makers at the time wanted to "satisfy" the Ottoman Empire in this way and limit a broad interpretation of the law due to possible conflicts that could have arisen from insufficient legal recognition. The lawmakers of the time explicitly retained the option that other Sunni legal schools could be recognized as well. The Habsburgs used the experiences of the imperial and royal monarchies in Bosnia to formulate the content of the law. In contrast to the Catholic community, the legislators understood that Muslims would need time to establish a religious community. Apart from that, the marriage law of the Muslims posed a challenge for the new rulers and could not simply be incorporated into the existing laws on monogamy. Other difficulties arising from the recognition of Islam were solved by Austrian lawmakers by limiting recognition to the Hanafi rite. It is very likely that the decision-makers at the time wanted to "satisfy" the Ottoman Empire in this way and limit a broad interpretation of the law due to possible conflicts that could have arisen from insufficient legal recognition. The lawmakers of the time explicitly retained the option that other Sunni legal schools could be recognized as well. (Cf. Heine et al. 2012, p. 49).

3   Current Developments

Islam is one of the largest world religions, with over 1.9 billion followers worldwide. In Austria, Islam is the second largest religion after Christianity and has gained a strong presence and importance in recent decades.[4] Currently, Turkish Muslims represent the largest group of followers of Sunni (Hanefi) Islam in Austria. This also becomes very clear with regard to Turkish-Islamic organizations that represent the interests of the Turkish-Muslim immigrant community. Before we focus on them, we will first cite current figures on Muslims in Austria. Currently, German citizens represent the largest immigration group in Austria.

---

[4] https://www.oesterreich.gv.at/themen/leben_in_oesterreich/kirchenein___austritt_und_rel igionen/3/Seite.820018.html Accessed 03.14.2023.

7 Alevis and Turkish-Muslims in Austria: History and Current Developments 119

According to the Austrian Integration Fund Report from 2021, internal EU migration has overtaken migration from third countries such as Turkey.[5] For example, 19,013 German citizens emigrated to Austria in 2020. The report also states that more than 2480 people from Turkey moved to Austria in 2020, and 2226 Turkish citizens left Austria (Cf. O A 2021, p. 38). These figures suggest that Austria also has a special attraction for many people from Turkey, and at the same time, just as many people with a Turkish migration background leave Austria again for another EU country or Turkey itself. However, these figures do not allow any conclusions to be drawn about the religious status of immigrants or emigrants. Rather, religious affiliation in Germany as well as Austria is statistically based on citizenship. In other words, people from Turkey are "automatically" certified as belonging to Islam (Cf. on this approach Rohe 2018, pp. 75–95).

Thus, Alevis, Kurds, or other minorities from Turkey in Germany as well as Austria are counted as part of the Islamic Turkish population, which leads to different ethnic groups being subsumed under one common denominator. This is an important reason why the statistics of the Austrian Integration Fund should be interpreted with caution. A reliable source of figures and data is still missing, and we have to operate with estimates which suggest that there are around 700,000 Muslims living in Austria.[6] Probably, the number of Muslims in Austria is higher than the mentioned figure, especially since people from Afghanistan, Syria, and other regions of the Middle East have migrated to Austria in recent years. It can also be assumed that some of the newly arrived migrants have not been registered until today.

Despite these shortcomings the Austrian Integration Fund's numbers on attitudes of immigrants towards Austria give a good picture of their sense of belonging to Austria. 41.8% of members of the Turkish community living in Austria feel at home in or native to the Alpine Republic. Only 2.8% of Turks believe that they do not feel at home at all (Cf. O A 2021, p. 97). The sense of belonging is also very strong among the group of recent immigrants. 53% of Afghans, Syrians, and Chechens stated that they feel "completely at home" or belong, according to the Austrian Integration Fund (Cf. O A 2021, p. 96). In other words, for many migrants of Muslim religiosity, feeling a sense of belonging to Austria is not a particular challenge.

It should be noted at the outset that all Turkish-Muslim groups or associations, as well as other Muslim groups or associations, are strongly committed to

---

[5] (cf. in more detail O A 2021, p. 35).

[6] https://www.statistik.at/statistiken/bevoelkerung-und-soziales/bevoelkerung/weiterfuehre nde-bevoelkerungsstatistiken/religionsbekenntnis.

integration and support state institutions (Cf. O A 2021, passim). At the same time, it should be noted that the individual associations also pursue their own interests, which in turn generates points of friction between the above mentioned associations. Even though many Muslims are not members of Turkish, Bosnian, or other Muslim organizations, many of these organizations claim to represent a large proportion of Muslims in Austria (Cf. Reiser 2000, p. 199). Detailed figures on the membership of Turkish associations and mosques are not available. Within Islamic communities, there is no formal act of acceptance into the faith community. It is common for the families of community members to be part of the mosque community as well. In recent years, detailed figures have begun to be collected with regard to Islamic religious education. Whether all Muslims feel represented by the existing organizations cannot be answered. At this point, a brief overview of the largest organizations representing Muslims will be given.

The Islamic Religious Community in Austria (IGGiÖ)[7] is subject to the Austrian legal system (new Islam Act 2015).[8] It was officially recognized as a corporate body in 1979. In 1987, the Constitutional Court ruled that the IGGiÖ must recognize all Muslim (Sunni or Shiite) schools of law and represent them. Thus, the IGGiÖ serves as the only hinterlocutor for the Austrian Republic; moreover, it is responsible for the religious issues of all Muslims living in Austria. In this context, the statutes of the IGGiÖ explicitly state that the IGGiÖ represents all Muslims living in Austria, regardless of origin, gender, or ethnicity. The IGGiÖ consists of four religious communities: Vienna, Linz, Graz, and Bregenz. These are responsible for representing the interests of Muslims at the federal level as well as at the state level. The community committee is the managing body of the respective religious community.[9] The IGGiÖ's claim to sole representation is repeatedly questioned by Muslim communities, especially Turkish ones.

The Turkish-Islamic Union for Cultural and Social Cooperation in Austria (ATİB) is one of the largest Turkish-Muslim umbrella organizations. Using the example of Vorarlberg, one of Austria's westernmost states, we will take a look at its structures and mosques. Vorarlberg is one of the regions in Austria most heavily populated by Turkish migrants.[10] In Vorarlberg[11] 13 associations belong

---

[7] http://www.derislam.at/.

[8] http://www.derislam.at/?c=content&cssid=Islamgesetz%202015&navid=1177&par=10, accessed 3.26.2023.

[9] http://www.derislam.at/?c=content&cssid=Rel.%20Gemeinden&navid=30&par=0, Accessed 02.02.2023.

[10] https://www.okay-line.at/Informationen/moschee-und-alevitische-cem-vereine-in-vorarl berg-kontaktdaten/ Accessed 25.3.2023.

[11] https://www.vol.at/von-atib-bis-zur-foederation/5924958 Accessed 25.03.2023.

7 Alevis and Turkish-Muslims in Austria: History and Current Developments   121

to the umbrella organization ATIB, namely Bezau, Bludenz, Bregenz, Dornbirn, Frastanz, Hard, Höchst, Hörbranz, Hohenems, Lustenau, Mäder, Nenzing and Rankweil. With 63 mosques and 65 imams, the ATIB is the largest Muslim association in Austria. In 1994, the ATIB[12] was founded in Austria. The close relations with the Turkish "Office for Religious Affairs" have for some time, or since the last failed coup in Turkey in 2016, been the cause of fierce criticism from Germany and Austria – the German equivalent to ATİB Austria is DİTİB in Germany.[13] The links between the Diyanet and the Turkish state go back to the state's founder, Mustafa Kemal Atatürk, who, in the course of his secular state policy, placed religion under a strict system of state regulation. The Cold War enabled secular nationalist and Islamic conservative groups in Turkey to converge on the basis of their shared anti-communist stance, alternating governments, and thus exerting considerable influence on the religious policy of the Turkish nation-state. The growing Turkish immigrant society and the certainty that many Turkish citizens would not leave their new homeland (beginning in the 1970s), as well as their interest in religious teachings as well as in the creation of places of worship prompted the Diyanet to take action in Germany and Austria beginning in the 1980s (Sunier and Landman 2015).

Since 2002, on the orders of the AKP (Adalet ve Kalkınma Partisi - Justice and Development Party or Justice and Development Party), the ATİB has been cooperating with all Turkish-Muslim as well as Turkish-nationalist associations or mosques and tried to bring them into line with its own political line. A famous slogan of the AKP, which is repeatedly encountered in Germany and Austria, is: "One flag, one people, one state." The ATİB as well as DİTİB mosques[14] in Germany are financed by the Diyanet office, donations, and membership fees.

A difficult relationship exists above all between the ATIB and the IF (Islamic Federation) – will be discussed below – and the IGGiÖ. ATIB is subordinate to the Diyanet, which in turn is politically controlled by the Turkish state. While ATİB wants to reach and win over Turkish associations or mosques primarily through their religious-national affiliation, the IGGiÖ's goal is to represent Muslims living in Austria regardless of their origin and without external political

---

[12] http://www.atib.at/index.php?id=43, accessed 2.20.2023.

[13] http://www.zeit.de/gesellschaft/zeitgeschehen/2017-01/spionage-verdacht-ditib-dachve rband-mosche
    e-community-investigations-federal-prosecutor's-office, accessed 2/20/2012; http://orf. at/stories/2378887/, accessed 2.20.2023.

[14] DITIB is the German equivalent of ATIB: Türkisch-Islamische Union der Anstalt für Religion e. V. (Diynet Isleri Türk Islam Birligi, DITIB). The Union is the umbrella organization for the coordination of Turkish-Islamic mosque communities in Germany.

influence. A solution to this problem is currently not in sight, especially since many Turkish Muslims from the ranks of the ATİB or the IF hold important positions in the IGGiÖ and thus want to carry their religious convictions into the Muslim immigrant society with the help of the IGGiÖ.

Detailed figures on the members of Turkish associations or mosques are not available. Within Islamic communities, there is no formal act of acceptance into the faith community. It is common that when an individual is a member of an association or mosque, the family of that individual is also part of the mosque community. In recent years, detailed figures have only begun to be collected with regard to Islamic religious education. Whether all Muslims feel represented by the existing organizations cannot be answered explicitly. According to the comprehensive study conducted by the German Islam Conference (DIK) in 2012, the Muslim umbrella organizations cannot be classified as representing all Muslims in Germany, nor should their influence be undererstimated (Cf. in more detail Halm et al. 2012). Analyses arrive at similar conclusions in Austria (Cf. Heine et al. 2012).

The Austrian Islamic Federation (Avusturya Islam Federasyonu / IF)[15] is another important Turkish-Islamic association that officially sees itself as part of Milli Görüş. Outside Turkey, organizations that were socialized in the political environment of the Welfare Party (Refah Partisi) or feel ideologically committed to it call themselves Milli Görüş. The most important leader of the Welfare Party was Necmettin Erbakan. From the 1970s on Erbakan was able to play a significant role in shaping Turkish politics and Turkish Islamism. Only the Turkish military was able to end Erbakan's political career time and again through interventions, most recently in 1997 (Reinkowski 2021, S. 193–221). Unlike some Islamist groups in the Middle East during the 1970s as well as 1980s, Erbakan opposed violence and was able to integrate Islamic teachings into Turkish educational policy. Most notably, he facilitated the establishment of religious educational institutions that trained Islamic preachers and Imams. He openly spoke out against secularism and laicism. In the course of the German-Turkish recruitment agreement in the 1960s, he was able to establish a large following in Germany and later in Austria. The current president of the IGGiÖ was socialized in the environment of Milli Görüş in terms of religious politics.

The umbrella group IF (Islamic Federation), is in charge of more than 60 groups in Austria, according to information from its own website.[16] Most of the time, the members of the federation finance it, but it cannot be ruled out that they

---

[15] https://islamfederasyonu.at/ Accessed 03.25.2023.

[16] https://islamfederasyonu.at/ Accessed 13.04.2023.

7 Alevis and Turkish-Muslims in Austria: History and Current Developments 123

are also financed from Turkey. In other words, their ideological brethren in Turkey could provide financial support. The IF's job – according to its homepage – is to give Muslims all the help they need to live their Islamic lives.[17] Even though some of the Turkish-Islamic groups have had ideological differences in the past, there have been different forms of cooperation since their foundation. For example, political fights between Turks and Kurds in Vorarlberg in during the 1990s show that Turkish-Islamic and Turkish groups work together. Since the 1990s, they have repeatedly used joint actions (protests, rallies, etc.) to ask the Austrian government to crack down on left-wing Turkish and Kurdish nationalist groups. They also appeared together in the course of the xenophobic attacks in Germany in the 1990s (Cf Volkshilfe Flüchtlings- & MigrantInnenbetreuung OÖ 2012, passim).

Islam Kültür Merkezleri Birligi / Association of Islamic Cultural Centers in the Austrian Alpine Region (VIKZ): The association is part of VIKZ Cologne and emerged from Islamisches Kulturzentrum e. V., which was founded in 1973 in Germany. In Austria, the association is assigned 16 mosques, seven of which are located in Vorarlberg: Dornbirn, Bludenz, Götzis, Hohenems, Kennelbach, Lustenau and Rankweil. They are largely financed by donations and membership fees. Their theology is a combination of mystical Sufi traditions and Sunni Hanafi Islam. However, the group's religious orientation is very traditional, so mystical impulses play only a limited role. Rather, the divine will is to be ascertained via the Sharia (Islamic law) and the Sunna (customs and instructions for action). It is no secret that the association rejects secular democracies.[18] At the same time, however, it maintains good relations with the Turkish state and its parties. The association's supporters are known as "Süleymancilar." The name goes back to the founder, Süleyman Hilmi Tunahan, and is used derogatorily for the group in Turkey. In general, it can be said that this group is convinced that classical views and interpretations still apply today.

Since the coup attempt in Turkey in 2016 the *Hizmet* movement also known as the Gülen movement – founded in Austria in the late 1980s– can be seen as diverging from the aforementioned organizations in terms of its orientation towards the Turkish state. *Hizmet* is a Turkish word of Arabic origin and can in this context be translated as both spiritual and social service to people. Currently, the community is accused by the Turkish state for the failed coup on July 15, 2016. In the late 1950s, F. Gülen became a member of the *Nurcu Cemaati*. Due

---

[17] https://islamfederasyonu.at/ Accessed 13.04.2023.

[18] https://www.stuttgarter-nachrichten.de/inhalt.islamverband-vikz-ilmihal-leitfaden-fuer-die-parallelwelt.6c6936fc-e16c-4682-aae3-c454d55f0737.html Accessed 13.04.2023.

to internal power struggles (there was disagreement over how to implement Said Nursi's theological guidelines, recommendations, and duties), F. Gülen decided to distance himself from the *Nurcu Cemaati* starting in the 1980s. Already in the 1990s, he was able to build a large network of people who followed him and had considerable power over the Turkish people, for example through daily newspapers like Zaman and TV stations like Samanyolu TV. At the end of the 1990s, different parts of the Turkish government accused him of trying to turn Turkey into an Islamist State. To escape state persecution, F. Gülen left for the United States. Apart from the media sector, the Gülen movement is very active in education and interfaith dialogue, but also in subsidizing mosque construction and Koranic courses (Cf. Rohe 2018, S. 147–149). Prior to the coup attempt the group owned hundreds of private schools in Turkey. After the coup, many of these schools were closed. Today the Gülen movement is very active abroad, for example in Russia, the Balkans, Asia, and Western Europe. In the U.S. alone, the movement operates 150 private educational institutions (Cf. Agai 2011, passim). Unlike ATIB/DITIB and Diyanet, the *Hizmet* movement is not subordinate to the Turkish state. Formally, according to the Gülen movement, the individual bodies and institutions are independent and can determine their own course of action, but the movement is nevertheless linked to one another through close media coverage or individual networks.

Austria is a special case with regard to Alevis. At present, there is an Islamic-Alevi association that is legally recognized by the state and a Free-Alevi community as a confessional community, which is expected to be recognized by the state within the next few years and will thereafter operate as a legally recognized association of Alevis in Austria.

The Alevis living in Turkey are also referred to (derogatorily) as "Kizilbaş" (Red Head). The Alevis live mainly in southeastern Turkey. At the same time, it should be noted that the industrialization of Turkey after World War II has led to mobilization, and a large part of the community is now found outside Anatolia. The Alevis are not a homogeneous group; some speak Zaza or Kurmanji (Kurdish dialects). According to various sources, the movement emerged between the fourteenth and fifteenth centuries on the territory of present-day Turkey (Cf. Yıldırım 2015, passim). In the Ottoman Empire, its members were persecuted as heretics (Cf. Karakaya-Stump 2020, passim). The latter led to the religious and social isolation of the Alevites. They do not possess holy books. At the center of their religious teachings is the Prophet's son-in-law, Ali. They refer to their house of prayer or gathering as *Cem* (where the worship of God takes place). They reject Sunni or Shiite religious teachings. Women and men sit together in a circle and celebrate their religious rituals. Since the 1990s, Alevis in Turkey and

7 Alevis and Turkish-Muslims in Austria: History and Current Developments 125

Europe have been trying to develop their own theology. The Turkish state refuses to recognize the group as a religious body or community.

The number of Alevis in Austria is estimated at 60,000 to 80,000.[19] As in practically all European countries, Alevi communities in Austria have also organized themselves outside the Islamic associations (Cf. Çiçek 2022, passim). In 1998, the "Federation of Alevi Communities in Austria" (AABF) was founded, which is a member of the European Alevi umbrella organization AABK.

A second grouping, irrespective of the differences in principle between Alevis and Sunnis, considers Alevism as a direction of Islam, comparable to the Sunnis and Shiites. It was represented by the Cultural Association of Alevis Vienna (VAKB), originally a partial association of the AABF, which left the umbrella association in 2009 and applied for registration as a religious confessional community. The VAKB, or "Alevi," are not members of the European umbrella organization AABK.

Because of the Islam Act from 1912, there is a particular situation in Austria when it comes to the integration of non-christian religious communities into each system of religious law. The Islam Law of 1912 fell outside the scheme for legally recognized churches and religious societies in two respects. First, only the legal equality of the followers of Islam with the members of the legally recognized churches and religious societies could be envisaged, since neither the existence of organizational structures (a religious community) necessary for recognition in the sense of the Recognition Act existed nor their formation had been foreseeable. Art. 11 of the Islam Law therefore provided that "[t]he external legal relationships of the followers of Islam [...] are to be regulated by ordinance on the basis of self-administration and self-determination, but subject to state supervision, as soon as the establishment and existence of at least one religious community is assured." Second, only the "recognition of the followers of Islam according to the Hanefitic rite as a religious society" was envisaged (Cf. Heine et al. 2012, S. 49–55). As historical developments make clear, organizational issues played a role in limiting recognition to the "Hanefitic rite," in addition to foreign policy considerations regarding the Ottoman Empire. The intention was to tie in with the uniform structure of Islam in Bosnia and Herzegovina.

In the 1970s, when Islam was being more recognised, both of these questions became important. The question of its extension to other schools of law also became virulent. Austria asked the Turkish government for an expert opinion. As

---

[19] https://www.wienerzeitung.at/nachrichten/politik/oesterreich/555279-Alevitentum-zwe igeteilt.html#:~:text=Seit%20dem%2022.,Bekenntnisgemeinschaft%20oder%20gar%20n icht%20anerkannt. Accessed 13.04.2023.

a result, a report from the Presidential Service for Religious Affairs of the Turkish Republic (Diyanet İşleri Başkanlığı) dated December 18, 1972, was submitted, which stated, among other things, that "All Muslims who count themselves among the four Sunni schools are orthodox." (Cf. Heine et al. 2012, S. 56).

The Turkish religious authority thus considered only the four Sunni schools of law as orthodox but not the Shiite schools. However, among those seeking state recognition were organizations that are part of Shiite schools such as the Twelver Shiites, Ibadites, and Zaidites, so the IGGiÖ amended its constitution in accordance with the conception of the recognized schools of law. The extension of recognition to non-Hanefites, and thus the scope of recognition, presented itself to the cult authority as an intra-religious society act that the state must take note of. The decision of the Constitutional Court in 1987 and the subsequent amendment to the Islam Act, Federal Law Gazette 1988/164, clarified that it is a matter of state religious law to determine the circle of addressees of a legal recognition but that the state may not exclude a part of the common confession in accordance with the self-image of the entire religious community (Cf. Heine et al. 2012, S. 57).

With this amendment to the Islamic Law, which may seem plausible at first glance, the question of how to classify those groups that do not conform to the Islamic mainstream in terms of cult, organization, and educational institutions and are not in a cultic community with it but derive at least in part from the Islamic tradition became virulent. All in all, it applies to Alevism to the same extent as it does to Islam—and, incidentally, to Judaism as well—that although uniform representation is desirable, it can by no means be enforced by the state. Accordingly, not only one group within Alevism may be granted a religious constitution and thus a de facto claim to sole representation. On the one hand, it is true that it is not a relevant question for the state which of these groups represents Alevism from a theological point of view. For the Austrian state, it is important that the linguistic differentiation criteria between the AABF, Free Alevis, and ALEVI are clearly emphasized so that there is no confusion.

The VAKB and the IGGiÖ, which have always emphasized their "being Islamic" - also in linguistic terms - as a distinguishing criterion from other Alevis, should rather have consistently called themselves Alevi Muslims.

In Austria, there is currently a legally recognized Islamic Alevi religious community with five registered associations and a Free Alevi Community, which was recognized as a confessional community (April 2022) and is also to be recognized as a religious community in the coming years. The Free Alevi Community includes 15 associations.

4 Outlook

The topic of integration, especially integration of "Muslims," has been high on the agenda in Austria for many years, and it appears to continue in the coming years. In this debate, it is needless to say that Muslims are stuck between two chairs. Not only is the government of the majority society telling them to integrate, but politicians in Turkey also intend to have an effect on the Turkish diaspora. Different groups within the two societies are also trying to take over the authority to interpret the issue of how to practice "true Islam". There is currently no sign of a decrease in tension.

The current majority of Muslim society in Vorarlberg comes from Turkey. In the discussion about integration, they are also always addressed directly by their geographic location not only by the Austrian government but also by the Turkish government. The political leadership of both countries considers integration necessary and important. For example, the current Turkish president calls on the Turkish immigrant community to learn German and also to get involved socially and culturally, to name just two points. At the same time, Erdogan says, the community should not forget its own roots. Erdogan claims that the concept of integration in European countries aims at assimilation (Cf. Erdogan urges O A o. J.). In other words, integration also serves to push Islamic religiosity and identity out of the public sphere and to secularize Muslims. However, Erdogan does not mention the fact that some of the Turkish immigrants are supportive of his party and that too strong an identification with the new homeland could mean a reduction in votes for him and his party.

When it comes to the Austrian federal government, Islam and integration are mostly about security policy. For this reason, a ban on headscarves in kindergartens was also enacted (Parlament Österreich 2018). The fact that there are no representative figures of girls wearing headscarves in kindergarten was not considered an obstacle in the process of making the law. Rather, the government frames this is a preventive measure against Islamist extremism (Parlament Österreich 2018). This approach is intended to open the way for social and cultural integration. In parallel, integration programs are intended to facilitate access to Austrian values.[20] The latter is also intended to prevent exclusion and curb radicalization.

---

[20] For more Information https://www.integrationsfonds.at/?gclid=CjwKCAjw0N6hBhAUEi wAXab-TR2RR8AvqIT7yu01jxAmaLOywShGPgsMJ_MTN-T809iIUtgbZ9jLghoC3rM QAvD_BwE Accessed 13.04.2023.

The IGGiÖ repeatedly takes part in public discussions about authentic Muslim life in Austria and Europe. It has also published a statement on veiling in Islam (Kurier 2017). Their way of argumentation is very problematic and dangerous. The reason: The IGGiÖ describes the wearing of a headscarf as an "absolute duty," as *fard*, and thus puts the dress requirement de facto on a par with the holy five pillars of Islam: covenant, prayer, almsgiving, fasting, and pilgrimage to Mecca.[21] According to Islamic religious doctrine, Muslims who do not live according to the absolute rules of faith will be punished by God in this world and/or the hereafter. The IGGiÖ's stance thus suggests that believers must wear a headscarf and those who do not must expect divine punishment, even though the statement itself emphasizes that "women and men who do not adhere to religious dress codes must not be devalued by others under any circumstances."(John 2023).

For many years, Turkish or ex-Yugoslav service providers in Austria (banks, theaters, sports clubs) have been competing with Austrian companies for customers. Turkish banks, theaters, and sports clubs are also part of Austrian life. Both immigrant groups have long been part of economic reality. People from the Turkish immigrant community are also politically active in Austrian political parties. In addition, there are two parties founded by Turkish immigrants in Vorarlberg, for example, that will run in the AK elections.[22] One of them even wants to represent all cultures.[23] At the same time, the party's cosmopolitan leadership supports presidents in Turkey who have repeatedly been criticized for undermining democracy.

Tensions will not decrease in the future. Not so much because immigrant societies do not want to integrate, but because integration is not a clear-cut process and presents itself differently depending on the situation.

---

[21] https://www.derstandard.at/story/2000053650450/kopftuch-islamische-glaubensgemeins chaft-raet-frauen-zur-verhuellung Accessed 13.04.2023.

[22] The Arbeiterkammer (Chamber of Labour) is a public institution in Austria that represents the interests of workers and employees in matters such as labour law, social security, and consumer protection. It provides various services such as legal advice, education, and support in disputes with employers. Every five years, the Arbeiterkammer holds elections, in which all employees in Austria are eligible to vote. The elected representatives serve as advocates for the interests of the employees they represent. The Arbeiterkammer plays an important role in shaping social and economic policies in Austria. https://www.arbeiterkammer.at/index.html Accessed 13.04.2023.

[23] https://vorarlberg.orf.at/v2/news/stories/2958764/ Accessed 13.04.2023.

References

Agai, Bekim. 2011. Von der Türkei in die Welt: Wie aus der Gülen-Bewegung in der Türkei eine weltweite Bildungsbewegung wurde. In *Bildung und gesellschaftlicher Wandel in der Türkei*, Eds. Arnd-Michael Nohl and Barbara Pusch, 177–196. Ergon Verlag.

Heine, Susanne, Rüdiger. Lohlker, and Richard Potz. 2012. *Muslime in Österreich: Geschichte, Lebenswelt, Religion: Grundlagen für den Dialog*. Innsbruck: Tyrolia-Verlag.

John, Gerald. 2023. Religionspädagoge Aslan: Was am Kopftuch-Gebot gefährlich ist. *der-Standard*, April 5 https://www.derstandard.at/story/2000053683761/religionspaedagoge-aslan-was-am-kopftuch-gebot-gefaehrlich-ist. Zugegriffen: 5. Apr. 2023.

Karakaya-Stump, Ayfer. 2020. *The Kizilbash-Alevis in Ottoman Anatolia: Sufism, politics and community*. Edinburgh: Edinburgh University Press.

Kurier. 2017. IGGiÖ rät muslimischen Frauen zum Kopftuch. *Kurier*, März 6 https://kurier.at/chronik/oesterreich/islamische-glaubensgemeinschaft-iggioe-raet-muslimischen-frauen-zum-kopftuch/250.185.996. Zugegriffen: 5. Apr. 2023.

O A. 2021. *Statistisches Jahrbuch Migration & Integration: Zahlen Daten, Indikatoren*. Wien: Österreichischer Integrationsfonds.

O A. o. J. Erdogan Urges Turks Not to Assimilate: „You Are Part of Germany, But Also Part of Our Great Turkey" - DER SPIEGEL. https://www.spiegel.de/international/europe/erdogan-urges-turks-not-to-assimilate-you-are-part-of-germany-but-also-part-of-our-great-turkey-a-748070.html. Zugegriffen: 13. Apr. 2023.

Parlament Österreich. 2018. Kopftuchverbot in Kindergärten einstimmig beschlossen. https://www.parlament.gv.at/aktuelles/pk/jahr_2018/pk1311. Zugegriffen: 5. April 2023.

Reinkowski, Maurus. 2021. *Geschichte der Türkei*, 2021st ed. München: C.H.BECK Literatur - Sachbuch - Wissenschaft.

Rohe, Mathias. 2018. *Der Islam in Deutschland: eine Bestandsaufnahme*. 2. München: C.H. Beck.

Sunier, Thijl, and Nico Landman. 2015. *Transnational turkish islam: Shifting geographies of religious activism and community building in Turkey and Europe*. Basingstoke: Palgrave Macmillan.

Volkshilfe Flüchtlings- & MigrantInnenbetreuung OÖ, Ed. 2012. *Grauer Wolf im Schafspelz: Rechtsextremismus in der Einwanderungsgesellschaft*. Grünbach: Steinmassl.

Yıldırım, Rıza. 2015. Sunni Orthodox vs Shiite Heterodox? A Reappraisal of Islamic Piety in Medieval Anatolia. In *Islam and Christianity in medieval Anatolia*, Ed. A. C. S. Peacock, Bruno De Nicola, and Sara Nur Yildiz, 287–307. Burlington, VT: Ashgate Publishing Company.

Internet sources:

Islam Law Amendment: IGGÖ with "clear no". *religion.ORF.at*. https://religion.orf.at/stories/3204426/. Accessed: 3. Mar. 2023.

https://www.integrationsfonds.at/wien/?gclid=CjwKCAiA3pugBhAwEiwAWFzwdYRGGrpZLYyDK7oxYW1fLOHzbFQtJP7kRT4bDob36sNgXYnCMm3X-hoCxw0QAvD_BwE Accessed: 3. Mar. 2023.

https://www.oesterreich.gv.at/themen/leben_in_oesterreich/kirchenein___austritt_und_rel
igionen/3/Seite.820018.html. Accessed: 14. Mar. 2023.
http://www.derislam.at/ Accessed: 3. Mar. 2023.
https://www.okay-line.at/Informationen/moschee-und-alevitische-cem-vereine-in-vorarl
berg-kontaktdaten/. Accessed: 25. Mar. 2023.
https://www.vol.at/von-atib-bis-zur-foederation/5924958. Accessed 25. Mar. 2023.
https://islamfederasyonu.at/. Accessed: 25. Mar. 2023.

Priv.-Doz Hüseyin Çiçek is a Senior Research Fellow at the Department for Religious Studies at the University of Vienna, a Fellow at Bonn Academy for International Affairs and a Fellow at the Center for Advanced Security, Strategic and Integration Studies (CASSIS), at the University of Bonn.

Part II
Southern Europe

Religious Freedom, Civil Rights, and Islam in Spain

8

Ana I. Planet and Johanna M. Lems

Abstract

Despite legislative attempts to facilitate freedom of religious practice for Muslims in Spain, the current challenges exceed the scope of legal recognition and lie within the political and social spheres, as well as education and research. In addition to the lack of compliance with civil and religious rights formally granted since 1992 – e.g., access to cemetery space for Islamic rite burials or the availability of halal menus at publicly funded schools—, a large part of Muslims in Spain face discriminatory practices such as foreignization and criminalization, which limit their capacity to participate like other citizens in Spanish society. Circumventing the sole interlocutor appointed by the State, a number of Muslim civil organisations have joined forces to fight anti-Muslim discrimination and secure recognition of their citizenship in law and practice. The State and its institutions should assume their responsibility in the construction of alterity of Muslims and guarantee compliance with the civil and religious rights of its Muslim population.

A. I. Planet (✉)
Professor, Universidad Autónoma de Madrid, Madrid, Spain
e-mail: ana.planet@uam.es

J. M. Lems
Assistant Professor, Universidad Complutense de Madrid, Madrid, Spain
e-mail: jmlems@ucm.es

© The Author(s), under exclusive license to Springer Fachmedien Wiesbaden GmbH, part of Springer Nature 2024
R. Ceylan and M. Mücke (eds.), *Muslims in Europe*, Islam in der Gesellschaft,
https://doi.org/10.1007/978-3-658-43044-3_8

Keywords

Religious freedom • Muslims in Spain • Civil rights • Discrimination • Islamic Commission of Spain • State legislation in security affairs • Challenges for the State and academia

As occurs in other European contexts, social and political dynamics in Spain related to Islam present a series of specific characteristics. In this sense, and despite legislative attempts to facilitate freedom of religious practice for Muslims in Spain, marked by a return to arguments that are also of a historical nature, the current challenges exceed the scope of legal recognition and lie within the political and social spheres, as well as education and research. Driving the construction of a plural society requires overcoming the existing obstacles and combating all forms of social and legal discrimination motivated by religion.

1   The Historical Development of Islam and Muslim Populations

As the famous 1960s slogan proclaimed ("Spain is different"), Spain did indeed differ from its neighbours, a characteristic that also extends to its relationship with Islamic culture. Although from a sociodemographic perspective, and as in other European countries, the presence of Islam in twenty-first century Spain is associated with the international migratory flows of the second half of the twentieth century, Spain's historical legacy with al-Ándalus and its geographical proximity to North Africa has forged historical and cultural ties with Islam dating back to the eighth century and which are reflected in the contemporary recognition and accommodation of Islam. In Spain, recourse to history is activated in a manner similar to that of the allegations regarding the 'Judeo-Christian' roots of European identity, namely in nationalist and discriminatory terms (Topolski 2020). This shared history is not just a period of co-existence and cultural hybridisation – the myth of al-Ándalus – but instead also has laid the foundations of a discriminatory national construct. This has essentialised the classic identification of Muslims as "others": they are seen as a menacing and dangerous presence, as evidenced by the interpellations Muslim citizens are subject to in their everyday lives (Lems 2021; Planet and Madonia 2022).

If there is a lesson to be learnt from the current scenario regarding the religious freedom and rights of Muslim groups in Spain, it is that the mere existence

8 Religious Freedom, Civil Rights, and Islam in Spain

within the law of the acknowledgement of religious pluralism that allows individuals to develop religious freedom fails to guarantee the effective exercise of these rights. In the wake of the 1978 Constitution, late twentieth century Spain was a secularised State in which the separation of Church and state was accompanied by the recognition of the population's religious beliefs and a mandate for cooperation between the authorities and religious entities in order to guarantee the effective exercise of individual and group rights. The constitutional mandate regarding religious freedom is clear: the State is the guarantor of religious freedom. In the case of Islam, it was therefore a matter of assuming control of the process of recognition and developing a legal framework in which to apply the aforementioned elements.

In legal terms, the 1978 Constitution allowed for the creation of a legal framework in Spain that regulated religious freedom and practice. This framework extended to both the rights of individuals and the nature of collective religious organisation and exercise. Individuals' ideological and religious liberty and freedom of worship was included as a fundamental right. Public powers were bound to its development and compliance under a system of accompaniment – or guardianship – of the religious confessions or communities. The later creation of a system of autonomous communities (regions) and the transfer of central State competences to these new administrations would further add to the complexities of this system.

The Spanish Ministry of Justice Advisory Committee's decision to declare Islam a consolidated religion in Spain, adopted on 14th July 1989, paved the way for a change to the status of Islam as a religion in the country. The significance of this recognition is twofold: on the one hand, it had a symbolic meaning, as it represented further progress in normalising the presence of Islam in the country after centuries of restricted religious practice, fuelled by a lack of recognition, intolerance and even persecution; on the other hand, it represented a clear step forward in terms of material and regulatory recognition, as it allowed for work to begin on a legal text that protected Islamic worship in Spain (Contreras Mazarío 2018). Indeed, the recognition of "the presence of the Islamic religion since the eighth century" and its "uninterrupted existence within the territory", included in the ruling of the aforementioned Advisory Committee, proved extremely important at the time. Furthermore, it came at a particularly significant moment for Spanish society, marked by the end of the Francoist dictatorship and progress in the transition towards democracy. Political change was speeding up the secularisation process that had begun several decades earlier, facilitating new forms of relations between the State, citizens, and the Catholic Church, and also marked the onset of religious pluralism (Pérez Agote 2022), fuelled by the economic transformation of Spain, which had become a new El Dorado for international migrations.

Although Islam had been present in Spain for many centuries, as acknowledged by the aforementioned ruling, the actual number of Muslims in Spain at the time of this legal recognition was relatively small, particularly in comparison with that of other neighbouring European countries and was characterised by a low level of visibility. The Francoist dictatorship, political isolation and economic factors meant that Spain was a later addition to the postcolonial international migratory flows that had fed Islam in Europe. The 1970s saw the arrival of the first flows of citizens from the MENA countries Spain had established cordial political relations with, namely Syria, Iraq, Egypt, and Morocco. A number of these immigrants studied at Spanish universities and ended up settling permanently in the country, obtaining Spanish citizenship. Together with the Muslim populations that lived in the Spanish cities of Melilla and Ceuta, situated on the North African coast, and a number of groups of Spaniards that had converted to Islam, they sowed the seeds of a religious minority. Indeed, during the 1980s and the 1990s in particular, Islam in Spain began to gain ground, thanks to the emergence of cultural and religious associative initiatives designed to provide simple spaces for worship and gatherings. Albeit to varying degrees, all these groups were involved in the institutionalisation of Islam in Spain, although it was the migratory flows from Morocco that would wield the greatest demographic weight (Planet 2014, 2018). However, the Muslim population resident in Spain is far from being a homogenous group. In just fifty years, a series of theological, ethnic, and generational visions have emerged, pointing to a clearly developing community reality. From a demographic perspective, there is no census or official instrument for quantification, and the only information in this sense are the approximate figures provided annually by the Andalusian Monitoring Centre (*Observatorio Andalusí*), dependent on the Union of Islamic Communities of Spain (*Union de Comunidades Islámicas de España*), a federation of Muslim entities (Muñoz-Comet 2022). According to its 2021 report (Observatorio Andalusí 2022), approximately 5% of the total population in Spain is Muslim and it is clear that Islam continues to be a minority religion in Spain.

The results of these joint efforts between the administration and religious communities include Law 26/1992, a Cooperation Agreement between the Spanish State and the Islamic Commission of Spain (*Comisión Islámica de España* or CIE in its Spanish initials), the contents of which will be discussed later. In terms of management and organisation, the ordered presence of Muslims proved crucial, including the creation of an interlocutory body, the Islamic Commission of Spain, which contained many of the existing Muslim religious associations,

8 Religious Freedom, Civil Rights, and Islam in Spain

based on two federations that had been formed during the recognition process. Since then, the number of Islamic religious associations has continued to grow, and today, the number listed on the State Register of Religious Entities stands at more than 1,700.[1] This Commission, an umbrella organisation for the two largest federations of associations, had a twofold purpose, as stated in its founding statutes. The Commission's dual objective was first and foremost political, as it attempted to become the sole interlocutor with the State for negotiating, signing, and monitoring the Cooperation Agreement, but it was also religious or doctrinal, as it undertook to facilitate the practice of Islam in Spain in accordance with the precepts of the Quran and Sunnah. Since then, the Islamic Commission of Spain has been responsible for working with the Spanish State on the process for the recognition of Islam. In 2015, its bylaws and working structure were reformed.

Despite the legal guarantees obtained through the recognition process, obstacles for the exercise of this freedom can still be observed among the so-called Muslim communities in Spain. However, these obstacles are hard to pinpoint exactly. A number of them stem from the legal problems involved in accommodating religious diversity in practice, whilst others are the result of prejudices regarding Islam and Muslims. It is therefore common to find a restrictive interpretation of a constitutional mandate, the use of a particular definition of 'public order' to limit a religious demonstration, or the adoption of an ultra-laic stance in political discourse and analysis that insists that religious expression must be limited to the private sphere when recognising a right that affects this religious minority. In all these instances, Islam is shown not as a religion recognised by the State, but rather as an alien religion opposed to western democracy, which, paradoxically, is to be protected by limiting the rights of certain individuals. An example of this can be found in the controversy that arises at the start of each academic year regarding the hijab and its use in schools. In this sense, we also wish to posit that the organisation framework created to guarantee the voice of Muslim communities with the State, based on a single interlocutor model of dialogue, has consistently reduced these communities' capacity for agency. Finally, there are also other laws which, despite not forming part of the actual framework for religious freedom, do exert a restrictive influence; examples include the Law on Foreigners or legal securitarian provisions.

---

[1] The updated number of these associations can be consulted at https://observatorioreligion.es/directorio-lugares-culto/ [Accessed: 25th November 2022].

2 The Structure of a Single Interlocutor with the State: A Need for Change?

As mentioned above, the Islamic Commission of Spain was founded in 1992 as the sole interlocutor with the Administration, acting on behalf and in representation of Spain's Islamic communities. Its main task was to sign the Cooperation Agreement with the State and monitor its compliance. Following several years of negotiations regarding its contents, the Cooperation Agreement signed between the Spanish State and the Commission in November 1992, which has the status of a law (Law 26/1992), grants a series of rights to Muslims resident in Spain – citizenship is not a requirement – related to their religion and the conservation and promotion of Islamic historical and artistic heritage. The Agreement includes both individual and collective rights, such as the recognition of marriages celebrated in accordance with Islamic rites; Islamic religious education and the availability of halal food in publicly funded schools (Contreras Mazarío 2018). Spain is divided territorially into municipalities, provinces, and autonomous communities, and therefore these rights are administered in accordance with the competences assigned to each. By way of an example, the administration of burials corresponds to the local authorities, whilst education falls to the autonomous communities (i.e., regional authorities).

Thirty years on from the entry into force of this Cooperation Agreement, many of the religious rights afforded to Muslim citizens and groups in Spain are not abided by in practice. According to the Union of Islamic Communities of Spain's *Observatorio* Andalusí (2022), 95% of the Muslim communities in Spain do not have access to cemeteries for Islamic burials, a situation which worsened during the COVID-19 pandemic. There are also numerous instances where Muslim families' requests for Islamic religious education are ignored, and the number of schools serving halal food is extremely low. Moreover, in 2022 there is only one imam in the whole of Spain – in the autonomous community of Madrid since 2021 – that provides religious assistance for the armed forces.

Discontent towards the Islamic Commission of Spain among the Muslim population has been growing for several years now, particularly among young people and new Muslims, who do not feel sufficiently represented by the model's single interlocutor structure. They consider that the Commission's passive attitude – despite receiving public funding[2] for its activities and organisation as the

---

[2] Over the period of 2017, 2018 and 2019, the Islamic Commission of Spain received funding totalling EUR 915,000 (FPyC 2017, 2018, 2019a, b).

representative of the Muslim minority in Spain – and the fact that it has occasionally hindered negotiations with the Administration regarding compliance with religious rights, have led to a loss of confidence in the persons that govern it. As a result, part of the Muslim communities no longer identifies with this representative body. Furthermore, a proportion of these Muslim populations have accused the Commission of a lack of transparency and technical expertise in a number of issues, and therefore, following Qureshi (2018), consider that it lacks the quality, veracity and independence required of an effective and reliable representative.

Over the last ten years and in various parts of Spain – e.g., in the La Rioja region and the cities of Vitoria or Madrid – a number of initiatives have been launched by associations, families or other Muslim actors, defending their rights on a local or regional level and on their own behalf, thereby circumventing the interlocutory structure designated by the State. In some cases, the negotiations reach a successful conclusion without the Commission's intervention, although on others the local and/or regional political leaders fail to heed the demands made by Muslim families, organisations, and NGOs, claiming that the Islamic Commission of Spain is the only valid interlocutor in discussions regarding religious rights. As a consequence, putting these rights into practice occurs at an uneven pace and degree across the various parts of the Spanish State. An example of such struggles can be found in La Rioja, where various organisations from Muslim communities resident in that region – migrant, worker and women's associations, religious entities, etc. – have mobilised to form a platform calling on the various administrations involved to guarantee their rights. Following successful negotiations to secure space in the municipal cemetery of Logroño – the capital of the La Rioja region – for burials in accordance with Islamic rituals, in 2022 their attention is centred on the right to Islamic education (ERI in its Spanish initials) and the availability of halal food in schools in La Rioja. Faced with administrative silence and the passive, or sometimes even blocking, attitude of the Islamic Commission of Spain, the families have taken their claims to court, with the backing of the aforementioned platform.

3   Fighting against anti-Muslim discrimination

As mentioned earlier, the history of Islam's presence in modern-day Spain is closely linked to a more complex, global process, namely the country's transformation into the recipient of international migratory flows. In recent decades, identifying the Muslim population as foreign has been a practically automatic process, and has a series of implications. The migratory origin of many Muslims – together with the country's history – has proved a determining factor for the social construct of Islam and Muslims as a foreign community (Moreras 2002). This condition has provided the basis for discourses of a xenophobic and Islamophobic nature that, as we shall see, find a response in political and associative spaces.

In this sense, and apart from the aforementioned incompliance with religious rights, Muslims in Spain face other disadvantages that affect numerous spheres of their daily lives, caused by a number of marginalisation practices. Different mechanisms hinder their capacity to act and participate like other citizens in Spanish society and the public sphere. From the disciplinary dynamics applied by some schools to female pupils wearing hijabs (Mijares 2014; Ramírez 2016) to difficulties in entering the job market –which in Spain is already precarious and characterised by high levels of unemployment –, where young Muslims and in particular women wearing a hijab find it especially hard to find employment (FRA 2017). Even those candidates with university degrees and good grade point averages are often overlooked (Lems 2021). Access to housing is another issue: renting an apartment is extremely difficult for racialized individuals and families, as the owners or real estate agencies have no qualms in rejecting them due to their condition of Muslims or foreigners of African origin (Lems and Mijares 2022). In addition, and as pointed out by Parvez (2017), arbitrary identification processes or the regular surveillance of mosques by the police are part of a global trend. In the case of Spain, young men in particular are frequently stopped by police due to ethnic profiling (Douhaibi and Amazian 2019). Other control mechanisms include the surveillance of mosques and community activities (Astor 2009; Lems and Mijares 2022; López Bargados 2014; Téllez Delgado 2018). A study conducted in Catalonia by SOS Racisme on police identification processes by ethnic profile revealed disproportionate figures between people with or without Spanish citizenship who were required to show their identification documents (SOS Racisme 2018). Practices such as these are one of the principal mechanisms for criminalising foreign and/or racialized groups (García Añón et al. 2013). In addition, legislation in security affairs also has a great impact on the construction of the alterity of Muslim groups. Through these laws, agreements, protocols, state, and regional plans, based mainly on supranational directives, the State contributes to the criminalisation of Muslims as "terrorism suspects" (Téllez Delgado 2018). In this sense, the threat of punishments in the form of fines or the withdrawal of residence or work permits and the risk of accusations of being a "terrorist" have a silencing effect on part of the Muslim population (Lems and Mijares 2022). In short, foreignization, invisibilization, and criminalisation are just three

8 Religious Freedom, Civil Rights, and Islam in Spain

of the practices that limit Muslims' capacity for action, restricting their options of reacting and rebelling against the discrimination exercised by institutions and citizens – almost always non-Muslims.

However, faced with these situations of discrimination, a number of Muslim civil organisations in various parts of Spain have joined forces to fight anti-Muslim racism and secure recognition of their citizenship in law and in practice, defending their civil and religious rights. The struggle against Islamophobia in Spain involves working to get the State and the various administrations to recognise the existence of anti-Muslim racism. Indeed, this is the first step in the creation and application of the measures needed to fight it. Their calls echo those of international organisations such as the Office for Democratic Institutions and Human Rights (ODIHR) – which is dependent on the Organization for Security and Co-operation in Europe (OSCE) –, the Fundamental Rights Agency (FRA) or the European Commission against Racism and Intolerance (ECRI), namely that the governments of the member states of these institutions must play an active role in monitoring hate crimes, establishing a distinct category for incidents of Islamophobia, separating them from other hate crimes in order to fight this form of racism in a more efficient manner by applying specific measures to each case. In Spain, despite the insistence of Muslim civil society, the ministry responsible for reporting hate crimes does not yet include a breakdown of incidents of Islamophobia in its data (ONDOD 2022).

Recording and monitoring islamophobic incidents is a challenging and precarious task that is almost always carried out voluntarily. The few initiatives include the Observatory of Islamophobia in Catalonia (ODIC in its Spanish initials). This organisation was set up in August 2020 by the *Stop als Fenomèns Islamòfobs* (Stop Islamophobic Phenomena) association, which in turn was created in 2017, in collaboration with Barcelona city and provincial councils. The aim was to monitor all reports of Islamophobia within the area governed by the Catalonian administration. The 2020 and 2021 reports by the Observatory and other recent reports on Islamophobia in Spain and Europe (Bayrackli and Hafez 2021, 2022; PCCI 2017, 2018) warn of an increase in anti-Muslim hate crimes and incidents, as well as the presence of Islamophobic discourse, spread in particular by certain politicians, journalists and media (Ali 2020; OIM 2019). Attempts are also being made by Muslim civil society to combat this discourse of hate with a series of measures, including the filing of complaints before the corresponding public prosecutors' offices. However, to date, the public prosecutors, judges, and courts in question have opted to close these cases related to alleged hate discourse without bringing them to trial. Furthermore, scholars and researchers also participate with discourse that occasionally legitimises the stereotyped image of Muslims, thereby underpinning the essentialisation of Muslims and Islam (Ramírez 2014).

Faced with this lack of legal, social, or political recognition, a section of Muslim society, and in particular young women, have mobilised to defend their Spanish citizenship and Muslimness in a country of religious freedom. In recent years, associations and initiatives have sprung up throughout Spain, led by young people who identify as Muslims and citizens *de jure* and de facto. Whilst some relate closely to the associative fabric related to immigration, others work from initiatives driven by Islamic religious associations, and others stem from associations of young Spanish Muslims. These young people insist that there is a lack of knowledge and recognition of Islam in Spain and feel that they are questioned within an increasingly hostile climate that converts them into the direct or indirect victims of certain discourses of hate or Islamophobic prejudices. They call for education in Islam in schools that will tackle both these issues: not only are their requests for Islamic education in schools overlooked, despite its inclusion in the Cooperation Agreement, but they also face numerous stereotyped situations in the classroom, textbooks, and the curricula. In this sense, they demand a review of the textbooks intended to teach the history of Islam and other religions. Based on their experience at school, they consider there is a need for greater symbolic and material recognition that will give them enhanced visibility as a group and strengthen the country's religious plurality, eliminating discriminatory aspects and stereotypes. Yet they also assume the demands for traditional burials and labour rights, the latter of which they perceive place Muslim women in a particularly vulnerable situation (Planet and Camarero 2022).

4 The State of Academic Research on Muslims and Islam

Spain continues to publish more books on Islam than any other European country. However, only a tiny proportion of these works address contemporary issues surrounding Islam and Muslims. The centuries of Islamic presence on the Iberian Peninsula are the object of historiographic study but, as we have seen, they are also present in discussions on the institutionalisation and organisation of Islamic worship, as well as the historical debate surrounding the construction of the Spanish nation (De Ayala and Palacios 2021; Martín Corrales 2002; Planet and Madonia 2022).

In addition, Spain's transformation into a country of immigration during the 1990s brought with it non-EU migratory flows that were rapidly perceived as a

8 Religious Freedom, Civil Rights, and Islam in Spain

problem in political and public debates. As Bravo (2006) explained, the Muslim immigrant – originating mainly from the neighbouring Morocco – would become the "sub-other" of the possible "others". Indeed, an ethnic filter would gradually emerge towards these migrants, whose religion and customs had historically opposed those of Spain's culture and identity. Within this context, a series of studies were conducted into the so-called "immigrated Islam" (the Islam of immigrant communities), focused initially on the question of the immigrants' origins. Despite the abundance of these studies, a paradigm would gradually emerge based on questions of culture and security, which in both cases limited the religious aspect to a negative, ethnic feature, portraying a homogenous and essentialised vision of both Islam and Spanish culture.

Turning to the process of the institutionalisation and accommodation of Islam in Spain, we find a further area of analysis addressed from a legal standpoint. In these cases, specialists in canon law and constitutional law have studied the institutionalisation of Islam, both in regulatory terms – the Agreement and its legal application – and from an administrative perspective. Apart from a few exceptions, these studies also fall within the paradigms referred to above. The regulatory process and the difficulties it entails – as discussed *supra* – are related to the foreignness of Muslims and Islam (Contreras Mazarío 2017, 2018) and tend to overlook the analysis of discrimination and the violation of rights, as well as their impact on people's daily lives.

As in other European contexts, the first decade of the twenty-first century witnessed the emergence of another research approach that we could term 'securitarian', which places national 'security' at its core and points to the country's Muslim population as the principal threat. The social and political climate, waves of crises and the actual funding of research in Europe, marked by an agenda centred on this approach, led to the prevalence of essentialist and reductionist perspectives. Yet these studies, which are based on culturalist and reductionist visions of Islam and/or Muslims, can easily be contested when the research moves beyond the generalised categories that comprise the Islam-Spain combination and all that stems from it. This occurs when attention is centred on (i) the difficulties the Muslim population faces in exercising their rights – such as the use of the hijab by young women, other forms of occupying the public space or death – or (ii) on the causes, needs and demands of the associations created by young Spanish Muslims, and as expressed by those young people who are ensnared in the categories that underpin the migratory and/or the securitarian paradigms, as well as (iii) the processes involved in building citizenship and the impediments to political action, through the description – and condemnation – of

the Islamophobia they encounter in their daily lives (Lems 2021; López Bargados 2016; Mijares and Lems 2018; Ramírez 2014; Téllez Delgado 2017). In our
opinion, the existence of critical studies, whose analysis is centred on the impact
of the legal and political system on citizens' lives, may well mark the start of
an epistemological change by academia that could contribute to the resolving
different challenges that exist within this sphere.

5   Future Challenges

The Spanish State faces a number of challenges regarding its Muslim population.
Based on our observation of the dynamics of recent years, a major challenge is
clearly the single interlocutory structure that has been in place since 1991. Considerable sections of Muslim communities are questioning the way the Islamic
Commission of Spain operates in terms of its representation of Spanish Muslims
before various administrations. As Topolski (2018) points out, forcing a heterogeneous population into a vertical and controlled homogenised power structure
is a political mechanism for managing minorities that seeks to disable the capacity of "the other" to act. This system of representation enables authorities to
silence those voices that attempt to speak out against their management methods.
Given the limited progress in religious rights for individual Muslims and Muslim groups in Spain following the creation of this model thirty years ago, there
is a clear need for improvement in methods currently used to manage religious
affairs. This is particularly true in the case of the demands of the communities
themselves, namely Islamic burials or religious education in schools and would
allow for continued progress towards the elimination of discrimination and the
infringement of religious rights.

Related to the above, we consider that a further question for the authorities
and ministries is admitting that anti-Muslim discrimination does indeed exist, as
has been indicated by a large number of international organisations. The State
must assume its responsibility for collecting and publishing specific information
on anti-Muslim racism in Spain, establishing a clearly differentiated category for
Islamophobia. This information is not only necessary in order to design policies
and apply efficient anti-discrimination measures, but also to determine the number
of hate crimes against Muslims that have been prosecuted and identify the extent
and seriousness of this form of racism. This aspect was highlighted by the UN
Human Rights Commission in the report published by its special rapporteur on

minority issues in March 2020,[3] which urged Spain to provide a breakdown of hate crimes targeting Muslims and other minorities. It remains to be seen whether the State will finally and in the short term adopt the recommendations made by a series of inter and supra national organisations with the twofold goal of combating Islamophobia and accepting the claims made in this sense by various Muslim and non-Muslim actors within civil society.

We would like to end by referring to a number of challenges facing academia. In our opinion, one of the greatest of these consists of not contributing to the problematisation of the "Muslim question", but rather of working from a critical perspective to encourage inclusive discourse that, instead of essentialising Islam and Muslims, will help to normalise a plural and diverse society. Academia has a certain responsibility for fomenting knowledge and respect for diversity, including religious freedom, in order to recognise the full citizenship of everyone residing in a country. Likewise, this task includes analysing the role and responsibility of the State and its institutions in enacting policies, regulations and strategies that together lay the foundations for the othering and marginalisation of certain population groups.

References

Ali, A. 2020. "Islamophobia in Spain: National Report 2019". In *European Islamophobia Report 2019*, Eds. E. Bayrackli and F. Hafez, 737–764. Istanbul: SETA.

Astor, A. 2009. "'¡Mezquita No!': The Origins of Mosque Opposition in Spain". GRITIM-UPF *Working Paper Series*, 3.

Bayrakli, E., and Hafez, F. Eds. 2021. *European Islamophobia Report 2020*. Viena: Leopold Weiss Institute.

Bayrakli, E., and Hafez, F., Eds. 2022. *European Islamophobia Report 2021*. Viena: Leopold Weiss Institute.

De Ayala, C., and J. S. Palacios, Eds. 2021. *Reconquista y guerra santa en la España medieval. Ayer y hoy*. Madrid: La Ergástula.

Bravo López, F. 2006. "Culturalismo e inmigración musulmana en Europa". In *Relaciones hispano-marroquíes: una vecindad en construcción*, Ed. A. I. Planet and F. Ramos, 304–350. Guadarrama: Ediciones del Oriente y el Mediterráneo.

Contreras Mazarío, J. M. 2018. "Muslims in Spain. The legal framework and status." In *Observing Islam in Spain. Contemporary Politics and Social Dynamics*, Ed. A. I. Planet Contreras, 23–61. Leiden: Brill.

Contreras Mazarío, J. M. 2017. *¿Hacia un islam español? Un estudio de derecho y política*. Valencia: Tirant Humanidades.

---

[3] Report on the official visit to Spain from 14 to 25th January 2019 https://undocs.org/es/A/HRC/43/47/Add.1 [Accessed: 4th October 2022].

Douhaibi, A. N., and S. Amazian. 2019. *La radicalización del racismo. Islamofobia de Estado y Prevención Antiterrorista.* Oviedo: Cambalache.

FRA Fundamental Rights Agency. 2017. *Fundamental Rights Report 2017.* Luxemburg: Publications Ofice of the European Union.

FPyC Fundación Pluralismo y Convivencia. 2019a. *Memoria 2017.* https://www.plural ismoyconvivencia.es/wp-content/uploads/2019/07/MEMORIA_2017.pdf. Accessed: 27 Sept. 2020.

FPyC Fundación Pluralismo y Convivencia. 2019b. *Memoria 2018.* https://www.pluralism oyconvivencia.es/wp-content/uploads/2019/07/Memoria-de-Actividades-FPyC-2018. pdf. Accessed: 27. Sept. 2020.

FPyC Fundación Pluralismo y Convivencia. 2020. *Memoria 2019.* https://www.pluralismoyc onvivencia.es/wp-content/uploads/2020/07/Memoria_2019_Pluralismo-1.pdf. Accessed: 27. Sept. 2020.

García Añón, J., Bradford, B., García Sáez, J. A., Gascón Cuenca A., and Llorente Ferreres, A. 2013. *Identificación policial por perfil étnico en España.* Valencia: Tirant lo Blanch.

Lems, J. M. 2021. Staying silent or speaking up: Reactions to racialization affecting Muslims in Madrid. *Ethnic and Racial Studies* 44(7):1192–1210. https://doi.org/10.1080/014 19870.2020.1779949.

Lems, J. M., and Mijares, L. 2022. "La securitización de la cotidianidad de las personas musulmanas en España: el silenciamiento como estrategia de control." In *Cambio, crisis y movilizaciones en el Mediterráneo occidental,* Eds. B. Azaola, T. Desrues, M. Larramendi, A. Planet, and A. Ramírez. Granada: Comares.

López Bargados, A. 2016. La amenaza yihadista en España: Viejos y nuevos orientalismos. *Revista De Estudios Internacionales Mediterráneos* 21:73–80. https://doi.org/10.15366/ reim2016.21.006.

López Bargados, A. 2014. "Autos de fe en un mundo de incrédulos: etnografiando la construcción del 'terror islámico' en Cataluña." In *La alteridad imaginada. El pánico moral y la construcción de lo musulmán en España y Francia,* Ed. A. Ramírez, 23–44. Barcelona: Bellaterra.

Martin Corrales, E. 2002. *La imagen del magrebí en España: Una perspectiva histórica, siglos XVI–XX.* Barcelona: Bellaterra.

Mijares, L. 2014. "El efecto *Persépolis*: procesos de domesticación y marginación de estudiantes musulmanas en los centros educativos." In *La alteridad imaginada. El pánico moral y la construcción de lo musulmán en España y Francia,* Ed. A. Ramírez, 189–217. Barcelona: Bellaterra.

Mijares, L., and J. M. Lems. 2018. Luchando contra la subalternidad: Reivindicaciones entre la población musulmana de Madrid. *Revista De Estudios Internacionales Mediterráneos* 24:109–128. https://doi.org/10.15366/reim2018.24.007.

Moreras, J. 2002. Muslims In Spain: Between the historical heritage and the minority construction. *The Muslim World* 92(1–2):129–142.

Muñoz-Comet, J. 2022. "Dificultades y retos para la cuantificación de las minorías religiosas en España." *Cuestiones de Pluralismo* 2(1) https://www.observatorioreligion.es/revista/ articulo/dficultades_y_retos_para_la_cuantificacion_de_las_minorias_religiosas_en_e spana/index.html. Accessed: 8. Nov. 2022.

8 Religious Freedom, Civil Rights, and Islam in Spain

Observatorio Andalusí. 2022. *Estudio demográfico de la población musulmana. Explotación estadística del censo de ciudadanos musulmanes en España referido a fecha 31/12/2021.* Madrid: UCIDE.

ODIC Observatori de la Islamofòbia a Catalunya. 2021. *Fent visible allò invisible. Informe anual 2020.* Barcelona.

ODIC Observatori de la Islamofòbia a Catalunya. 2022. *Quan venen de matinada. Informe anual 2021.* Barcelona.

OIM Observatorio de la Islamofobia en los Medios. 2019. *Un cambio a nuestro alcance: Islamofobia en los medios.* http://www.observatorioislamofobia.org/2019/09/19/informe-2018-cambio-alcance-islamofobia-los-medios/. Accessed: 31 Aug. 2020.

ONDOD Oficina Nacional de Delitos de Odio. 2022. *Informe sobre la evolución de los delitos de odio en España 2021.* Ministerio del Interior. Gobierno de España.

Parvez, F. Z. 2017. *Politicizing Islam. The Islamic revival in France and India.* New York: Oxford University Press.

Pérez Agote, A. 2022. "The Processes of Religion in Modern Spain". In *Religious landscapes in contemporary Spain. The impact of secularization on religious pluralism,* Eds. A. I. Planet Contreras, J. de la Cueva, and M. Hernando de Larramendi, 7–30. Sussex Academic Press.

Planet Contreras, A. I. 2014. Chapter 7: Islam in Spain. In *Handbook on European Islam,* Ed. J. Cesari, 311–349. Oxford: Oxford University Press.

Planet Contreras, A. I. 2018. "Islam in Spain. From historical question to social debate." In *Observing Islam in Spain. Contemporary Politics and Social Dynamics,* Ed. A. I. Planet Contreras, 1–22. Leiden: Brill.

Planet Contreras, A. I., and R. Camarero. 2022. Las políticas de diáspora en cuestión: El caso de Marruecos. In *Cambio, crisis y movilizaciones en el Mediterráneo occidental,* Eds. B. Azaola, T. Desrues, M.H. Larramendi, A. Planet, and A. Ramírez, 117–133. Comares: Granada.

Planet Contreras, A. I., and S. Madonia. 2022. "Thinking about contemporary Islam in Spain". In *Religious landscapes in contemporary Spain. The impact of secularization on religious pluralism,* Eds. A. I. Planet, J. de la Cueva, and M. Hernando de Larramendi, 179–207. Sussex Academic Press.

PCCI Plataforma Ciudadana Contra la Islamofobia. 2017. *Informe Anual Islamofobia en España 2016,* http://mezquitadesevilla.com/wp-content/uploads/2017/11/Informe-sobre-la-islamofobia-en-Espa%C3%B1a-2016.pdf. Accessed: 2. Oct. 2020.

PCCI Plataforma Ciudadana Contra la Islamofobia. 2018. *Informe Anual Islamofobia en España 2017,* http://pccislamofobia.org/wp-content/uploads/2018/03/Informe-Islamofobia-en-España.-PCCI-Informe-Anual-2018.pdf. Accessed: 27. Apr. 2018.

Qureshi, A. 2018. *The virtue of disobedience.* United Kingdom: Byline Books.

Ramírez Fernández, Á. 2016. La construcción del problema musulmán. Radicalización, islam y pobreza. *Viento Sur* 144:21–30.

Ramírez Fernández, Á. 2014. "Introducción y estructura de la obra." In *La alteridad imaginada. El pánico moral y la construcción de lo musulmán en España y Francia,* Ed. A. Ramírez, 9–19. Barcelona: Bellaterra.

Sos Racisme Catalunya & Parad de pararme. 2018. *La apariencia no es motivo. Identificaciones policiales por perfil étnico en Cataluña. Informe 2018.*

Téllez Delgado, V. 2018. El 'Pacto Antiyihadista' y las estrategias de lucha contra la 'radicalización violenta': Implicaciones jurídicas, políticas y sociales. *Revista De Estudios Internacionales Mediterráneos* 24:9–30. https://doi.org/10.15366/reim2018.24.002.

Téllez Delgado, V. 2017. "Embodying religiosities and subjectivities: The responses of young Spanish muslims to violence and terrorism in the name of Islam". In *Secularisms In A Postsecular Age?: Religiosities And Subjectivities In Comparative Perspective*, Eds. J. Mapril, R. Blanes, E. Giumbelli, and E. K. Wilson, 87–106. Palgrave McMillan. (open access: https://link.springer.com/chapter/doi.org/10.1007/978-3-319-43726-2_5).

Topolski, A. 2018. Good Jew, bad Jew…good Muslim, bad Muslim: Managing Europe's others. *Ethnic and Racial Studies* 41(12):2179–2196. https://doi.org/10.1080/01419870. 2018.1391402.

Topolski, A. 2020. The dangerous discourse of the 'Judaeo-Christian' myth: Masking the race–religion constellation in Europe. *Patterns of Prejudice* 54(1–2):71–90. https://doi. org/10.1080/0031322X.2019.1696049.

Ana I. Planet is Professor of Sociology of Islam at the *Universidad Autónoma de Madrid* (Spain). Director of research group *Taller de Estudios Internacionales Mediterráneos* and Editorial Board director of the *Revista de Estudios Internacionales Mediterráneos*. She has edited and published numerous works on Islam in contemporary Spain, including *Religious landscapes in contemporary Spain. The impact of secularization on religious pluralism*, Sussex Academic Press (2022) and the coordinated volume *Observing Islam in Spain: Contemporary politics and social dynamics*, Brill, Leiden (2018).

Johanna M. Lems is assistant professor at the Department of Linguistics and Oriental Studies, *Universidad Complutense de Madrid* (UCM) in Spain. Prior to this she was post-doctoral researcher *Margarita Salas* and honorary professor at the *Universidad Autónoma de Madrid*. Editorial Board member of the *Revista de Estudios Internacionales Mediterráneos* and member of research group GRAIS (UCM). She has publications in *Ethnic and Racial Studies*, *Revista Internacional de Sociología* and the *Routledge Handbook of Islam and Race* (forthcoming 2024).

An Unacknowledged Presence—Islam in the Italian Public Space: History, Reactions, Perspectives

9

Stefano Allievi

Abstract

Historical documentation of Muslim presence dates back to 652 AD. Later, Muslim domination of Sicily lasted for two centuries, even though Islamic influence lasted far longer, included during the Norman domination. Traces of Arab Muslims in costumes, arts and architecture, toponymy, language, etymologies, continue to permeate Sicilian culture.

On the other side of the Italian peninsula Venice reveals a different relationship with Islam. Here we have a cosmopolitan city that was capable to forge a relationship with the Muslim world, influencing it and being influenced by it. Sicily and Venice show two different ways of influence: the former in terms of domination; the latter, as a place of contact, exchange, and reciprocal cultural permeability. Islam has also left its traces in more recent Italian history through the country's colonial adventures and the attempts to build an Italian Empire, during the Fascist period. From the Eighties Islam has returned to Italy through peaceful means, as the unexpected consequence of different waves of immigration, that now include close to two million Muslims. The passage from a first generation of immigrants to a second generation of Italian Muslims is involving important transformations, that often produce reactions, conflicts and hermeneutic incidents.

S. Allievi (✉)
Università di Padova – FISPPA, Padova, Italy
e-mail: stefano.allievi@unipd.it

© The Author(s), under exclusive license to Springer Fachmedien Wiesbaden GmbH, part of Springer Nature 2024
R. Ceylan and M. Mücke (eds.), *Muslims in Europe*, Islam in der Gesellschaft,
https://doi.org/10.1007/978-3-658-43044-3_9

Keywords

Islam • Muslims in Italy • Immigration • Sociology of Religion • Cultural Conflicts

1 Historical Notes

Islam had already made its presence felt in Italy by the seventh century, when the very history of Islam began, first as isolated episodes (historical documentation of Muslim presence goes back to 652 AD) and later due to the Muslim conquerors in Sicily (firmly established on the island, but with strongholds also on the mainland, with the Emirates of Bari and Taranto). During the following centuries, many raids by Barbary pirates reached the coasts of Southern Italy and the islands, becoming a common threat for the coastal populations: some of them even nearly reached the banks of the Tiber and the city of Rome.

By the second half of the fifteenth century, several groups of Ottoman pirates penetrated inland, into Veneto and what is now Friuli. Their arrival had a disproportionate effect. Ippolito Nievo, in his *Confessioni d'un italiano*, a masterpiece of the literature of unified Italy, recalls that "the short-lived forays of the Turks at the end of the century had filled this province of Italy with an overriding and almost superstitious fear" (Nievo 2014). This fear of the Turks pervaded the whole of Europe (as Jean Delumeau 1978, has documented in his history of fear in the West), and the expression "*Mamma, li Turchi!*" (which could be loosely translated as "Heaven save us, the Turks!") became popular, together with the prayer "*a furore Turchorum libera nos Domine*", a fear that is recalled even in a youthful text by Italian writer Pier Paolo Pasolini called *I Turcs tal Friúl* (Pasolini 1995). The expansion of the Ottoman Empire reached its peak in the two sieges of Vienna in 1529 and 1683, which risked reaching Italy, but which above all involved the country through the role undertaken on the second occasion by a monk from Pordenone, Marco D'Aviano, beatified by Pope John Paul II, whose name has been used as an ideological reference in today's anti-Islam movements, such as the *Lega Nord* political party (the founder of the party, Umberto Bossi, has even acted in a movie, *11 settembre 1683*, which reconstructs the story of the second siege, that, given the date, has an undoubted symbolical fascination).

During this long period, which ranged from the Arab domination of Sicily to the abandonment of any possible idea of Ottoman conquest, groups of Muslims came into occasional contact with the Italian peninsula, greatly influencing the image of Islam in Italy, for a range of reasons. Prisoners, merchants, travellers, but above all, as already mentioned, Saracen pirates and, among them, the first converts to Islam (Bennassar 1989), who sometimes constitute a reference and an example for today's converts (Allievi 1998). Still visible on the Italian coastline are the remains of 'Saracen towers' used for defence and as lookout posts, and 'Saracen jousts' and similar events are still alive in local folklore. And, of course, the country's historical imagery of Islam has been built around the Crusades.

Islam has also left its traces in more recent Italian history through the country's colonial adventures and the attempts to build an Italian Empire. This was a period in which Italy had rather more interest in the Islamic world, particularly as regards to its religious dimension. For example, a special statute was granted from 1919 onwards to the Muslims of Tripolitania and Cyrenaica. However, this statute, not often applied, was suspended in 1922 and finally cancelled in 1928. During the Fascist period, another significant episode involved the relationships with local Muslims during the conquest of Ethiopia in 1935–1936. The symbolically most important occasion was the 'spontaneous' consignment of the 'Sword of Islam' to Mussolini, visiting Tripoli on March 18 1937, by some of the local chiefs. Mussolini liked to have his equestrian portrait taken with this gift and had responded to its presentation vehemently: "Fascist Italy intends to assure the Muslim populations of Libya and Ethiopia peace, justice, wellbeing, and respect for the laws of the Prophet, and also wishes to demonstrate its empathy with the Muslims and with Islam throughout the world". Obviously, these words must be set in the context of the period of colonisation. Already ten years earlier, in a speech on the foreign policy of his regime, on June 5 1928, Mussolini had even declared to the Senate that Italy was "a friend of the Islamic world and conscious of its functions as a great Muslim Power ...." (both quotations in Allievi 2003; see also Mazzuca 2017). It is interesting to note that some contemporary converts to Islam, particularly those coming from a background referring to a militant engagement in extreme right-wing movements, openly refer to Mussolini's 'sympathy' towards Islam as a model, to contrast anti-Islamic propaganda coming from the same political area at present day.

At the time, Italy did in fact have a true Muslim policy, which did not fail to arouse some concern amongst other colonial powers. Examples were Radio Bari's broadcastings in Arabic, which started in May 1934, even before the BBC's Arabic Service; the support of and penetration into the Arabic press; the important funding allocated to the *Istituto per l'Oriente* in Rome and the *Istituto Orientale di Napoli*, which were prominent and represented in that period a point of reference for European Orientalism; the relations with the Mufti of Jerusalem, Amir Al-Husayni (known for his position pro Nazi-Fascist regimes and their anti-Judaism), who spent long periods in Rome before and after the beginning of the Second World War. All this activity refers to relations of strength and spheres of influence with respect to the other chancelleries of Europe, particularly the British, and is openly based on a rhetoric of Italy being a bridge between East and West and, in the Mediterranean, between North Africa and Europe, and even as a possible "Western school" (still a Mussolini's quote) for the new Islamic nations which were coming into being. Later, Italy no longer aspired to this role. After the fall of fascism, this policy was abandoned and so, progressively, were the studies, culture, knowledge, and awareness acquired during these years.

2 Between Sicily and Venice

From north to south, Islam eventually influenced all regions of Italy to some extent. Symbolically, for different reasons and at different times, we can underline its presence in two places diametrically opposed to each other: Sicily and Venice; the former in terms of domination; the latter, as a place of contact, exchange, and reciprocal cultural permeability.

The most important case is, of course, that of Sicily. Muslim domination lasted for two centuries, but its influence lasted far longer. In a certain sense, Sicily was 'invented' with Islam, or rather, with the Arabs, who gave the island history, dignity, and extraordinary material and artistic wealth, all of which was certainly not inferior to the vestiges left by the Greeks. As the writer Leonardo Sciascia noted, "the inhabitants of the island of Sicily began to behave like Sicilians after the Arab conquest" (ibidem). Traces of Arab Muslims in costumes, arts and architecture, toponymy, language, etymologies, and other cultural aspects were to remain: two centuries of domination, and an even longer lasting cultural influence, thanks to the opening of the Norman court to Arab civilization and language, did not pass in vain (Metcalfe 2009; Nef 2015; Tramontana 2014).

Within Italy, Sicily was to remain the area most influenced by Islam: from Mazara del Vallo, a Sicilian outpost facing Tunisia, the ancient Ifriqiya (from which we define the entire continent of Africa, but which, for several Arab geographers and historians, is a term which also comprises Sicily), to Palermo, that comes from the Arabic *Balarm* (it had previously been the Greek *Panormos*), the court capital, and the "city of three hundred mosques" as it was called by Ibn Hawqal, an Arab traveller of Norman times, in his chronicle of 973. But reference to the Arab-Islamic past, as shown by local place names, is to be found everywhere: from the port, or *marsa Alì* (or *Allah*), now Marsala, the western cape Trinacria, the gorges of Alcantara (*al-qantara* means "bridge"), to various names such as Caltanissetta, Caltabellotta, Caltagirone, Calatafimi and Calascibetta, which refer to the Arab *qal'a*, a castle, but also a fortress or stronghold,

9 An Unacknowledged Presence—Islam in the Italian ...   153

to Canicattì (*al-qattah*), Favara (from *fawar*, a "spring"), Sciacca (*as-saqqah*, a "split" or a "crevice") and Alcamo (the Arab *manzil al-qamah*). Sometimes the same linguistic derivation serves to denominate a place: like the Latin *mons* or the Arabic *giabal*, both meaning "mountain", which led to the invention of Mongiabal, now Mongibello, which is simply Mount Etna (Gibellina and Gibilmanna have the same derivation).

Beyond the place names, surnames, and the Sicilian language itself, the presence of Arabo-Islamic traditions and mores remained alive also in the material development (for example, wells and waterwheels, fountains—linked both to practical use and liturgical necessities linked to ablutions—and the import and introduction of the date palm, oranges, pistachios, bananas, myrrh, saffron, cotton and sugarcane), and in folklore (the popular stories of Giufà, for example, that come directly from the Arabic Giuha). This cultural presence of Islam lasted far beyond the two centuries of direct Arab domination, and continued throughout the Norman period, thanks to the extraordinary figure of Federico II, *stupor mundi* (for the Arabs *al-Imbiratur*—the Emperor) and his successors.

Yet Venice reveals a different relationship with Islam. Here we have a cosmopolitan city that was capable to forge a relationship with the Muslim world, influencing it and being influenced by it. Not a great deal of what is truly Islamic has remained in Venice. Yet one of its many visitors, Marcel Proust, in his *Recherche,* describes "palaces disguised as sultans". There are not many architectural features, which can be clearly identified with Islamic traditions. But several buildings have absorbed Ottoman influences, at the extent that visitors to Venice feel that they are in some way in the Orient. This impression is reinforced by the city's history, which included the arrival of Jews from the Ottoman empire, Armenians, and later a few Bosnian, Persian and Turkish merchants. Above all, for the latter, the Fondaco dei Turchi (from *funduq*, which is to this day the Arab word for 'hotel'), the Palazzo Palmieri da Pesaro, on the Canal Grande, was re-adapted for them as an 'institutional' building. Perhaps it was not by chance that it was placed in almost exact topographic symmetry with the ghetto, which is on the other side of the canal. Inside this building, there were 24 storerooms, 52 bedrooms and, of course, a small mosque with a nearby space for ablutions. The Fondaco was inaugurated in 1621, and its history finished when the last remaining Turk, a certain Saddo-Drisdi, refused to leave the *palazzo* which he believed he had a right to inhabit, although it had been acquired in 1838 by a builder who wanted to restructure it and, despite an ongoing court case for eviction, finally left the building and the city without leaving any further traces. The Fondaco is now the city's Museum of Natural History (Allievi 2003; Pedani 2010).

It is interesting to note, as sometimes still happens these days in Europe, that even on the Fondaco dei Turchi, and despite the long, peaceful and 'integrated' history that has been described, fear was widespread. On 13 April 1602, worried about the destiny of the *Serenissima* Republic, a Venetian citizen started a petition against the proposal to create the Fondaco. This was because the great numbers of Turks would inevitably lead to the building of a mosque (which did happen), in itself a motive for scandal, as the Turks were "adorers of Mohamed" (as Muslims were perceived then) and associated with the corruption which the dissolute behaviour of the Turks would involve. However, other Turks lived outside the Fondaco, in spite of the severe laws which obliged them to live there as foreigners. Perhaps this may be explained (as it can today) by the state of marginality of many of these people: slaves who worked on building defensive fortifications, or others, more fortunate, including servants in noble houses, and convicts of all sorts, sailors, and yet more helping in kitchens or in gondolas. The best these men could do was to offer their services for humble, tiring work. Jobs not too different from the ones in which new immigrants from Muslim countries are involved. Yet as the punctilious registers of foreigners' deaths compiled by the *Provveditorato alla Sanità della Serenissima* shows, there were also some *hoca*, or masters, soldiers who were members of the Sultan's guard, a couple of *agà*, "signori" a title which indicated some kind of wealth, and also a couple of members of Sufi confraternities, a *fakir* and a dervish.

Venice, with its celebrated printed works and relative freedom, also became one of the major sources of Arab works, both in translation and in various Oriental languages. It was also one of the first places where Arabic was printed with mobile character: the Koran was printed for the first time in 1537. The first translation of the *L'Alcorano di Macometto* was printed in 1547 by Andrea Arrivabene, while another version—of historical importance for the role it was later to play—did not appear until 1698, 150 years later, in Padova, and was translated by Father Ludovico Marracci. Venice played a decisive role also in promoting a fashion for Turkish carpets (marketing them throughout Europe), ceramics, goldworks, tissues even used as sacred liturgical Catholic vestments, and other luxuries.

But it was the city of Venice itself which revealed its relationship with the Islamic world. Examples include the *Fondamenta dei Mori* and the *Campo dei Mori* and, of course, the two '*mori di Venezia*' which, for more than four centuries, have marked the hours by ringing the bells of St. Mark. And think to St. Mark itself. In the year 828, two Venetian merchants, Rustico da Torcello and Bon da Malamocco—not without irony and indeed with a certain spirit of initiative, and with the complicity of an Alexandrine priest—managed to steal the

9 An Unacknowledged Presence—Islam in the Italian ...   155

mortal remains of St Mark the Evangelist from under the noses of the guards of Alexandria, where they had originally been buried, by concealing them in a cart loaded with pork, impure for Muslims, and which the customs officers therefore avoided checking. The precious relic then underwent a dangerous sea voyage to Venice, and was miraculously saved from shipwreck during a storm. Justinian ordered the building of a church next to the Ducal Palace, destined to become the doge's chapel and official church. It is now universally known as St. Mark's Basilica. Of all this, little has been transmitted into mainstream historical legacy, yet this history is beginning to be rediscovered thanks to the present-day Muslim presence in Italy.

3   The Return of Islam

It was to give justice to this neglected history that when Felice Dassetto and I conducted the first research carried out on migrant Muslims in Italy during the early 1990s we decided to title it *Il ritorno dell'islam (The return of Islam*, Allievi and Dassetto 1993). What was intended to be a recognition of, and a homage to, a forgotten memory, sounded as a sort of provocation, how great the ignorance of this past was widespread. Yet Islam in Italy today, which is frequently under discussion, receives far more attention than the historical facts and background which, as the title of this paper suggests, is an 'unacknowledged' presence. There is much talk and frequent rumours about Islam, but Muslims are still relatively little-known: the debate is *about* Muslims, but it is not often addressed *to* them and even less is a conversation *with* them. In fact, the actual production of research on Muslims in Italy, even from the viewpoint of quantity, cannot be compared with that in countries such as France, the United Kingdom or Germany, or Belgium, Holland, Scandinavian countries and even Spain.

That said, there *is* something worthy of discussion, not only sociologically but also historically. Through immigration, Islam reached Italy far later than other European countries because immigrants arrived much later. The reason is that while Central and Northern European countries were already well established labour-importing economies as a result of post-Second World War reconstruction and the subsequent economic boom, Italy, together with other Mediterranean countries such as Spain, Greece and Portugal, were still sending countries, with significant percentages of emigrants. Only since the 1970s has Italy become—officially, we might say—a country of immigration and religious pluralism. But the country has had great difficulty in acknowledging this change, even in its legislation, and it has done its best to avoid recognising and accepting the cultural and religious implications of this process of pluralisation, particularly as far as Islam is concerned. Because of this lack of recognition, Italy has not produced a specific model of cultural politics to favour immigrant integration. Instead, anti-multiculturalist discourses created debate in the public space even before multiculturalist policies had been implemented (Allievi 2010), due to the actions of important political entrepreneurs of fear (such as the *Lega Nord*, and what at present is named *Fratelli d'Italia*, the party that won the elections in 2022, whose leader, Giorgia Meloni, is, while we are writing, the Italian prime minister). In this sense, Italy may be viewed as a country without an established model of pluralism, and different governments have produced contradictory laws, depending on the majorities supporting them in power. Nevertheless, cultural and religious pluralism has flourished in the country. Through what we might call a silent revolution, Italy is no longer "the Pope's country" and Catholicism "the religion of the Italians" (Allievi 2014b). A new and more complex religious landscape is emerging, of which Islam, being more statistically important and more 'debated' by mass media than other non-Christian minorities, is an important, if not crucial, part. In fact, unlike other European countries, which already had internal religious pluralism and in which immigration started decades earlier, Italy is now discovering a hitherto unknown pluralism in the presence of Islam. Therefore pluralism may be perceived as more difficult to understand and being accepted.

4 The Present Situation: Quantitative and Qualitative Data

From a demographic-statistical viewpoint, the Islamic presence in Italy shows considerable consistency. For about a quarter of a century now, Islam has been and still is the religion of about one-third of immigrants. In 2021 there were 5.193.669 legal foreign residents (8,8% of the population living in Italy): the estimate of Muslim population (based on the country of origin, including second generations) is 1.800.000, 34,2% of the foreign population, and a bit more of 3% of total population. If we add a percentage of irregular residents without legal permit (an estimate of 500.000, in which the percentage of Muslims is higher than one-third), those who have obtained the Italian citizenship in recent years, and Italian converts to Islam, we can roughly estimate 2,2–2,5 millions of Muslims in Italy. Their origin varies from Morocco (the most important foreign community, with more than 400.000 legal residents, roughly one fifth of Muslims) to Albania (very close in numbers to Moroccans, but with few practising and many nominal Muslims): Egypt and Bangladesh count 150.000 presences each;

9 An Unacknowledged Presence—Islam in the Italian ... 157

Pakistan 130.000; Tunisia, Senegal and Nigeria around 100.000; continuing to very different countries such as Kosovo 44.000, Turkey, Bosnia, Algeria and Mali all counting around 20.000 residents, Gambia, Afghanistan and Iran 15.000, and many others minor groups (IDOS 2022), included an estimate of 20.000 Italian converts to Islam, including those involved in sufi groups and converted because of a marriage with a Muslim partner. It is the image of a large ethnic, national and linguistic diversity, to which we must add various traditions and interpretation of religion (Sunnites belonging to different juridical schools or *madhab*, Shiites and other Muslim minorities), political attitudes and transnational affiliations. This plurality, differently from other European countries (at least in the initial phase of their Muslim presences: Algerians in France, Turks in Germany, Indopakistanis in the UK, etc.), characterized from the beginning the Muslim presence in Italy. The transformations in the demographic stratification, must be added to the figure: we are not talking anymore of young adult males, as in the classic image of the migratory chain. Increasingly, we are now talking of families, women, second and third generations, old people and retired workers who do not return to their countries of origin anymore (Saint-Blancat 2015).

Some of these migrants, mainly the members of the early generations, still hark back to their countries of origin, linguistically but also relationally, keeping a close contact with their enlarged original families for emotional, symbolic, and even economic and political reasons, purchasing houses, investing in land or commercial ventures. Many others definitely aim to integrate in the country they have chosen to live in, or in which they are obliged to live in not having succeeded in migrating further north within Europe (as many try to do: onward migrations increase when they get the Italian citizenship and, with it, the freedom to circulate within the EU). In both cases, the focus for interpretation is *change*, not *continuity*. This is not only because living conditions change, but also opinions and even beliefs and theologies, subjected in the same way to the pressures of radical transformations (van Bruinessen and Allievi 2011; Allievi 2022).

The Muslim presence in Italy is scattered all over the country. Unlike other European countries, it cannot be identified only with communities in large cities, although they are mediatised almost exclusively. In Italy, Islam (as immigration) is also largely present—even with places of worship, although often small and precarious—in medium-sized and small towns, and in the countryside and rural areas. It is what we could call 'dialectal' Islam, locally integrated: in a certain sense more 'localised' than 'nationalised', but it often shows processes of integration and acceptance which are higher than those visible in some large cities (and lower levels of radicalization: even the number of foreign fighters during the period of ISIS capacity of attractions has been among the lowest compared to other European countries: see Allievi 2021).

However, the fact that this is still essentially a first-generation Islam in its organised, visible forms still means that it is 'backward-looking'. Many first-generation Muslim representatives still speak Arabic (or another mother tongue) better than Italian, and refer to their origins, often losing sight of the aim of integration. However, the situation is rapidly evolving: Muslims are no longer newcomers and are rapidly passing from the status of foreigners to that of neighbours, even if not yet citizens. Islam in Italy is beginning to enter what we may call phase two of its presence: stabilisation, and partly institutionalisation.

Among the various characteristics of Islam in Italy, with respect to other European countries, we can refer to several key aspects. First, the variety of countries of origin prevents identification, also in terms of perception from Italian observers and institutions, with only one Muslim country. Second, Muslims have been able to build their associations and mosques quite rapidly, compared to other European countries, where Muslims have arrived several decades before, but have been slower in the process of visibility and institutionalisation, and Islam has been confined for a long initial period in the private sphere. Third, more recent arrivals are characterised by the fact that even in countries of origin the reference to Islam is much more central to public discourses, and in the construction of public space, on religious, political, and cultural planes (much more than in the 1970s and early 1980s, for example, in which large-scale immigration occurred in central and northern Europe). Fourth, the presence of Islam has become visible in the public space—through mosques and organisations—already with the first generation, in the early years of their migration, when Islamic leadership still had little experience of the country and a modest knowledge of the Italian language and culture: and this has led to frequent conflicts and misunderstandings, that has had a negative influence on the perception of Islam. Fifth, the greater frequency of irregular presence (immigrants without legal permits), partly due to illegal entry but also to current laws, and by the slowness and malfunctioning of the bureaucratic apparatus required to apply them, constitutes a severe obstacle to integration, even in cultural and religious terms. Sixth, the presence of Islam in Italy is marred by the scarcity of people arriving from ex-colonies with pre-existing cultural and linguistic links with Italy, and a tradition of reciprocal knowledge, and thus also the consequent lack of a post-colonial debate. Seventh, the important role played by converts in what we might call the social production and the cultural transmission of Islam (mass media visibility, Muslim press, websites, translations) and the political milieux (lobbying in favour of agreements with state authorities and the promotion of Islam on both local and

9 An Unacknowledged Presence—Islam in the Italian ...   159

national scales), with a more general role of substitution for the organisational shortcomings of Muslim immigrants. Eighth, the greater working and residential dispersion, and the weakness, at least at present, of secular ethnic and cultural interlocutors with sufficient claim to representation, which makes the social and religious role played by mosques even more important (Allievi 2009; Bombardieri 2010; Degiorgis 2014).

5 Hermeneutical Incidents: The Perception of Islam Through Conflict

One of the main problems affecting Muslims, epistemological in nature, is that Islam enters discussion in the public space primarily through conflicts. From terrorism to cultural conflicts about books or cartoons; from occasional clashes of behaviour in contrast with the law or traditions (polygamy, female circumcision, forced marriages, but also a simple veil) to problematic or violent declarations against the West or some aspects of its culture (tolerance towards homosexuality, women rights). But conflicts are even more often raised from the side of the hosting societies: what goes more or less correctly under the name of Islamophobia, which in Italy for a certain period has become mainstream particularly through Oriana Fallaci's influence, with her trilogy against Islam and Muslims in Europe, sold in million copies of each book, is part of the issue (Allievi 2017; Burdett 2015).

These hermeneutic incidents, interpretative conflicts which concern the limits of rights which are always and inevitably subject to interpretation, have had as a consequence the fact that the very image of Islam is linked to conflict. This produces the paradox that processes of integration (as it happens for immigrants in general) find their way in society (through schools, working environment, institutions, and even jurisprudence); but in the case of Islam, we must acknowledge a generalized conflictual perception which—even though regarding a sentiment of unspecific xenophobia—in its forms and heightened sensitivity is peculiar only to Muslims.

We can observe a substantial integration because there is no single empirically analysable indicator which tells us that Muslims are less integrated than other immigrants or members of other religious communities (if we refer to classic indicators such as levels of literacy or infantile mortality, the percentage of self-employed persons, levels of education, *pro capita* GNP, social and relational capital, statistics on imprisonment, etc.). In these cases, significant differences can be eventually based on citizenship or other social indicators (rural or urban background, for instance), whereas religious variables are far less significant and demonstrable. However, conflictual perception is visible in the fact that Islam, and thus Muslims, despite their real diversity and cultural distance, are perceived as more "different" (if not totally other, and then enemy) than other religious and ethnic groups, even more 'Eastern' and 'Oriental'. Differently from what happened in Spain concerning *al-Andalus*, the fact that Islam has been part of Italy's history has been widely forgotten and thus has not produced consequences in terms of inclusion. Instead, Islam is often perceived as an external enemy rather than as an internal actor: allochthonous, not autochthonous, and exogenous, not indigenous.

The organisation and institutionalisation and, more generally, the levels of co-inclusion of Italian Islam, are affected by this situation. It is almost as if Islam in Italy was obliged to exist in an eternally minor(-ity) condition, in some way on the defensive.

6 How Islamic Presence is Transforming Italian Society?

Islam does not develop in a vacuum, and integration processes are promoted not only by internal dynamics, but also by the environment in which they take place. Integration—whether the word is correctly describing the ongoing processes or not—is, like marriage, an equation with two factors (and many unknowns): it does not work if only one of its two main actors does want to make it work.

What characterizes the Islamic presence in Italy today is not stability and continuity but change and transformation. This is happening for various reasons, affecting both the Italian part of the *umma* and the perception of it in the country.

On the Islamic side, the most interesting phenomena are the following: the gradual emergence, even in the public space, of second generations and their social and cultural visibility, with the accentuated activism of younger generations, through organisations such as the GMI (*Giovani Musulmani d'Italia*; Young Muslims in Italy), but also more secular groups; to a lesser extent than for young people, the greater visibility of women's Islam; the partial decline in representativeness of the traditional social actors of organized Islam and the emergence of new social actors of a certain dynamism, with good capacity for mobilisation and acceptable investment in organisational, financial and human capital resources; some (slow and partial) leadership turnover (with the emergence of a younger leadership that is different from the "founding fathers" of Italian Islam: not immigrated, but born in Italy, and thinking their future in the country, not

9 An Unacknowledged Presence—Islam in the Italian ... 161

"back" to somewhere else); the greater presence—financial but not only—of some transnational or governmental bodies, capable of affecting, in various directions, the evolution of Italian Islam (from the charities of Qatar to the government of Morocco, being the Moroccan diaspora the main organised ethno-national component of Italian Islam); a greater ability to organize and also to react to what is happening or what is talked about in the media; greater activism in the production of Islamic culture, in various forms and declinations, and through artistic expression; a greater awareness of the need to form leaderships that are also professionally better equipped than in the past, to respond to the needs of the community but also to the challenges of radicalism and terrorism.

On the side of Italian society and institutions there are equally interesting changes, not all of which go in the same direction. Going in the direction of greater closure with respect to Islam is the exaggerated if not hysterical mediatization of issues concerning Islam (which continues to have few parallels, in this form, in other European countries): from TV talk shows to the national press to the local media. Political Islamophobia is linked to it, with the effect of a lack of respect for individual and collective rights of Muslims (for example, regarding places of worship in some municipalities). There are also cases of a selective application of the law (for example, safety and fire regulations which, in their strictest form can lead to the immediate closure of Muslim prayer halls), or what we could call Islamic "exceptionalism", that consider Muslims to be exceptional cases and thus ordinary laws do not apply to them and thus for whom specific conditions are required. All this occurs within a cultural setting that continues to be unfavourable to good relations with Islam. One example could be the pervasive and extremely effective press campaign initiated by the already quoted reporter Oriana Fallaci, whose books de facto set the agenda of Italian politics for many years, from 9/11 until today (Burdett 2015). For instance, the regions of Lombardy (in 2015) and Veneto (in 2016), ruled by majorities in which the *Lega*, the party of Matteo Salvini, known for his tough anti-immigrant and anti-Islam politics, has passed highly problematic laws on mosques (partly refused by the Constitutional Court), glossing over the fact that the exercise of religion is a constitutionally guaranteed right. The continuous and intentional overlapping with the refugee emergency in the Mediterranean equally pushes towards a confrontational and closed perspective with respect to Islam, producing chain effects at the local level. Yet there is a more general political climate which also consented to the use of a public language towards Muslims (in mainstream politics and journalism), which has no parallel to that used for other religious communities or ethnic groups (and elsewhere is used only by extremist and openly xenophobic groups and newspapers).

On the other hand there is a development in the direction of greater awareness, institutional caution, and the opening of a more in-depth reflection than in the past on the things to be done by the Ministry of the Interior (three or four governments ago…), which activated a Table of Islam (composed of representatives of the various tendencies of Italian Islam, in 2015) and a Council for Italian Islam (composed of experts, in 2016): which led to the signing, in 2017, of a Pact with Italian Islam, by Interior Minister Minniti and the organizations that are part of the Table: these institutions are still active, but with no other signs of novelty. The emergence of ISIS and the risk of attacks in Italy as well has therefore led to the need to identify representative instances of Islam and the search for interlocutors in the Islamic world. The feeling that Italian Islam is characterized by a substantial push for integration would, for now, be, after all, confirmed by the fact that Italy has not suffered any major terrorist attacks so far, and the number of foreign fighters and sympathizers of the Caliphate seems to be much lower, even in percentage terms, than in most European countries-which would seem to indicate that cooperation, prevention and control, and the moderate repression linked to a certain number of expulsions of radicalized individuals and imams, seem to be working (although it would only take one attack to change climate and perception, and we do not venture into predictions).

At the religious level, too (both on the part of the Catholic church and Protestant minorities), there is a deeper activism and capacity for dialogue, even at the local level. We can observe processes of effective integration due to an averagely positive role, dialogical and inclusive, played by the religions long present in the country, major and minor: the Catholic Church, and actors as the Waldesian (Protestant) Church (very active on migration issues and religious rights), as well as the Lutherans, Adventists, and the Jewish communities. We are far from some premature enthusiasms of the past (usually followed by early disappointments), but also from the aprioristic rejection of parts of Catholic hierarchies, and attitudes seem now more inclined to a daily long-term activity of involvement in discussion, in fact inclusive, and capable of influencing important parts of public opinion with messages other than those conveyed by the media.

In this sense, the fact that Italy had not yet made time to elaborate a strong model for integrating Islam (or even immigrants, it must be said), identifying itself neither with the French-style assimilationist and ostentatiously secularist model nor with the Anglo-Saxon-style multiculturalist model, could for once prove to be a competitive advantage, allowing to avoid the mistakes or extremes of either, while learning some useful preventive lessons, in order to build an original road to mutual understanding. But whether this really happens, we wait to see it confirmed by what will happen in the near future.

References

Allievi Stefano. 1998. *Les convertis à l'islam. Les nouveaux musulmans d'Europe*. Paris: L'Harmattan.

Allievi Stefano. 2003. *Islam italiano. Viaggio nella seconda religione del paese*. Torino: Einaudi.

Allievi Stefano. 2009. *Conflicts over Mosques in Europe. Policy issues and trends*. London: Alliance Publishing Trust.

Allievi Stefano. 2010. *Immigration and cultural pluralism in Italy: Multiculturalism as a missing model*. in Italian culture, vol. XXVIII, n. 2, sept., pp. 85–103

Allievi Stefano. 2014. 'Immigration, religious diversity and recognition of differences: The Italian way to multiculturalism', *Identities. Global studies in culture and power* 21(6):724–737.

Allievi Stefano. 2014b. 'Silent Revolution in the Country of the Pope: From Catholicism as "The Religion of Italians" to the Pluralistic "Italy of Religions"'. In *Beyond Catholicism. Heresy, Mysticism, and Apocalypse in Italian Culture*, Eds. F. De Donno and S. Gilson, 287–313. New York: Palgrave-McMillan.

Allievi Stefano. 2017. *Il burkini come metafora. Conflitti simbolici sull'islam in Europa*. Roma: Castelvecchi.

Allievi Stefano. 2021. *Senza terrore. Perché l'Italia era potenzialmente il terreno di coltura ideale del radicalismo islamico: e perché è andata altrimenti. Un bilancio*. In *"Jihadismo e carcere in Italia. Analisi, strategie e pratiche di gestione tra sicurezza e diritti"*, Eds. M. Bernardini, E. Francesca, and S. Borrillo e N. Di Mauro (a cura di), 47–62. Roma: Istituto per l'Oriente C. A. Nallino.

Allievi Stefano. 2022. *Islamic knowledge in Europe: Where does it come from? Transformation as a structural condition*, Eds. R. Tottoli (a cura di), 301–313 "Routledge Handbook of Islam in the West". Abingdon-New York: Routledge.

Allievi Stefano, and Dassetto Felice. 1993. *Il ritorno dell'islam. I musulmani in Italia*. Roma: Edizioni Lavoro.

Bennassar Bartolomé and Lucile. 1989. *Chrétiens d'Allah*. Paris: Perrin.

Bombardieri Maria. 2010. 'Why Italian mosques are inflaming the social and political debate'. In *Mosques in Europe. Why a solution has become a problem*, Ed. S. Allievi, 269–299. London: Alliance Publishing Trust.

Burdett Charles. 2015. *Italy, Islam and the Islamic World. Representations and reflections, from 9/11 to the Arab Uprising*. Bern: Peter Lang.

Degiorgis Niccolò. 2014. *Hidden Islam*. Bozen: Rorhof.

Delumeau Jacques. 1978. *La peur en Occident (XIV–XVIII siécles). Une cité assiégée*. Paris: Fayard,

IDOS. 2022. *Dossier statistico immigrazione 2021*. Roma: Idos.

Mazzuca Giancarlo. 2017. *Mussolini e i musulmani*. Milano: Mondadori.

Metcalfe Alex. 2009. *The Muslims of medieval Italy*. Edinburgh: Edinburgh University Press.

Nef Annliese. 2015. Muslims and Islam in Sicily from the mid-eleventh to the end of the twelfth century: Contemporary perceptions and today's interpretations. In *Routledge Handbook of Islam in the West*, Ed. R. Tottoli, 55–69. Abingdon-New York: Routledge.

Nievo Ippolito. 2014. *Le confessioni d'un italiano (1867), trans.* Frederika Randall, London: Penguin.

Pasolini Pier Paolo. 1995. *I Turcs tal Friul.* Udine: Società Filogica Friulana.

Pedani Maria Pia. 2010. *Venezia porta d'Oriente.* Bologna: il Mulino.

Saint-Blancat Chantal. 2015. Italy. In *The Oxford handbook of European Islam*, Ed. J. Cesari, 265–310. Oxford: Oxford University Press.

Tramontana Salvatore. 2014. *L'isola di Allah. Luoghi, uomini e cose di Sicilia nei secoli IX–XI.* Torino: Einaudi,

van Bruinessen Martin, and Allievi Stefano. 2011. *Producing Islamic knowledge. Transmission and dissemination in Western Europe.* New York: Routledge.

Stefano Allievi is Full Professor of Sociology at the University of Padua. He has founded and directed the Master's Degree Course in "Cultural Pluralism, Social Change and Migrations", and a Master on "Religions, Politics and Global Society" (in English and Arabic). He is specialized on migration issues, in sociology of religion and cultural change, and has particularly focused his studies and researches on the presence of Islam in Italy and Europe, on which he has extensively published in different languages (www.stefanoallievi.it). He has been member of the "Council for Italian Islam" at the Ministry of Interior, and of the "Commission on Jihadism and the prevention of radicalization" at the Presidency of the Council of Ministers.

Part III
Southeast Europe

Islam and Muslims in the Perspective of Croatian Historiography

10

Dino Mujadžević

Abstract

This chapter deals with the perception of Islam and Muslims in Croatian historiographic sources in the period between c. 1500 and c. 1990. Already in the early modern period Croatian narrative sources, in the context of ongoing Ottoman wars, some very negative perceptions about Islam, and particularly about converts to Islam, became widespread, but there were relatively numerous exceptions to these attitudes. In the nineteenth century, closely related to the development of activities of South Slavic national integration ideologies centred in Croatia, negative stereotypes about converts to Islam persisted and even became more prominent. Croatian historians of the nineteenth century often use extremely negative constructions about Bosnian and Croatian converts to Islam, sometimes under the influence of Orientalist travelogues and folk oral tradition. Between end of the nineteenth century and 1930s, under the influence of social and political changes in Croatia and wider context, the open anti-Islamic discourse disappeared—including the vilification of converts—while anti-Ottoman attitudes in general remained. After the Second World War, research of Bosnia and Herzegovina's history, especially on issues such as Islamization, declined in Croatia.

D. Mujadžević (✉)
Hrvatski institut za povijest, Zagreb, Croatia
e-mail: Dino.Mujadzevic@hu-berlin.de

© The Author(s), under exclusive license to Springer Fachmedien Wiesbaden GmbH, part of Springer Nature 2024
R. Ceylan and M. Mücke (eds.), *Muslims in Europe*, Islam in der Gesellschaft,
https://doi.org/10.1007/978-3-658-43044-3_10

168 D. Mujadžević

Keywords

Croatia • Islam • Bosnia • Ottoman Empire • Habsburg Empire •
Austria-Hungary

1 Introduction

The Ottoman rule in parts of what is now the Republic of Croatia (later in the text: Croatia)—its parts today known as Slavonia, Banija, Kordun, Lika, and inner Dalmatia—came as the result of military conquest and lasted between the early sixteenth and early eighteenth century. Nevertheless, as Ottomans impacted or controlled territories of Croatia's immediate eastern neighbour Bosnia from the first half of the fifteenth until the beginning of the twentieth century, the Ottoman presence in many aspects of the life of Croatia was even stronger and more durable. Ottoman-controlled regions in what are now Bosnia and Herzegovina and Croatia were from the 1580s for the most part administratively united in the Bosnian province of the Ottoman Empire (eyalet). The Ottoman incursions and conquests in Croatia in the fifteenth and sixteenth centuries were a time of great material and human destruction as well as demographic changes. In this context, catastrophic territorial and other losses that were inflicted by Ottomans on predominantly Roman Catholic kingdoms of Croatia and Slavonia—initially parts of the Hungarian Kingdom, after 1526 a part of Habsburg Monarchy, and today mostly within the Republic of Croatia—were also reflected in the literature of the era, sometimes augmented to serve the purposes of anti-Ottoman mobilization and other contemporary purposes. Additionally, even after the Ottoman danger subsided by the late seventeenth century, the invocation of the era of defeat and destruction of previous centuries in the works of later historians continued until the twentieth century. Also, Anti-Ottoman as well as anti-Islamic discourse persisted but was also transformed within these works, as will be explained later in this chapter.

Apart from the destructiveness associated with the incursions and conquests and despite the anti-Ottoman views of Croatian historiography, the Ottoman rule in Croatia and the territory of contemporary Bosnia and Herzegovina should be also viewed in the light of some other constructive developments associated with it. Bosnia experienced a previously unseen level of the development of urban life, both in terms of the numbers of settlements and urban population in general (Handžić 1994, p. 161–168), while the Ottoman-ruled cities and towns between

10 Islam and Muslims in the Perspective of Croatian Historiography

the rivers of Sava, Drava and Danube changed their previous late mediaeval outlook to the Ottoman one and remained approximately at the same level of population numbers (Moačanin 1997, 2001). Also, largely as the result of the development/change of urban life under Ottoman influence, these cities and towns became the home to a relatively large Muslim population with its religious life and institutions. In eastern Croatia (Slavonia and parts of Syrmia), the largest chunk of Croatian territory under Ottomans, the Muslim population was also to be found in villages and approached one-third of the entire population of the region in the seventeenth century (the overall population of eastern Croatia under Ottomans in the seventeenth century could have been around 150 000). Nevertheless, Muslims there and in other parts of what is now Croatia disappeared around 1700 due to Habsburg and Venetian Reconquista. This series of successful military counteroffensives and post-war anti-Islamic policies of Venetians and Habsburgs systematically and thoroughly erased traces of Muslim and Islamic life in Croatia. The material heritage of early modern Muslims in what is now Croatia was destroyed or transformed beyond recognition in virtually all cases. The great majority of Muslims were evacuated before the advance of Christian forces or were sometimes enslaved and kept in captivity as the so-called *Beutetürken*. As new Christian rulers of these regions did not allow any permanent Muslim population within their realms, in Dalmatia and, especially, Lika, a part of the formerly Muslim population chose to convert to Christianity to be able to stay (Kaser 2003; Mujadžević 2021). In Bosnia, the percentage of Muslims varied but stabilized around one-third in the nineteenth century. While the Muslim population in Bosnia retained continuity from the fifteenth century to contemporary days, the Croatian Muslim population started to very slowly renew only after Bosnia was incorporated into the Habsburg Monarchy in 1878.

This chapter is dedicated to questioning the relationship of Croatian historiography in the period between sixteenth and twentieth centuries to Islam and Muslims in Croatia and Bosnia during Ottoman rule. This topic has not been the subject of research until now. In this context, we will not look into the attitudes of the modern era and contemporary Croatian historiography towards the Ottoman Empire and its rule and warfare in Croatia and neighbouring countries, which of course prominently included local and foreign Muslim governing personnel and soldiers. Instead, we will focus on the early modern and modern historiographical discourses about the religion of Islam and the presence of its believers in this area with an emphasis on the Islamization (i.e. conversion to Islam) of the local South Slavic Muslim population.

2 Origins of Modern-Era Anti-Islamic Discourse (C. 1500–C. 1840)

Already in the sixteenth century, Croatian writers and historians depicted contemporary Croatian and Bosnian Islam and Muslims in a predominantly simplified, often negatively caricatured, fashion although there were also neutral and even affirmative views about them. These attitudes arose in the context of the ongoing Ottoman-Habsburg and Ottoman-Venetian wars which brought general devastation and depopulation. Croatian Christian authors of that era, writing mostly in Latin and, sometimes, Croatian vernacular, lived mainly within Habsburg and Venitian realms or other Christian states (Papal States or Dubrovnik) and naturally adhered to anti-Ottoman and anti-Muslim discourses. The vast majority of writers came from the ranks of the clergy giving a special stamp to these works, which are, at least in part, the products of religious apologetics, but also state propaganda. However, there were some deviations from these norms. According to Dukić (2004), the motif of converts to Islam is common in Croatian literary and historiographic works of the era and is the most frequent one associated with the religion of Islam itself. His observations are based on multiple examples of writings by Croatian authors about Islamization (i.e. conversions to Islam) as well as local South Slavic converts to Islam and their decedents (often described as so-called Turcified persons: in Croatian/Bosnian/Serbian language "poturčenici" or "poturice"). Dukić's analysis points to the sometimes complicated and contradictory stereotypes that were used in their works. These early-modern stereotypes include negative ones (early heretical Christian origins of Islam; pressures to convert to Islam; special hate of converts towards Christianity; treacherous nature of converts, etc.) associated with the conversion or converts to Islam, but also there are positive ones (place of converts in the Ottoman meritocratic system and its superiority in comparison to Christian feudal system, etc.), sometimes completely contradictory to the thematically related negative ones (religious tolerance of Ottomans vs. persecution of Christians). There were early modern Croatian authors who used both positive and negative stereotypes about Islam.

Croatian-Hungarian writer, church prelate and diplomat Antun Vrančić (1504–1573) in his work "Iter Buda Hadrianopolim" (Travel from Buda to Edirne, 1553) brought the testimony of a Serb from Plovdiv, who claimed that under the Ottoman rule he was not deprived of religion in the slightest, adding that those who had to maintain and spread Christianity were slowly converting to Islam. On the other hand, Humanist writer Fran Trankvil Andreis (1490–1571) points out that converts especially hate Christians. He pointed out that the Turks entrusted the care of military and civil affairs to Islamized Christians because,

10 Islam and Muslims in the Perspective of Croatian Historiography 171

as he put it, somebody's origin is not important for the Ottomans but ability. The former Ottoman captive Bartol Đurđević (1506–1566) talks about voluntary, but also, as he sees it, forced "Turkification" which supposedly happened under Ottomans "because of the too heavy Turkish yoke and the burden of tribute". The trope of forced Islamization of not only Christian captives but Ottoman Christian subjects—by and large historically baseless except in the case of the devşirme regrutation—will nevertheless remain pervasive until the twentieth century. The Franciscan writer Filip Grabovac (1698–1748) considered conversion to Islam to be religious treason to Christianity, a trope very often present in works by other authors. In his poetic works, Grabovac calls converts to Islam to return to Christianity. With respect to conversions, he also went beyond Croatia and the South Slavic area. In his Croatian-language poems, as a prominent "poturčenik" he also singles out the Syrian monk Sergius, with whom Prophet Muhammad came into contact in his childhood and who was in the view of Grabovac the founder of Ottoman laws and customs. Contrary to this, the Jesuit Bartol Kašić, in his memoirs from 1612, describes a pleasant meeting with sancakbey Hasan of Syrmia, a converted Christian from Dalmatia who hosted him and his entourage well. The very influential Franciscan writer Andrija Kačić Miošić (1704–1760), the author of the poem "Razgovori ugodni naroda slovinskog" (Pleasant conversations of the Slavonic people; 1756) did not hesitate to celebrate the Muslim epic heroes from Bosnia for their virtues, emphasizing their "Slavonic" origin. This part of Kačić's song is one of the places where the most tolerant attitude towards the "Turkified" neighbours—South Slavs of a different religion—in Croatian early modern literature is found (Ibid., p. 33, 178, 208–209, 213, 239).

In the late sixteenth and seventeenth centuries, in north-western Croatia, the conversion to Islam of Franjo Filipović, a canon of the Zagreb cathedral church, resonated sensationally. It was remembered in later early modern historiography as a particularly shameful and incomprehensible act of betrayal by a high-ranking Zagreb Catholic priest. In 1573, Filipović was captured by the Ottomans during the battles near the town of Ivanić and was taken to the interior of the Ottoman Empire and, despite the attempts of the church and Habsburg dignitaries to free him, he converted to Islam and took the name Mehmed. According to the much later account by the Zagreb-based historian Adam Baltazar Krčelić (1715–1778), after converting to Islam, Filipović boasted that he would conquer Zagreb within three days and emphasized that his knowledge of the area and the Habsburg defence system in Croatia posed a great danger. Krčelić emphasizes that the then bishop of Zagreb, Juraj Drašković, excommunicated Filipović and burned all the movables he owned and confiscated all real estate, having his house painted black and taking away his vineyards "while sending a message to a wide audience that some possible future defectors are waiting" (Krčelić 1994, 282–283).

3 The Birth of Croatian Modern Historiography and Anti-Islamic Discourse (C. 1840–C. 1900)

The advent of bourgeois society in the nineteenth century in much of Europe also deeply impacted Croatia. At the time, the territories belonged to the Habsburg Monarchy (from 1867 known as Austria-Hungary). Around the middle of the nineteenth century, in connection with the appearance of South Slavic national integration movements with the centre in Croatia (Illyrism, and later Croato-centric Yugoslavism) there has been a sudden development of historiography, now predominantly in the Croat language. The historiography became increasingly academic, institutionalized, and professional. Historians could now be found more and more often outside the church and noble circles, although the authors affiliated with the Catholic Church, still had a significant influence. Generally, in addition to various nationalist concepts and impulses that radiated from the political context, the Croatian historiography of the nineteenth century was influenced mainly by the historiographic trends from German-speaking countries and Hungary. The development of the modern university in Zagreb (1874), as well as the Yugoslav Academy of Sciences and Arts (JAZU) in the same town, were also important factors in the development of historiography.[1]

The negative depiction of the Ottoman historical and contemporary presence in the Balkans was the **crucial** element in the new nationalist discourses in Croatia that aimed to culturally and potentially politically unite South Slavs in the nineteenth century. Additionally, vilifying the role of Islam as an inseparable part of the Ottoman rule, especially with respect to the Ottoman-era converts ("poturice") and their descendants (also sometimes described by the same term) was seen as integral to the creation of the useful anti-Ottoman narrative. Aware of their influence on wider readership—some of the historical works were published in increasingly popular daily newspapers—Croatian historians of the much of nineteenth century tried to mobilize citizens around their national integration ideas using, among other topics, anti-Islamic and anti-Ottoman rhetoric with its strong

---

[1] For the South Slavic national integration movements with the center in the nineteenth century Croatia see Tomljanovich (2001) and Stančić (2002). For the development of Croatian historiography in the 19th c. see Gross (1996).

10 Islam and Muslims in the Perspective of Croatian Historiography

emotional appeal could help in this project. The Ottomans including local Muslims of South Slavic origin—primarily Bosnian Muslims—were considered the main enemy of South Slavs and Croats and their defeat and expulsion seen as the best medium of national unification.[2] The anti-Ottoman and anti-Islamic attitudes were considered especially important when appealing to the Catholic population in Bosnia and Herzegovina. Even more important for the leaders of the Illyrian and Yugoslav nationalist movements and their historiographic followers in Croatia was to make a common cause with the Serb leadership, intellectuals, and population in the Habsburg Monarchy and the Principality of Serbia.[3] The anti-Islamic discourse of the South Slavic unification movements with the centre in Croatia and related historiography were aimed to resonate well with Serb anti-Ottoman aspirations as many Serbs were during most of the nineteenth century Ottoman subjects, both in Serbia and elsewhere, i.e. in Bosnia. The overthrow of the Ottoman "yoke" was seen as the main goal of Serb nationalists. Especially, the crisis and the uprising of part of the Christian (predominantly Serb) population and the Austro-Hungarian occupation of Bosnia and Herzegovina in the 1870s fuelled anti-Ottoman attitudes in Croatian historiography and other elements of public life.[4] These events boosted hopes for the disappearance of Islam in the Croatian neighbourhood and the annexation of this province to Croatia or Serbia. In this particular period, Bosnian and Croatian converts to Islam were targeted in Croatian historiography unusually vehemently as a treacherous, morally corrupt, and a violent element.[5] Paradoxically, the first-hand knowledge of the Ottomans and Muslims of South Slavic origin was scarcer among historians of the nineteenth century than the above-discussed writers of the sixteenth and seventeenth centuries, many of whom travelled to the Ottoman Empire as diplomats or missionaries and had personal experiences with Muslims. The depiction of Ottomans including the Bosnian Muslim population in Croatian historical narratives of the nineteenth century was based on the politically charged interpretation of much older historical and epic poetry accounts and, mostly foreign, contemporary Orientalist travel literature. As a result of this, albeit the Ottoman danger to Croatia at the time was non-existent, the Bosnian Muslims were during the nineteenth

---

[2] Such contemporay attitudes on Islam and Muslims are epitomized in some of the private letters of the leader and patron of the Yugoslav movement as well as the main benefactor of the JAZU, bishop Josip Juraj Strossmaye, see Strossmayer & Rački (1924–1933) and Strossmayer and Vanutelli (1999).

[3] For attempts by the bishop Strossmayer to work with Serbian leadership in order to annex Bosnia see Ciliga (1972).

[4] For the reception of the Bosnian uprising 1875–1878 see Pavličević (1973).

[5] See my analysis of Vjekoslav Klaić's and Tadija Smičiklas' works later in thischapter.

century in historiography portrayed arguably in an even more negative way than in previous centuries.

Among the first historians of this period modernization period was, Ivan Švear, a village priest from the vicinity of Požega. His multivolume work "Ogledalo Ilirie" (The Mirror of Illyria; 1842), dedicated to the history of South Slavic countries from the earliest times to the nineteenth century, although written in Croat language and eager to represent the Illyrian ideology of South Slavic togetherness, was without substantial academic background reflecting contemporary developments in historiography. In the depictions of the Ottoman rule over Slavonia, this author's narration is often at the level of unrelated anecdotes, which seem to be intended for the broadest class of readers, and even for those who cannot read, but someone literate will read them stories from the book just as if it were oral literature. Švear's book could be seen as a sort of link between the early-modern and modern periods. This work takes a relatively extensive look at the period of Ottoman rule, especially Slavonia, and some accounts of converts to Islam can also be found. For the events of the Ottoman era in Slavonia, there is no indication of sources this author used but it is supposed that Švear often used now-lost chronicles of Catholic monasteries in Slavonia. The fact is that the origin of this information cannot be verified in any source near to the time of Ottoman rule. Having in mind all that is said about Švear and his approach, it is no surprise that Muslims and especially the conversion to Islam are presented exclusively in an extremely negative way. According to Švear, refusing offers to convert to Islam is a true act of Christian heroism. For example, he relates the story of the bey of the Slavonian town of Valpovo who wanted to reward his servant for saving his life by offering "the brave Illyrian his daughter as a wife, if he turns Turkish". However, "this one didn't want it … He, like a true Croat, showed what can be done even in slavery; because the same oppressors were afraid of him". While describing the heroism of another Slavonian Christian under Ottoman rule, a certain Franje Ilinić, Švear personifies the alleged Ottoman cruelty and moral depravity in the characters of converts to Islam ("poturice"): one who kidnapped Ilinić's wife and a jailer who released Ilinić from the dungeon in exchange for a bribe (1842, vol. 4, p. 424–425, 428).

A leading Croatian historian and geographer Vjekoslav Klaić (1849–1928) completed his studies in Vienna in 1872 and published in 1878—in the context of the Bosnian-Herzegovinian crisis that led to the occupation of this country by Austria-Hungary the same year—the book "Bosna. Podatci o zemljopisu i poviesti Bosne i Hercegovine" (Bosnia. Data on geography and history of Bosnia and Herzegovina). Among other things, Klaić in this book presents a short summary of the historical origin and ethnographic description of Bosnian Muslims which is

10 Islam and Muslims in the Perspective of Croatian Historiography

distinguished by virulent anti-Islamic sentiment. As sources for the contemporary situation of Bosnian Muslims the author uses the orientalist accounts of the nineteenth century European travellers (A. F. Hilferding, Cyprian Robert, Karl Sax, Matija Mažuranić). Klaić sees Bosnian Muslims as "Mahometan Croats". After the Ottoman conquest of Bosnia in 1463, he narrates, a large part of the Bosnian population—Croats, as he would like it—converted to Islam. Among them, there were a lot of magnates—for whom Klaić assumes that they were largely heterodox Bosnian Christians—and their servants accepting Islam to keep their estates and freedom respectively. The Islam in Bosnia is described as "aristocratic" in nature and this would-be fact is according to Klaić something unique in the whole Islamic world. Some of the peasants converted, too. The scholarship of the second half of the twentieth century rejected the claim that Bosnian Muslims were largely originating from the mediaeval ruling strata.[6] According to Klaić, in Bosnia "poturice" took all the power while Bosnian Christians became "their slaves, a herd without any rights" and this situation had remained the same until the time Klaić was writing his tractate. It is insisted that there have been only two areas where Islam is professed by "a European tribe"—Albania and Bosnia. While Albanian Muslims are described as less diligent in their faith, Bosnian ones are seen as more fervent believers. Klaić notes the apparent paradox in this due to the supposed materialistic reasons of the first generation Bosnian Muslims to "become Turks". Nevertheless, he insists that adherence of Bosnian Muslims to Islam is outward and the reinstallation of the Christian rule in Bosnia would cause their return to Christianity for selfish reasons. Also, Klaić completely maligned Islam in Bosnia as having contributed only "fanaticism and the lack of spiritual power" albeit he accepts in a rather self-racist fashion that Slavic peoples are "generally prone to fanaticism". In Klaić's disparaging view, Bosnian Muslims were possibly even greater fanatics than Arabs or Turks, certainly than any inhabitant of "the European Turkey", because they supposedly combined Islamic and Slavic fanaticisms, although he admits they are less so in recent times supposedly due to the enforced sultanic reforms and the presence of foreign consulates. The reason for the ostensible phenomenon of Bosnian Muslim fanaticism—which itself is not clearly defined—is found in something he called "the spirit of renegacy". In other words, as Klaić imagines, they tended to be fanatics to warrant before themselves the betrayal of Christianity. It is admitted that Islam in the Arabic and Turkish context created periods of glory and greatness, but Klaić tendentiously concludes that this religion in Bosnia "created nothing". Bosnian Muslims are presented as more phlegmatic—"doing nothing", sitting, smoking and drinking

---

[6] For the overview of this problem see Lopasic (1994).

coffee—and more conservative than even "Orientals" resulting in fierce resistance to the progressive Tanzimat reforms and supposed complete stagnation in Ottoman Bosnia. The ethnographic description of Bosnian Muslims doesn't depart much from Klaić's previously mentioned views: they are "distinguished by proud, upright, sometimes brazen posture", in sharp contrast to allegedly "fearful" Bosnian Christians; they are superficially showing "a much more noble character" but this is often a false impression caused by their better social position, it is claimed; for Klaić, it is more befitting to describe them as "arrogant renegades" having "somehow morose, unpleasant and suspicious temperament" who hate both Ottoman Turks and South Slavic Christians; supposedly they are pious Muslims upholding the prescriptions about cleanliness but still having dirty houses. The fact that Bosnian Muslims are predominantly monogamous, something hailed by some European travellers, does not impress Klaić who claims that this phenomenon originates not in "virtue" but in the poverty of Bosnian Muslims (Klaić 1878, p. 84–90).

Tadija Smičiklas (1843–1914), one of the most prominent Croatian historians of the 19th and early twentieth centuries and the long-term president of the JAZU, can be seen as a typical example of anti-Islamic attitudes of his era. He has published several books in which he touches on Ottoman themes including one of the first syntheses of Croatian history, a two-volume work entitled "Poviest Hrvatska" (Croatian History; published in 1879 and 1882). Smičiklas, who graduated in history in Vienna in 1869, was well aware of the methodology of modern historiography and used a number of published and unpublished sources known at the time, and was also familiar with historiographical literature from the German and Hungarian speaking areas. Regardless of the modernity of his historiographic approach, he was deeply involved in the movement of Croato-centric Yugoslav cultural and political nationalism led by the influential and wealthy bishop of Đakovo (in Slavonia) Josip Juraj Strossmayer. Smičiklas' texts, despite the elements of modern academic scholarship, are sometimes deeply impacted by national-integration myths that romantically celebrate the heroism and civilizational successes of the Croat—and sometimes Serb—people embodied in selected members of the elite. In his vision, the main historical enemy of the Croats is, as expected, the Ottomans. Smičiklas, like his predecessors in historiography, continued to consider the conversion to Islam as an act of national and religious treason which, he believed, was carried out mainly under coercion. In the "Poviest Hrvatska", the famous conversion to Islam of the canon of the Zagreb church Franjo Filipović, after he was captured in 1573 by the Ottomans is accordingly attributed to "torture". (1879, vol. 2, p. 94–95; later Croatian historians dismissed this allegation, see later in this chapter).

10 Islam and Muslims in the Perspective of Croatian Historiography 177

Also, he continued to attribute the worst of Ottoman rule to the South Slavic converts to Islam. His still-often-quoted two-volume work "Dvjestogodišnjica oslobođenja Slavonije" (Bicentenary of the Liberation of Slavonia; 1891) focuses on the Ottoman rule and, especially, Habsburg Reconquista in eastern Croatia at the end of seventeenth century. In this work, he heavily quoted from the works of Austrian and Hungarian Orientalist literature, but also made use of Habsburg primary sources. Smičiklas was one of the first historians to use a Habsburg early post-census to point to the existence of not only the Muslim urban population but also to substantial Muslim peasant population, mainly around the town of Požega in Slavonia. He concluded—without any documentary sources—that Muslim peasants there were "our Bosnian poturice" (Smičiklas 1891, vol. 1, p. 6–7), or in other words, they were settlers from Bosnia not indigenous to Slavonia. On the other hand, he also uses material from unreliable sources, primarily Švear, to describe alleged Ottoman atrocities against Christians in Slavonia including graphic depictions of the murdering of children, body mutilation and impaling of whole families together (Ibid., p. 16). According to Smičiklas, the religion of Islam is associated with violence. He insists that Islam demands from its believers to kill Christians until they submit quoting—without any historical context—passages from a German translation of the Qur'an. Smičiklas goes so far as to fraudulently claim that "according to Muhammed's teachings the violence comes from God" and that Muslims despise Jews so much that they wouldn't allow them to convert to Islam. (Ibid., p. 64–65). Reality and fiction are mixed in Smičiklas' depiction of the life of Christians and the Catholic Church under Sharia law in the Ottoman Empire: there was a general ban to build new churches, but Christians and especially their priests were also supposedly constantly humiliated and blackmailed by the Ottoman government (Ibid., p. 66–69). Additionally, Smičiklas devoted himself in this book to the issue of the conversion of Christians from Croatia to Islam under Ottoman rule and gave vent to his intolerance towards the "poturice" like never before. As a special oddity of this work, it should be noted that for the purposes of dealing with Ottoman rule, but especially with the "poturice", Smičiklas temporarily abandoned the historiographical methodology, which should be based on the critical evaluation of material, documentary and contemporary narrative sources, and used instead the popular oral epics as supposedly reliable historical evidence to depict the supposed reality about converts to Islam. He mentions a certain Stjepan Maljković, who appeared in several folk epic songs, as a typical example of a "horrible poturica" or "real poturica" in the seventeenth century. Smičiklas accepted without hesitation the almost caricatured descriptions of the wickedness of this villain—"poturica"—from folk epic poetry on the Christian side of the Ottoman-Habsburg border. Thus, he reports that Maljković defected to the "Turks" only "because of one slap from his master", whom he later, even though he was only an old man, "slaughtered" together with his wife and four sons, and took his daughter "to disgrace with the Turks". As a reward, the Ottomans named him to the position of commander in the Lika region. According to Smičiklas, he was present "wherever it was necessary not only to fight, but also to angrily slaughter and kidnap girls". Maljković had "an inhuman heart" and didn't cry when his sons died in battle against Christians (Ibid., p. 64).

4 The Demise of the Anti-Islamic Discourse

From the beginning of the twentieth century, the weakening of the anti-Islamic, and less often anti-Ottoman, attitude of Croatian historiography is noticeable. In this period, the presence of Bosnian-Herzegovinian Muslims in the Austro-Hungarian Monarchy was normalized and the process of integration has begun. The ideas about Islam originating in the Croat nationalist movement of "pravaši" became increasingly influential in the wider society. This movement was advocating the integration of Bosnian-Herzegovinian Muslims—without renouncing Islam—into the Croatian nation. In 1916, the Croatian Parliament passed a decision on the official recognition of Islam in Croatia. In this period, the Catholic Church gradually lost its influence on the scientific and cultural public in Croatia. At the same time, some Muslim authors began to work on the Croatian cultural and scientific scene, advocating the rejection of religiously based prejudices towards Islam, as well as the Ottoman past. During the interwar period of Croatian history (1918–1941) the small Muslim community was established in the Croatian capital of Zagreb and its leaders took the prominent place in the cultural life of the city. These developments additionally opened the door for a more accepting view of Islam and Muslims in the Croatian society of that era.[7]

A typical example of this new approach to Islam and Muslims, is the transformation of the discourse of the previously mentioned Vjekoslav Klaić. Since his already discussed 1878 book in which he wrote dismissively against "poturice", Klaić became university professor and rector of Zagreb University. By the end of the century he had grown into the most respected representative of

---

[7] For the attitudes of the pravaši movement on Islam including the Islamophile writings of their early leader Ante Starčević and reappearance of Muslim community in Croatia in early twentieth century see Hasanbegović (2007) and Mujadžević (2014).

10 Islam and Muslims in the Perspective of Croatian Historiography

erudition-genetic historiography in Croatia and the author of the extremely popular multivolume synthesis "Pov(i)est Hrvata" (The History of Croats; first edition 1899–1922), whose parts about the fifteenth and sixteenth centuries are still often used in historiography. In this work, he uses an exceptional number of previously known documentary and narrative sources, as well as relevant literature from the German, Italian, Hungarian and South Slavic speaking areas. In some places in this book, he spoke about prominent converts to Islam using the Croat language verb "poturčiti se" (to turcify himself/herself; to become a Turk) for their act, like his predecessors. However, the condemnation of conversion to Islam, common to his predecessors and his earlier work, was absent. Thus, without any emotion or additional comments, he talks about the nobleman Mihajlo Svetački, who in the second half of the sixteenth century "became a Turk and moved to Turkish Slavonia, where his descendants then lived in Orahovica" (Klaić 1911, vol. 5, p. 427). Although he considers the late sixteenth century-Bosnian governor Hasan Pasha Predojević "belligerent and bloodthirsty", Klaić mentions without negative comments the claims of some sources that he was born a Christian, moreover that he was allegedly a Benedictine monk, and later "turned Turkish" (Ibid., 367). In contrast to his older contemporary Smičiklas, Klaić emphasizes that, according to contemporary sources, the already mentioned Zagreb canon Franjo Filipović "voluntarily ... renounced the Christian faith, and turned Turkish" (Ibid., 280). It is also mentioned without comment that the Croatian nobles Krsto Svetački, Ladislav More and Franjo Bebek "became Turks" in the sixteenth century. (Ibid.). Nevertheless, Klaić also believes, without any evidence, that some Christian prisoners "were forced to turn to the Turks, left their homeland and, having escaped ... returned to the fold of the Christian faith" (Ibid., 18).

Already after Klaić's death in 1928, the interest of mainstream Croatian historiography in researching the Ottoman past in Bosnia and Herzegovina and Croatia waned. While most important documents from the era of Ottoman-Habsburg/Venitian wars related to Croatia were already analysed or published by Croatian historians, the researchers from Croatia who could study Ottoman-Turkish documents as well as manuscripts in Arabic and Persian languages were extremely scarce and there was no institution to educate them. Therefore, during the interwar period, Croatia's capital Zagreb lagged behind established centres of Ottoman scholarship in Central Europe (Vienna, Budapest) and the Balkans (Sofia, Belgrade, Sarajevo). At the same time, some Bosnian Muslim historians and orientalists like Safvet-beg Bašagić, Hamdija Kreševljaković, and Hazim Šabanović, most of them versed in the Ottoman-Turkish language, became increasingly influential in the Croatian scholarly life of the Interwar period. They were accepting Croat national identification for at least part of their lives but did not accept either anti-Islamic or anti-Ottoman discourse in their works. The 1930s and the first half of the 1940s were also the pinnacle of the influence of the exclusivist Croat nationalism (as opposed to the Croatian Yugoslavism), inheriting the Islamophile tendencies of the older "pravaši" tradition on Croatian culture and science in the nineteenth and twentieth centuries. Around this period, Croatian historiography for the most part abandoned the terminology that described the Islamization of the South Slavic population under the Ottoman rule as "poturčivanje" (Turcification) and converts to Islam as "poturice". These terms have been ever since been considered derogatory in Croatian public life. The most prominent examples of the influence of Bosnian Muslim historians in Croatia include the publication of Bašagić's biographical lexicon of illustrious Bosnian Muslims perceived as Croats from the Ottoman times ("Znameniti Hrvati, Bošnjaci i Hercegovci u Turskoj carevini") in 1931 by the leading Croatian national cultural institution "Matica Hrvatska" as well as the noted participation of Kreševljaković (as one of the editors) and Šabanović in the preparation of the "Hrvatska enciklopedija" (the Croatian Encyclopedia), a multivolume lexicographic project started in the era of Kingdom of Yugoslavia (1939) and abandoned unfinished at the end of the existence of the pro-axis WWII-era Ustasha-led Independent State of Croatia (1945).

After the establishment of socialist Yugoslavia at the end of WWII, conditions were initially not conducive to the study of the Ottoman past within Croatian historiography. In this new context, the study of the history of Bosnia and Herzegovina, a major Ottoman-related topic, by historians in socialist Croatia was not encouraged and was rare until 1990. Until the 1980s and the start of the career of Nenad Moačanin, there were no Ottoman historians *stricto* sensu in Croatia, which can partly be attributed to the lack of a tradition of relevant specialist education and a small body of pre-existing research, as well as to the inter-republic division of duties within the Yugoslav federal science and scholarship system, according to which Bosnia and Herzegovina and the eastern republics were supposed to develop orientalist studies and research into the Ottoman past. Also, in socialist Yugoslavia, Bosnia's statehood was re-established and Bosnian Muslims' separate ethnicity was gradually officially recognized. In this context, the attempts of the WWII-period Ustasha regime to annex Bosnia and Herzegovina and to incorporate Bosnian Muslims into the ranks of Croat nation were vilified. The interest in Bosnian history, especially Bosnian Muslim one, attracted suspicion and was avoided by most historians in Croatia during the socialist era (1945–1990).

Nevertheless, even in the period up to the 1980s, there was limited interest in the Ottoman past, including Islamization, within the Croatian scholarship of the pre-1980 socialist period. But this interest was now mostly focused on the history of Islam within the territories that were part of socialist-era Croatia (these borders are identical to those of the contemporary Republic of Croatia). In his book "Porijeklo naselja i govora u Slavoniji" (The origin of Croatian and Serbian settlements and dialects in Slavonia; 1953), Croatian linguist and geographer Stjepan Pavičić (1887–1973) tried to give an original account of the origin of the Muslim population of Slavonia and Srijem under Ottoman rule, mainly on the basis of Western sources and their own, sometimes quite free, estimates. According to Pavičić, a large number of indigenous Catholics converted to Islam after the establishment of Ottoman rule in in the region between rivers of Sava and Drava. As he points out, the "vast majority" of Muslims in this area were of indigenous origin. Pavičić did not cite sources for these claims and it is not clear how he came to these conclusions. On the other hand, Pavičić expressly asserted that there was no Muslim rural population, which later studies based on Ottoman archival material would rightly reject. Pavičić also made a pioneering estimate of the number of the Muslim population at the end of Ottoman rule (around 1680): 115,000 out of a total of 222,000 (so as much as 51%, which would represent an absolute majority). Here, too, he did not state how he calculated this number (1953, p. 307–308). According to later research on basis of the Ottoman cadastral and tax records, Pavičić's calculation overestimates the share of Muslims in the population in this period, and a maximum of 33% would be more realistic (Moačanin 2001, p. 43).

Croatian historian Jaroslav Šidak (1903–1986), as part of his several studies on the history of the late mediaeval heterodox Bosnian Church, marginally touched on the history of the Islamization of broad strata in Bosnia and Herzegovina, becoming the first historian from the Republic of Croatia to touch on this topic at all. According to Šidak, who did not contribute original research to the issue of the relationship between Bosnian Christians and Islamization, but referred to the work of noted Bosnian scholar of the Ottoman period Nedim Filipović, the original material does not support the thesis that after the Ottoman conquest, the Bosnian inhabitants "suddenly decided to convert *en masse* to Islam". He emphasized that Islamization took place equally regardless of religion and did not take place everywhere at the same speed (1974, p. 182). Church historians in Croatia, operating on the margins of science in the socialist period, also dealt with issues related to the Ottoman history of Croatia including, sometimes, Islamization. One of them was Josip Buturac (1905–1993), the author of the study "Katolička crkva u Slavoniji pod turskom vlašću" (Catholic Church in Slavonia under Turkish rule; 1970), which largely used Western sources. Some information on the history of Slavonia from the relevant Ottoman archival material was made available to the author, as he pointed out, by the Bosnian-Herzegovinian orientalist Hazim Šabanović. Buturac, just like Pavičić, believed that the Muslims of Ottoman Slavonia and Srijem were "mostly natives, fewer immigrants from Bosnia and Serbia, and rarely real Turks and Arabs" and made up "about half of the population". There is no reference or explanation for this claim, but it is apparently based on Pavičić's book. It is interesting that Buturac, without clearly indicated sources, claims that around 1680 there were 108,000 Muslims (48.5%) in Slavonia and Srijem out of a total population of 222,000, which is a slightly lower estimate than the one Pavičić presented in the conclusion of his book. Apart from the cities, Buturac notes, Muslims lived in the surroundings of Požega and in the villages. Although it is not indicated, this claim probably originates from the Ottoman archival information supplied to him by Hazim Šabanović (1970, p. 54–55).

5 Conclusion

Already in the early modern period Croatian narrative sources, in the context of ongoing Ottoman-Habsburg and Ottoman-Venetian wars, some very negative perceptions about Islam, and particularly about converts to Islam from Croatia and Bosnia, came to prominence, but at the same time, one can come across examples of a balanced view of people who accepted Islam. The dominant view on conversion is that it is a kind of betrayal of one's faith and moral decline. In the nineteenth century, closely related to the development of bourgeois society and activities of South Slavic national integration ideologies centred in Croatia, negative stereotypes about converts to Islam ("poturice") persisted and, to some extent, despite the disappearance of the direct Ottoman danger and little contact with real Muslims and Ottomans it became even more extreme. Despite the gradual adaptation to the discourse of academic genetic historiography, Croatian historians of the nineteenth century often use tendentious constructions about "poturice", which are sometimes brought to the point of bizarreness under the influence of Orientalist travelogues and folk oral tradition. In this and earlier periods, most historians dealt with "Turkified" individuals, rarely with the broader problem of Islamization of a larger number of inhabitants. From the end of the nineteenth century, under the influence of social and political changes in Croatia, Austria-Hungary and the South Slavic state, the open anti-Islamic discourse faded, disappearing from the Croatian scientific public until the 1930s. At the same time, the fundamental anti-Ottoman attitudes of Croatian historiography persisted. Conversion to Islam in this period was no longer publicly condemned

10 Islam and Muslims in the Perspective of Croatian Historiography

as a morally repugnant act. During the socialist period (1945–1990), interest in Bosnia and Herzegovina's history, especially on issues such as Islamization, declined in Croatia. At the same time, there was a fringe interest in research of Islamization in the context of studying the history of Slavonia and Srijem, but without sufficient knowledge of Ottoman archival material.

References

Bašagić, Safvet-beg. 1931. *Znameniti Hrvati, Bošnjaci i Hercegovci u Turskoj carevini.* Zagreb: Matica hrvatska.

Buturac, Josip. 1970. *Katolička crkva u Slavoniji za turskog vladanja.* Zagreb: Kršćanska sadašnjost.

Ciliga, Vera. 1972. Josip Juraj Strossmayer i pitanje Bosne i Hercegovine 1870–1878. *Časopis Za Suvremenu Povijest* 4(1):47–60.

Dukić, Davor. 2004. *Sultanova djeca. Predodžbe Turaka u hrvatskoj književnosti ranog novovjekovlja.* Zagreb—Zadar: Thema i.d./ Ibis grafika.

Handžić, Adem. 1994. *Studije o Bosni: historijski prilozi iz Osmansko-Turskog perioda.* Istanbul: OIC & IRCICA.

Hasanbegović, Zlatko. 2007. *Muslimani u Zagrebu 1878.—1945. Doba utemeljenja.* Zagreb: Institut društvenih znanosti Ivo Pilar—Islamska zajednica Zagreb.

Gross, Mirjana. 1996. *Suvremena historiografija.* Zagreb: Novi liber.

Kaser, Karl. 2003. *Popis Like i Krbave.* Zagreb: SKD Prosvjeta.

Klaić, Vjekoslav. 1899–1922. (prvo izdanje; 8 editions to 1988). *Pov(i)jest Hrvata od najstarijih vremena do svršetka XIX. stoljeća,* 1–6. Zagreb: Matica hrvatska.

Krčelić, Baltazar Adam. 1994. *Povijest stolne crkve zagrebačke.* Translated by Zlatko Šešelj. Zagreb: Institut za suvremenu povijest.

Lopasic, Alexander. 1994. Islamization of the Balkans with special reference to Bosnia. *Journal of Islamic Studies* 5(2):163–186.

Moačanin, Nenad. 1997. *Požega i Požeština u sklopu Osmanlijskog Carstva.* Jastrebarsko: Slap.

Moačanin, Nenad. *Slavonija i Srijem u razdoblju osmanske vladavine.* Slavonski Brod, Hrvatski institut za povijest—Podružnica za povijest Slavonije, Srijema i Baranje, 2001.

Mujadžević, Dino. 2014. The consolidation of the Islamic community in modern Croatia: A unique path to the acceptance of Islam in a traditionally Catholic European country. *Journal of Muslims in Europe* 3:66–93.

Mujadžević, Dino. 2021. Croatia. In *Yearbook of Muslims in Europe*, vol. 13, Eds. Stephanie Müssig, Egdūnas Račius, Samim Akgönül, Ahmet Alibašić, Jørgen S. Nielsen, and Oliver Scharbrodt, 144–159. Leiden—Boston: Brill.

Pavičić, Stjepan. 1953. *Podrijetlo hrvatskih i srpskih naselja i govora u Slavoniji.* Zagreb: JAZU.

Pavličević, Dragutin. 1973. Odjek bosanskog ustanka (1875–1878) u sjevernoj Hrvatskoj. *Radovi Zavoda Za Hrvatsku Povijest* 4(1):121–196.

Smičiklas, Tadija. 1882 & 1879. *Poviest Hrvatska.* Sv. 1–2. Zagreb, Matica hrvatska.

Smičiklas, Tadija. 1991. *Dvjestogodišnjica oslobođenja Slavonije*. Sv. 1–2. Zagreb: JAZU.

Stančić, Nikša. 2002. *Hrvatska nacija i nacionalizam u 19. i 20. stoljeću*. Zagreb: Barbat.

Strossmayer, Josip Juraj & Rački, Franjo. 1928–1933. *Korespondencija Rački—Strossmayer*. Vol. 1–5. Zagreb: JAZU.

Strossmayer, Josip Juraj, and Vannutelli, Serafin. 1999. *Korespondencija Josip Juraj Strossmayer-Serafin Vannutelli 1881–1887*. Redacted by Josip Balabanić and Josip Kolanović. Zagreb: Hrvatski institut za povijest, Kršćanska sadašnjost & Dom i svijet.

Šidak, Jaroslav. 1977. Heretička "Crkva bosanska". *Slovo: časopis Staroslavenskoga instituta u Zagrebu* 27:149–184.

Švear, Ivan. 1842, *Ogledalo Ilirie ili dogodovština, Ilirah, zatim Slavinah, a najposlè Horvatah i Serbljah zvanih ...* Vol. 1–4. Zagreb: Franjo Župan.

Tomljanovich, W. B. 2001. Biskup Josip Juraj Strossmayer: Nacionalizam i moderni katolicizam u Hrvatskoj. Zagreb: Dom i svijet.

Dino Mujadžević is senior researcher at the Croatian Institute of History. In 2000, he graduated from the Faculty of Philosophy in Zagreb (Croatia) with degrees in history and turkology. He has worked at the Lexicographic Institute in Zagreb (2002–2007) and the Croatian Institute of History (2008–13, 2021). He was a Humboldt post-doctoral researcher at the Ruhr University Bochum (2013–2016) as well as a Humboldt, DFG and Gerda Henkel fellow at the Humboldt University (2019–2021). He is the author and editor of the volume *Annotated Legal Documents on Islam in Europe: Croatia* (Leiden: Brill: 2015) and *Digital Historical Research on Southeast Europe and the Ottoman Space* (Berlin: Peter Lang 2021) as well as the author of the book *Asserting Turkey in Bosnia 2002–2014* (Wiesbaden: Harrassowitz: 2017).

The Position of the Mufti in Greece. New and Old Ambiguities

11

Konstantinos Tsitselikis

Abstract

The Muftis in Greece, religious leaders of the Muslim communities and judges applying parts of Sharia law, acquired a key importance throughout time. The implementation of the Treaty of Lausanne since 1923 and the fluctuating Greek-Turkish relations framed the legal and political position of the Muftis. Two major issues became field of tensions: First, the mode of selection, namely election by the community or appointment by the government; second, the extent, content and procedures in relation to Sharia law (regarding family and inheritance law) and the respect of the principle of non-discrimination on the grounds of religion and sex. The legal arrangements dealing with the position of the Mufti in Greece seem more to serve political concerns than to apply effectively fundamental human and minority rights.

Keywords

Minorities • Muslims • Sharia • Mufti • Greece • Turkey • Jurisdiction • ECtHR

K. Tsitselikis (✉)
Professor, University of Macedonia, Thessaloniki, Greece
e-mail: kt@uom.edu.gr

© The Author(s), under exclusive license to Springer Fachmedien Wiesbaden GmbH, part of Springer Nature 2024
R. Ceylan and M. Mücke (eds.), *Muslims in Europe*, Islam in der Gesellschaft, https://doi.org/10.1007/978-3-658-43044-3_11

1 Introduction[1]

The legal and social structures of Greece's Muslim communities have continuously had a strong communal profile. After the annexation of Thessaly (1881) and the Balkan Wars (1912–1913), community organizational structures, community schools and foundations (waqfs), as well as religious hierarchies (Muftis) were integrated into a modern legal system. The Mufti became a person with important political influence. Before the Greek-Turkish mandatory population exchange that took place at the end of the Greek-Turkish war of 1919–1922 and the fall of the Ottoman Empire, the Muftis enjoyed the status of the head of the communities. Since 1923, the Muftis continued to possess an important position within the Muslim communities, have the authority interpret Sharia law and exert jurisdictional competences pertaining to disputes among Muslim Greek citizens involving personal status, namely of family and inheritance character.[2]

The members of the Muslim minority of Thrace are subject to the Greek Constitution and international human rights treaties in the same way as any other Greek citizen. On top of that legal nexus, since 1923 the minority of Thrace has been governed by the chapter of the Treaty of Lausanne on minority protection (Articles 37–45) which creates mirror obligations for Turkey and Greece regarding non-Muslims and Muslims respectively. This legal protection system reflects once again a *millet*-like (or "neo-millet") precept regarding the attribution of religious and linguistic rights through religion. Two major issues pertain to the position of the Muftis in Greece:

a. The mode of selection of the Muftis, who are religious leaders but also very influential political figures. It became an issue of major importance and the subject of national (Greek-Turkish) confrontation and legal controversy. Three Muftis are appointed in Thrace by the government, heading the Mufti Office and the Sacred Court. Two more Muftis have been elected by Muslims, with no official authority. The Muftis appointed by the government keep a very low profile on national ethnic issues, while the elected Muftis voice strong national Turkish feelings.

b. The Mufti as religious leader and judge. The three Muftis appointed by the government are the religious authority in their respective region and exert

---

[1] The present article draws from previous published works by the author (Tsitselikis 2019a, b, 2021), reshaped and amended in accordance with recent legal developments.

[2] The Muftis in Greece have been granted jurisdiction over personal status issues of the Muslims with Greek citizenship since the treaties of Constantinople (1881), Athens (1913), and Lausanne (1923). Before the population exchange, there were about fifty Mufti Offices throughout Greece.

special jurisdiction over Muslims on family and inheritance matters. The officially recognized Muftis are granted special jurisdiction on family and inheritance law disputes among Muslims of Thrace. However, Sharia law applied by the Muftis of Thrace would need to submit to comprehensive reforms as compatibility with fundamental human rights is questionable (Tsitselikis 2019a).

The law governing the position of the Mufti was rooted in Act 2345/1920. Seventy-one years later, it was replaced by Act 1920/1991, as a result of the major turbulences that hit and reshaped the relations between the Turkish/Muslim minority of Thrace and the Greek governments in late 1980s and early 1990s. In 2022, the Act 4964/2022 (Gazette A' 150) codified all previous legal norms and introduced a series of novelties, as an attempt to rationalize the position of Thracian Islam in Greece. However, the main characteristics dealing with the role of the Muftis within the Greek legal order remained untouched.

2 The Mufti Offices as State Bodies and the Selection of the Mufti

The ongoing political dispute since the late 1980s over the control of the Mufti offices of Thrace makes the legal system of this Greek minority a field of contention within the broader Greek-Turkish antagonism. Before 1990, the Muftis were, in practice, appointed following an agreement between the minority's elders and the government (Aarbakke 2000). In the period from 1985 to 1990, Greek governments became concerned about controlling the influence of the Turkish government on the Muftis, and passed Act 1920 (1991), which provided for Greek government appointment of the Muftis. The appointment process for Muftis by the Greek government has renewed a Greek-Turkish confrontation.

Turkey has maintained a strong interest and involvement in Turkish-Muslim minority issues in Greece, as has Greece in Greek Orthodox issues in Turkey though the ill-implemented principle of reciprocity. In the 1930s and 1950s, Turkey had suggested the abolition of the Mufti's jurisdiction, whereas after the late-1980s, Turkey politically supported the election of pro-Turkish Muftis.

According to Article 137 of Act 4964/2022, the Mufti Offices of Didymoteiho, Komotini and Xanthi constitute decentralized public services belonging to the Ministry of Education and Religious Affairs. The Muftis are civil servants as head of general directorate and exert jurisdiction (Art. 143). They are the highest-ranking administrative officials for the Muslim communities within their jurisdiction. They supervise the mosques and religious officials in each place of worship, as well as its cemeteries and religious foundations (waqfs). They also issue exhortations and legal advice to the faithful, direct charity work and perform marriages (Art. 146, par. 1–7).

The qualifications and competence of Muftis are not on a par with those required for other judges, causing the system to come under criticism. In practice, the three Muftis of Thrace are not trained in official judicial procedures before they are appointed by the government. Moreover, as they are also not necessarily well-educated in Islamic law, they adjudicate cases on the basis of a vague understanding of Islamic law: There are no textual sources that the Muftis can refer to; There is no guidance in the Greek legislation; There is no guidance from Greek courts or from foreign courts where Sharia law of Hanafi tradition is applied.

The Mufti selection process has also triggered strong political reactions among pro-Turkish circles of the Greek Muslim minority, starting in the 1980s and existing even to this day. This led to an intense stand-off, with the minority rallying around the then-independent deputies elected in the Greek parliament (1989–1993), invoking their Turkish identity. Since then, along with the three officially recognized Muftis (in Xanthi, Komotini and Didymotyho), there are two parallel Muftis (in Xanthi and Komotini) elected by a limited electorate. These parallel Muftis control most of Thrace's mosques and act as political leaders.

The issue of the election of two "parallel" Muftis, not recognized by the government, ended up in the European Court of Human Rights (ECHR) after lengthy processes before the penal and administrative Greek courts. A series of rulings in the Serif and Agga cases concluded that Greece had violated Articles 9 and 6 of the European Convention on Human Rights (ECHR) by "usurping the functions of a minister of a 'known religion.' through the criminal prosecution of the two elected Muftis."[3] The ECtHR, in upholding the applicants' rights to manifest their religion, recognized that social tensions may arise in situations where a religious or any other community becomes divided; it suggested that this was one of the unavoidable consequences of pluralism.[4]

The ambiguous and dual selection methods for Muftis reflect the tension in the dual nature of this position. On the one hand, the Muftis' appointment by

---

[3] Serif v. Greece, 1999-IX Eur. Ct. H.R., http://hudoc.echr.coe.int/sites/eng/pages/search. aspx?i=001-58518; Agga v. Greece (No. 2), Eur. Ct. H.R. (2002), http://hudoc.echr.coe.int/ sites/eng/pages/search.aspx?i=001-60690; Agga v. Greece (No. 3), Eur. Ct. H.R. (2006), http://hudoc.echr.coe.int/sites/eng/pages/search.aspx?i=001-76317; Agga v. Greece (No. 4), Eur. Ct. H.R. (2006), http://hudoc.echr.coe.int/sites/eng/pages/search.aspx?i=001-76319.

[4] . Serif, 1999-IX 53. In a similar case concerning the *Mufti* of Bulgaria, the Court held that "In democratic societies the State does not need to take measures to ensure that religious communities are brought under a unified leadership," Hasan v. Bulgaria, 2000-XI Eur. Ct. H.R. 78, http://hudoc.echr.coe.int/sites/eng/pages/search.aspx?i=001-58921.

11 The Position of the Mufti in Greece. New and Old Ambiguities

the state may infringe on the moral obligation to respect the community's will to choose a religious leader. On the other, since he is a judge, election of the Mufti by the community contravenes the fundamental constitutional rules of Greece about the status of judges as founded in the European legal order.[5]

In 2018, the age of retirement of the muftis was set at 67 (Act 4559/2018, Gazette A 142). As a result, the Muftis of Xanthi and Komotini had to retire and be replaced. Thus, a long tradition according to which the Muftis served with no age limitations was broken. New ad interim Muftis have been appointed in all three Mufti Offices. The discussion over a liberal or/and communitarian selection mode was triggered by Resolution 2253 (2019) adopted by the Parliamentary Assembly of the Council of Europe that called upon Greece to "allow the Muslim minority to choose freely its muftis as purely religious leaders (that is, without judicial powers), through election, thereby abolishing the application of sharia law [...]"(par 13).

According to the new Act of 2022, the present Muftis will serve for another 5 years and new procedures will be implemented in order to select each of the three Muftis. The Minister of Education and Religious Affairs will appoint the Mufti, among the candidates who fulfil the requirements set by the law, namely: To be residents of Thrace, member of the Muslim minority, aged less than 62, graduates of the theological school of Thessaloniki, especially from the branch of Islamic studies, or graduates from any theological school from abroad and having served at least 5 years as registered imams, or from the Islamic high schools of Thrace and served at least 10 years as registered imams or religious teachers at minority schools (Art. 148).

The novelty introduced by the new law of 2022 is that a 33-membered Consultative Committee comprised by knowledgeable Muslims of different categories (serving imams, teachers etc.) will finalise the candidates' list and comment on their individual competence to assume the post of Mufti. However, the Committee has not authority to evaluate the candidates and suggest who are the most qualified ones. The Minister has the absolute discretion to choose among the ones of the list. Therefore, the selection modalities again are upon the discretion of the government and the autonomy of the minority to select the Mufti by their own means is very limited.

---

[5] In most European countries a judge cannot be elected; he must be appointed by the state and must enjoy independence from community pressure. According to the Greek Constitution, article 88, judges are appointed for life term.

The Greek government seemed to have considered only how Sharia court would comply with procedural norms aligned with human rights instead of abolishing them. The status of the Mufti-judge would be subject more and more to norms that govern civil servants, and the Mufti Offices would become more and more state-like authorities. In June 2019, according to Presidential Decree No 52 (Gazette A 90), each Mufti Office acquired an administrative structure, the "Directorate of Cases under the Jurisdiction of the Mufti" and a series of public servants in order to staff the Directorates. New structures are created within the Mufti Offices to the expenses of the state. These structures have been re-established by Act 4964/2022. The Secretariat of the Sharia courts is being standardised and staffed for the assistance to the Mufti-judge. It could be arguable whether it surpasses the border line that guarantees the institutional autonomy to a minority religious community under both the ECHR and the Treaty of Lausanne (Takis and Tsigaridas 2019). On the other hand, these courts have become closer to the state-court model than to the community andinstitution-based character. Last, it is ambivalent that the Sharia courts are put under the administration of the Ministry of Education and Religious Affairs and not under the Ministry of Justice. The High Administrative Court (StE, judgment No 1822/2020) adjudicated an appeal filed by a member of the Muslim minority and finally ratified the constitutionality of the Presidential Decree No 52 and rejected the appeal (Tsitselikis 2021).

3   The Mufti as Judge and Sharia Law

The Treaty of Lausanne (signed in July 1923) guarantees special minority rights to non-Muslim Turkish citizens in Turkey and to Muslim citizens in Greece who were exempt from the mandatory population exchange. Article 42 par. 1 states: "The [Greek] government undertakes, as regards [Muslim] minorities in so far as concerns their family law or personal status, measures permitting the settlement of these questions in accordance with the customs of those minorities." This article has been interpreted as allowing the jurisdiction of the Mufti which remained untouched for long decades.

The legal content of Act 2345/1920 on the authority and status of the Muftis did not change even when the law was replaced by Act 1920/1991. The Mufti courts have survived, albeit with some limitations. Therefore, within their areas of jurisdiction, the three officially appointed Muftis of Thrace have jurisdiction on restricted issues of family and inheritance disputes between Muslim Greek citizens (Art. 146.8, Act 4964/2022).

11 The Position of the Mufti in Greece. New and Old Ambiguities

The codifying Act 4964/2022, in fact codifies pre-existing regulations and introduced new ones as regards the Muftis and the Mufti Offices in Thrace retained the Sharia courts. The adoption of the act takes into account the *Molla Sali* judgment by the European Court of Human Rights[6] (see hereinafter) as regards the jurisdiction on inheritance matters and most of all it establishes the optional character of Islamic jurisdiction. Until then, the Greek civil courts very often remanded an appeal filed by one of the Muslim litigants to the Sharia court, on the basis that disputes among Muslims on family and inheritance matters should be adjudicated by the Mufti. Therefore, until 2018, the possibility of choosing between the two jurisdictions was not clear and at last resort in many cases the Court of Cassation said that Sharia was mandatorily implemented to Muslims. The *Molla Sali* case triggered a series of changes dealing with the Sharia courts of Thrace ensuring the right to opt out and a series of procedural regulations.

An amendment to the Mufti's law was submitted in December 2017 before the Parliament a few days before the hearing of the *Molla Sali* case took place before the Grand Chamber of the ECtHR. The new law adopted in January 2018 (Act 4511/2018, Gazette A 2)[7] made clear that the civil courts will have competence by default for all civil disputes, unless both of the litigants make an agreement to have their case heard by the Mufti. The same regulation was retained by the Act 4964/2022. According to Art. 146.10 of the latter, both Muslim litigants have to sign an agreement in order to file their case before the Sharia court. Otherwise, the civil courts have full jurisdiction. According to Act 4511/2018 wills drafted by a Muslim can be subject to civil law, clarifying an ambiguity that lasted long. Art. 146 par.10b of Act 4964/2022 reiterated this provision.

Although the implementation of the 2018 law was dependent on the adoption of procedural norms as regards the process before the Mufti-judge, in October a new amendment (Act 4569/2018, Art. 48.3) made immediate the implementation of the new law before the adoption of procedural rules. These amendments anticipated the ruling of the European Court on Human Rights that in December 2018 found a violation of the right to property in combination with discrimination in the case *Molla Sali v Greece*[8] on the ground that the Greek Court of Cassation

---

[6] ECtHR, judgment *Molla Sali v Greece*, 20,452/14, 19.12.2018.

[7] Amendment of article 5 of the Legislative Act of December 24, 1990 On Muslim religious officials (A 182), certified through the article of law 1920/1991 (A 11).

[8] https://hudoc.echr.coe.int/eng#{%22itemid%22:[%22001-188985%22]}, accessed: 27 December 2021.

had imposed Sharia law without the explicit wish of the members of the Muslim minority of Thrace.[9]

The coexistence of two legal systems in Thrace, applying both Islamic law and the Greek Civil Code, creates a number of discrepancies (Tsitselikis 2010, p. 673; Ktistakis, 2013). These discrepancies arise from the dual authority of the Muftis as judges and religious leaders, creating procedural problems, raising competence and authority issues, resulting in jurisdictional ambiguities related to mixed marriages, and problems of enforceability by foreign courts. Equality of sexes represent a common denominator of these issues. In inheritance cases, per instance, the male heir gets twice the share of the female heir thus breaking the principle of equality endorsed by both the Greek and European legal order (Tsaoussi and Zervogianni, 2008, p. 209, 219). In practice, after 1985, such cases became rare, as Muslim heirs, members of the minority of Thrace, are using the Mufti's opinions (*fetva*) on the inheritance before the notary and the taxation office in order to register and apply for the necessary transactions. However, certain cases of dispute reach the courts. In some cases, the Civil Courts said that the Mufti had exclusive jurisdiction, and the *Molla Sali case*[10] that ended up to the court of Strasbourg is one of them.

4   The Molla Sali Case (Greek Courts—ECtHR)

A Muslim man drafted a public will before a notary. He passed away, and according to the will his wife acquired his properties. His two sisters appealed before the courts, and finally in cassation claiming that the will drafted by their brother could not be valid as it is not in harmony with Sharia law and that only the Mufti Court would have jurisdiction over the case. The Court upheld the appeal and said that the Mufti Court has exclusive jurisdiction over property left by a deceased member of the Muslim minority of Thrace and that a Muslim could not have the right to draft a will before a notary according to the civil law, as *lex specialis*, namely article 5 of law 1920/1991 is the only applicable law (Cassation Court, *AP*, judgment 1862/2013). The widow filed an application before the ECtHR on the grounds of right to a fair trial (Art. 6), right to property (Art. 1, Pr. 1) and discrimination (Art. 14). The case was adjudicated by the Grand Chamber of the

---

[9] The Court however was reluctant to examine the alleged violation of Art. 6 of the ECHR, so the denial of justice by the Court of cassation, which would put straight forward the issue of non-adjudication of a case on the ground of religion.

[10] On different approaches to the case, see: Kalambakou, 2019; Tsavousoglou, 2019; Iakovidis and McDonough, 2019.

Court (*Molla Sali v Greece*, Application no 20152/14, judgment of 19.12.2018). The Court upheld that there was violation of the right to property of the applicant in conjunction to the prohibition of discrimination "by association" on the basis of religion of the deceased husband. The Court said that the right to self-identification of the member of a minority means also the right to opting out from the minority protection framework. According to the Court, "Refusing members of a religious minority the right to voluntarily opt for and benefit from ordinary law amounts not only to discriminatory treatment but also to a breach of a right of cardinal importance in the field of protection of minorities, that is to say the right to free self-identification" (para. 157).

It is not only substantial law but also sharia procedural law that raises issues of compatibility with constitutional principles, such as fair trial. There is still large room for improvement as regards the rights of the litigants. One of the most important issues is that no second instance (appeal) which would guarantee the review of the Mufti judgment is available to the litigants.

In the past 25 years major issues of concern that accumulated criticism: a) the right to fair trial, under article 6 of the ECHR, when equality of the litigants is not safeguarded, and neither representation through a lawyer nor predictability and visibility of the applicable law is provided; b) lack of efficient control of the merits of the Mufti's decision, and lack of effective means to control the constitutionality of such decisions; c) lack of the possibility to resort to civil courts and conflicts resulting from parties making different choices of forums d) lack of the right to appeal against the Mufti's decision.

Among these points a), b) and c) have been satisfactorily resolved by Presidential Decree No 52 which was adopted in June 2019 (Gazette A 90) on the regularisation of the Mufti's court procedure in the context of the Molla Sali case. For the first time, the Sharia courts of Thrace are subject to procedural norms set by the state. The main points of the reform regard:

- The presence of a lawyer who represents the litigants is obligatory.
- The enforceability of the mufti's judgment by the civil courts is depended on the compatibility of the judgment to the Constitution (non-discrimination clause) and the ECHR.
- The procedure through which the litigants have to sign an agreement of choice for the Sharia court is set out in detail.
- The judgment has to be properly justified. It has to be written in both Greek and Ottoman (*sic*) languages. Official translation can be delivered upon request in Arabic, Turkish or English.

Sharia law can be directly applied only by the Mufti or taken into consideration by a civil court while testing the constitutionality of the sacred court's decision. The decisions of the Mufti can only be executed after being ratified by the Civil Court of First Instance (Act 4964/2022, Article 146. 9). Consequently, civil courts (should) monitor the compliance of the Muftis' decisions with the constitution and the ECHR. However, most of the Mufti decisions are ratified by the Greek Courts even if they infringe women's and children's rights. The UN Human Rights Committee has commented on this issue, urging Greece "to increase the awareness of Muslim women of their rights and the availability of remedies, and to ensure that they benefit from the provisions of Greek civil law" (Human Rights Committee 2005, par. 8). These decisions are subject to appeal before the First Instance Court (*Polymeles Protodikeio*), concerning, solely, the extent of the Mufti's jurisdiction. There is no second instance within the Mufti's court. Since it is not submitted to any corrective control from a higher court, the Mufti's decision endangers not only the legal interests of citizens who come under his jurisdiction, but also the authority and importance of this Muslim institution. Therefore, the question of incompatibility of the content of the applicable law by the Mufti with human rights standards is remaining open.

5 Time to Reform Again?

Stemming from the institutional Ottoman legacy of the *millet* system, today's minority protection granted to the Muslim minority of Thrace (Tsitselikis, 2012) could serve as a strong case for legal pluralism. At the same time, inflexible societal segregation and problematic legal norms infringe on fundamental legal principles. Juridical procedures and law applied by the Muftis of Thrace had to take a generous leap forward. On the other hand, it was only since 2019 that the law clarifies the modalities of applicability of Sharia law by the Mufti's Courts according to the choice of the Muslim litigants.

The discussion of the status of the Mufti within the Greek and European legal order and the compliance of Sharia law to human rights law inevitably touches upon the issue of how to accommodate community-based laws within a uniform legal context. The discrepancies between Sharia as applied by the Muftis' courts and fundamental principles of human rights could be remedied in two different ways: either by abolishing the Mufti's jurisdiction, or by channelling the development of Sharia in a direction that will not contradict public policy (*ordre*

11 The Position of the Mufti in Greece. New and Old Ambiguities

public).[11] That would require the development of this legal system in consonance with the Greek constitution and the European Convention of Human Rights.

Not surprisingly, a series of international and national bodies have expressed their concern about the noncompliance of the Mufti courts with human rights standards. For instance, the Commissioner for Human Rights in the Council of Europe has made recommendations that Greece should consider withdrawing the judicial competence of the Muftis, given the courts' incompatibility with international human rights standards; strengthening the substantial review of the Mufti's judicial decisions by domestic courts; and/or formalizing an open and continuous dialogue with representatives of the Muslim minority in order to start the process of achieving compliance (Hammarberg 2009).[12]

As said, the *Molla Sali* case has triggered a series of amendments to the law on the Sharia courts. The new rules adopted in 2018–2022 quashed a series of procedural deficiencies in a positive direction. However, attempts at reform must consider the political situation first and foremost, if an overall harmonization with international human rights norms is to be achieved. The survival over decades of the Mufti's jurisdiction constitutes a supreme example of instrumentalized resistance to attempts at liberal reform. The reasons for this resistance stem from the competitive political and ideological embrace of the Muslim minority by both the Greek and the Turkish governments going back to 1923, and the implementation of the Lausanne Treaty, still considered an immutable legal foundation of minority protection today.

Sharia law could develop new approaches encompassing legal principles which establish the foundations of the European legal order. If that were to happen in Greece, Sharia law implemented by the Mufti courts and reformed from within, could comply with fundamental human rights principles; and Greek law could accommodate Islamic law. At last, implementation of Sharia law became optional, and thus legal discrepancies were limited to cases in which both litigants willingly take their case before the Sharia courts.

---

[11] The *ordre public* (public policy) consists of a series of fundamental norms and principles that supersede and reflect the legal, social, economic, religious, ethical, and other beliefs that govern legal relations. The concept is related to norms that are so fundamental for the legal order that they have to be respected, regardless of procedural obstacles. Overriding of the *ordre public* occurs when these beliefs are offended and legal relations are disrupted.

[12] Resolution 1704 (2010), Parliamentary Assembly, Council of Europe and Hunault 2009, p. 48.

6   Conclusions

Ideological antagonism between the *community of citizens* and the *community of the nation* affects the position of Muslims of Greece in a fragmented and incoherent way. That would be the challenge for law and policy as regards the muftis, religious eminent figures among the Muslim communities who retain jurisdiction in personal status matters.

The discussion of the status of the Mufti within the Greek and European legal order inevitably touches upon the issue of how to accommodate the non-liberal laws (Sharia), the excessive limitations by the state of a community structure (Mufti Offices) and religious freedom to select a religious leader (Mufti) in a liberal legal context. To move forward, this discussion must maneuver between the demands for integration, and the preservation of minority, collective and individual identity, as potential fields of normative action.

There is increasing criticism—not unjustified—that Sharia law as the Mufti courts apply it does not comply with human rights norms, such as equality of the sexes and the right to fair trial. The religious and political elite of the Thracian minority counters this criticism by pointing to the central importance of the adjudication by the Mufti for the enjoyment of minority rights. What could serve as a strong case for legal pluralism and minority protection infringes upon fundamental legal principles. The *Molla Sali* case triggered already a series of changes in procedural law, in compliance with human rights. As the Court said, no disadvantage shall result from the choice to belong or not to belong from the exercise of the rights which are connected to that choice (par 67–68).

On the other hand, the Greek-Turkish antagonisms in relation to whom would assume the position of the Mufti screens the liberty for the community to arrange their own affairs. For all above aspects a genuine reform is needed as the Act of 2022 cannot resolve all above-mentioned issues. An alternative, culturally accommodating, structure of adjudication and administration could be put forward as a democratic paradigm, along with a comprehensive and inclusive selection mode of the Muftis.

References

Aarbakke, Vemund. 2000. *The Muslim minority of Greek Thrace*. Bergen: University of Bergen [Ph.D. dissertation].

Hammarberg, Thomas. 2009. Report by the commissioner for human rights of following his visit to Greece on 8–10 December 2008, CommDH(2009)9. Strasbourg: Council of Europe.

Hunault, Michel. 2009. *Freedom of religion and other human rights for non-Muslim minorities in Turkey and for the Muslim minority in Thrace (Eastern Greece)*, Parliamentary Assembly, Committee on Legal Affairs and Human Rights, Report, Doc 11860/21.4.2009, Strasbourg: Council of Europe 2009.

Kalambakou, Eleni. 2019. Is there a right to choose a religious jurisdiction over the civil courts? The application of Sharia in the Muslim minority of Western Thrace, Greece, *Religions* 10:1–7. file:///C:/Users/user/Downloads/Is_There_a_Right_to_Choose_a_Religious_J.pdf. Accessed: 12. Oct. 2022.

Tsavousoglou, İlker. 2019. *The curious case of Molla Sali v. Greece: Legal pluralism through the lens of the ECtHR*, Strasbourg Observers. https://strasbourgobservers.com/2019/01/11/the-curious-case-of-molla-sali-v-greece-legal-pluralism-through-the-lens-of-the-ecthr/. Accessed: 12. Oct. 2022.

Iakovidis, Iakovos, and Paul McDonough. 2019. The Molla Sali case: How the European court of human rights escaped a legal Labyrinth while holding the thread of human rights, Oxford *Journal of Law and Religion* 1–20. https://doi.org/10.1093/ojlr/rwz017.

Ktistakis, Yannis. 2013. *Charia, Tribunaux religieux et droit grec*. Istanbul: Istos.

Takis, Andreas, and Vasilis Tsigaridas. 2019. The organizational requirements of fair trial and the Mufti's jurisdiction [Οργανωτικές προϋποθέσεις της δίκαιης δίκης και η δικαιοδοσία του Μουφτή]. *Journal of Public Law [in Greek]* 6:770–771.

Tsitselikis, Konstantinos. 2012. *Old and New Islam in Greece. From historical minorities to immigrant newcomers*. Boston: Martinus Nijhoff.

Tsitselikis, Konstantinos. 2019a. Muslims of Greece: A legal paradox *and* a political failure. In *Legal pluralism in Muslim Context*. Eds. N. Oberauer, Y. Prief, and U. Qubaja, 63–82. Boston: Brill.

Tsitselikis Konstantinos. 2019b. Sharīʿa in Greece, Part 1, Between communal autonomy and individual human rights, islamiclawblog. *Journal in Islamic Law Harvard Law School*. https://islamiclaw.blog/2019/10/01/shari%ca%bfa-in-greece-part-1-between-communal-autonomy-and-individual-human-rights/. [also: Part 1–2–3–4], https://islamiclaw.blog/category/greece/. Accessed: 15. Oct. 2022.

Konstantinos, Tsitselikis. 2021. The autonomy of the minority of Thrace and the establishment of the sharia courts. A commentary of the judgment No 1822/2020 by the High Administrative Court [Η αυτονομία της μειονότητας της Θράκης και η οργάνωση των μουφτειακών δικαστηρίων. Σχόλιο στην απόφαση ΣτΕ Ολ. 1822/2020]. *Theory and Praxis of Administrative Law [in Greek]* 2–3:236–249.

Tsaoussi, Aspasia, and Eleni Zervogianni. 2008. Multiculturalism and family law: The case of Greek Muslims. In *European Challenges in contemporary family law*. Ed. K. Boele-Woelki and T. Sverdrup, 200–225. Antwerp: Intersentia.

Human Rights Committee. 2005. Greece. In Concluding Observations, ICCPR, 25/04/2005, CCPR/CO/83/GRC. Geneva: United Nations.

Konstantinos Tsitselikis Professor in Human Rights and International Organizations at the University of Macedonia (Thessaloniki, Greece). Dean of the School of Economic and Regional Studies (2018–2023). Author of a series of books, studies and articles on human rights, minorities, refugee and migrant rights. He has also taught at the Universities of Thrace and Bilgi (Istanbul) and cooperated with the universities of Harvard, Sorbonne II, Tampere, Aix-en–Provence, SOAS, Aga Khan (London), Erlangen, Suleymaniye (Kurdish Region, Iraq), among others. He has worked for the Council of Europe (1992–95), the OSCE, the UN and the EU (1997–1999) in human rights and democratisation field missions. Member of the Secretariat of the Research Centre for Minority Groups (KEMO) and chairman of the Hellenic League for Human Rights (2011–2017). Co-director of the Series of Studies of KEMO at Vivliorama pub. (Athens). Member of the Bar Association of Thessaloniki, lawyer before the European Court of Human Rights.

Part IV

Northern Europe

Muslims in Sweden: Historical Developments, Present Issues, and Future Challenges

12

Göran Larsson and Simon Sorgenfrei

> **Abstract**
>
> The present chapter is a literature review that focuses on the study of Islam and Muslims in Sweden in both the past and the present. The aim of the chapter is threefold. First, we provide a brief background to the history of Islam and Muslims in Sweden. Secondly, we give a bibliographical overview of existing research on Muslims in Sweden. Finally, we discuss some potential areas that should be studied in the future if we want to acquire a more informed understanding of Islam and Muslims in Sweden.

> **Keywords**
>
> Islam · Muslims · Sweden · Tatars · Mosques

G. Larsson
Faculty of Humanities, Department of Literature, History of Ideas, Religion, University of Gothenburg, Gothenburg, Sweden
e-mail: goran.larsson@lir.gu.se

S. Sorgenfrei (✉)
Historical and Contemporary Studies, Södertörn University, Huddinge, Sweden
e-mail: simon.sorgenfrei@sh.se

© The Author(s), under exclusive license to Springer Fachmedien Wiesbaden GmbH, part of Springer Nature 2024
R. Ceylan and M. Mücke (eds.), *Muslims in Europe*, Islam in der Gesellschaft,
https://doi.org/10.1007/978-3-658-43044-3_12

201

1 Introduction

The present chapter is a literature review that focuses on the study of Islam and Muslims in Sweden in both the past and the present. The aim of the chapter is threefold. First, we provide a brief background to the history of Islam and Muslims in Sweden. Secondly, we give a bibliographical overview of existing research on Muslims in Sweden. Finally, we discuss some potential areas that should be studied in the future if we want to acquire a more informed understanding of Islam and Muslims in Sweden.

While we focus on Sweden, it is important to stress that there are regional and geographical similarities that should be highlighted when we study the history of Islam and Muslims in the West. Instead of being limited by national or local frameworks, as has often been the case the case in earlier studies, it is important to place the study of Islam and Muslims in Sweden in its proper global context (see, for instance, Mausen 2007). Muslims have primarily established themselves in Europe as migrants and therefore often belong to transnational networks that both entangle European nations in a global web and make national borders as well as religious identities increasingly porous (e.g., Tweed 2006). The 'production of Islam' (i.e., how Islam is being interpreted and 'lived', as well as how it is being understood or discussed by both Muslims and non-Muslims) is consequently not something that can be limited by a national framework or by Sweden as a country. For instance, processes like globalization and transnationalism are vital forces that should be considered if we want to understand Islam and Muslims in Sweden (e.g., Green 2020).

With this critical remark, the chapter starts by providing a short description of early encounters and ends by looking into the future to see how the study of Islam and Muslims in Sweden ought to be developed.

2 Early Encounters

It has been established that Scandinavians had extensive interactions with Muslim cultures in the so-called Viking Age (ca. 700–1100). Reports of such interactions occur on runestone inscriptions and archeological findings, but also and in particular in a more detailed manner in Persian and Arabic chronicles. One of these describes the visit of the Arab envoy Ibn al-Ghazal to Denmark (or possibly Ireland) in the 840s. Primarily, however, these reports tell us about encounters between so-called Vikings (often identified as *al-Rus*) and Muslims outside Scandinavia, in what are today Russia, Azerbaijan, Iraq or Andalusia (Birkeland 1954;

12 Muslims in Sweden: Historical Developments ...

Duczko 2004; Mikkelsen 2008; Jonsson Hraundal 2013). A more famous example is the travel report by Ibn Fadlan from the Volga region in the tenth century (Lunde and Stone 2012). Even though large amounts of Arabic coins and other archeological findings connected to the so-called Muslim world have been found in Swedish soil (e.g., Arne 1952), there is no evidence for any Muslim presence in what is today called Sweden in the Viking age, whether as visitors, slaves, or possible converts (Sorgenfrei 2018, p. 9–16).

However, the first documented Muslims to arrive in Sweden are of a later date and almost as old as the nation itself. In 1523 Gustav Ericsson (d. 1560) became King Gustav I of Sweden. Gustav Vasa, as he has become known, also began the process of reforming Sweden as a Lutheran nation, a process which would lead to the country developing into a religiously quite homogeneous nation. To be a Swedish citizen, you has to be a member of the national Lutheran church. Even so, King Vasa already had diplomatic relations with non-Lutheran countries. In 1556, while war was raging between Sweden and Muscovite Russia, Vasa personally met with a Tatar Muslim, in the Swedish archives called 'Bissura', to discuss the possibilities of a Swedish–Tatar alliance against Russia (Sorgenfrei 2018, p. 33–34; also Jarring 1987 and Zetterstéen 1952).

Even though the proposal for a Swedish–Tatar alliance came to nothing, the meetings between Gustav Vasa and the Tatar envoy Bissura introduced a new element in Swedish politics—that is, diplomatic relations with Muslim states. Throughout the seventeenth to nineteenth centuries, Tatar, Ottoman and Persian embassies regularly visited Sweden, and Sweden also sent diplomats to various Muslim states (Jarring 1987; Zetterstéen 1952). Swedish-Ottoman relations were particularly strong throughout the seventeenth and eighteenth centuries, and between 1709–1714 Sweden was even ruled from Ottoman territory, after King Karl XII fled Macedonia after being defeated by the Russians at Poltava in 1709. In a way like Gustav Vasa, Karl XII now hoped to be able to convince the Ottomans to join forces with him against the Russians. This, however, also came to nothing, and after a few years the Ottomans forced the Swedes to leave their territory and head back to Sweden (Kronberg et al. 2016). By then the Swedes owed both the Sultan and individual creditors large amounts of money, and some of these creditors therefore decided to follow the king back to Sweden. Hence, between 1714–1722 several Ottoman lenders, of which the majority were Muslims, lived in Sweden and were also allowed to practice their religions if this was done 'behind closed doors' (Sorgenfrei 2018, p. 43–47; 2020a, b).

Charles XII's affairs with the Ottomans also resulted in a Muslim embassy in Sweden, as the Ottomans wanted to make sure they had their loans reimbursed.

The first Ottoman emissary, Mehmet Pasha, came to Stockholm in 1733, and the last, Cherif Pasha, left in 1908 (Sorgenfrei 2018, p. 46–51).

2.1 The First Swedish Muslims

However, the first known Muslim not only to come to Sweden, but also stay and become a Swedish citizen while keeping his Muslim faith and practice arrived later. This was the Tatar furrier Ebrahim Umerkajeff (1877–1954), who came to Stockholm in 1897 to visit a fair that was being held in the city that summer. At the fair he met a Swedish seamstress by the name Elisabeth Hult (1876–1955), and they started a relationship. In 1901 their son Hussein (d. 1989) was born, and Umerkajeff decided to settle for good in Stockholm, where he became a successful merchant in the fur business.

Then in 1930 a Turkish family by the name of Arhan moved from Istanbul to Stockholm. Akif Arhan (1905–1981) opened a carpet shop on the same street as Umerkajeff's fur store, on Birger Jarlsgatan in central Stockholm, and the two seem to have socialized and celebrated the central Muslim holidays together.

By the end of the second World War, further Tatar and Turkish refugees came to Sweden, and they all were helped by Umerkajeff to establish themselves in the Stockholm area. They also met regularly at a café that was located between Umerkajeff's and Arhan's shops, where they decided to establish a Muslim organization and congregation. Therefore, in 1948, they wrote to a Turkish citizen living among Tatars in Finland by the name of Osman Soukkan (1903–1975) and asked him to join them in Sweden to become their imam. Soukkan was from İzmir in Turkey, but earlier he had moved to Järvenpää outside Helsinki in Finland, where he had started a family and worked as a teacher and Imam among the Tatars living there. The Soukkan family now moved to Stockholm, and in October 1949 Osman Soukkan was among the small group of migrants who founded the first Swedish Muslim organization and congregation at Kjellson's Café in Stockholm.

The organization called itself the Turk-Islam Organization in Sweden for Religion and Culture and gathered together a small group of Tatars and Turks living in Stockholm. They were soon able to establish a Muslim burial ground in Stockholm and arranged for Muslims to be able to celebrate Id al-Fitr, Id al-Adha and Mawlid an-Nabi together in the city. The small group of Muslims established themselves as an organization rather than a congregation, since Sweden had no law of religious freedom until 1951. Some years after such law was in force, the

12 Muslims in Sweden: Historical Developments …

organization changed its name to the Islam Congregation in Sweden (for these first Muslims, see Sorgenfrei 2020a, b, 2022).

In the fifties, two converts joined the congregation, one of whom, Björn Ismail Ericsson, also founded what seems to be the first so-called cellar mosque in the Stockholm suburb of Kärrtorp in 1959. The other early convert, Gunnar Saif-ul-Islam Eriksson, later joined the Ahmadiyya community, which established itself in Sweden through the agency of the missionary Kamal Yousuf in the mid-1960s (Sorgenfrei 2018, p. 88–102; see also Arly Jacobsen et al. 2014).

From the 1950s onwards, the number of Muslims living in Sweden saw a small but steady increase through growing labour immigration. Among the migrants who moved to Sweden, many came from the former Yugoslavia and primarily from the Kulu district in Turkey; they ended up in Sweden's larger cities, or in cities with larger industries in need of labour. Some of these migrants were Muslim and joined the congregation in Stockholm or formed their own congregations around Sweden (Sorgenfrei 2018, 2022).

2.2 Muslims in Multi-Religious Sweden

In 1975, due to a policy change leading to greater support for religious minorities, Muslim organizations were able to acquire state subsidies because they had more than 3000 members. The congregation in Stockholm, together with congregations from other cities, then formed the first Swedish national Muslim organization, the FIFS (United Islamic Congregations of Sweden).

With FIFS, Swedish Muslims were included in the neo-corporatist Swedish Model, and FIFS was to represent Muslims in their relations with the state authorities. Pretty soon, however, a rift emerged in the FIFS, and in 1982 it split in two competing national organizations, the split-off being the SMF (the Muslim Union of Sweden). Since then, due primarily to refugee migration, both the number and heterogeneity of Muslims of Sweden has grown, and new congregations have usually been formed following ethnic and sometimes denominational divides. Some of these have also joined in founding new national organizations, and today there are seven Muslim national organizations receiving financial support from the state, as well as others that do not cooperate officially (i.e., they do not receive financial support from the state), with the state authority handling the support to faith communities (SST) (This section relies primarily on Sorgenfrei 2018 and 2022).

The relatively generous migration of refugees in recent decades has resulted in large demographic changes in Sweden. Today approximately a fourth of the population have a migrant background, and about 800 000 to 1,000 000 Swedes have a Muslim family background (PEW 2017). This also means that most Muslim traditions found globally are also to be found in Sweden (e.g., Larsson and Sorgenfrei 2022).

2.3 Making Muslim Space in Sweden

In 1976, the Ahmadiyya community built the first proper Swedish mosque in Göteborg. In 1983 a Sunni Mosque was built in Malmö with funding from the Muslim World League in Saudi Arabia and from Lybia, and in 1985 a Shi'ite Mosque was built in the city of Trollhättan by so-called Khoja Muslims, who had come from Uganda a decade earlier (on Shia Muslims in Sweden, see Larsson and Thurfjell 2013). It was not until 2000 that the Swedish capital, Stockholm, saw its first purpose-built Sunni mosque (Sorgenfrei 2018, p. 233–244).

At the time of writing there are nine purpose-built mosques in Sweden. The ones in Uppsala and Göteborg, and two respectively in Stockholm and Malmö, are run by Sunni congregations. There is one purpose-built Shi'ite mosque in Trollhättan, and two Ahmadiyya mosques, one in Göteborg and one Malmö. In Stockholm, Gävle, Västerås and Sundsvall, Muslims have also bought old churches and converted them into mosques, one example being the large Shi'ite Imam Ali Center in Järfälla outside Stockholm. There are also several mosques in the planning. However, most Muslim prayer rooms and congregational centres are to be found in basements, flats, or warehouses, and there is no reliable figure for how many they are (Larsson and Sorgenfrei 2022).

Resembling most other European countries, the building of mosques in Sweden has been met with varied responses. In the 1970s and 1980s, mosques did not receive much attention, but from the mid-1980s and early 1990s, mosques have often been met with great suspicion and even open hostility (Karlsson and Svanberg 1995; Larsson 2011). For instance, the Shi'ite mosque in Trollhättan, mentioned above, was destroyed by arson in 1993, and the Shi'ite mosque in Järfälla, Stockholm, was severely damaged by arson in 2017. There are several reports indicating that many mosques have received threats and suffered from various forms of hate crimes, especially anti-Muslim graffiti, but many have also been desecrated by pig's blood or pig's carcasses (see Larsson 2011; Gardell 2018).

Besides mosques, Muslim burial places can be regarded as important 'Muslim spaces' in Sweden. The first thing the first Muslim congregation did, after settling on the name of their organization, was to decide on an Islamic burial ground in

Stockholm. This was inaugurated in the early 1950s, and the first person to have an official Muslim burial in Sweden was the Senegalese citizen Mamadou Gueye, who died in a workplace accident in 1952 and was buried in the Muslim burial ground at Skogskyrkogården in Stockholm (Sorgenfrei 2022, p. 169–176).

Today most larger cities in Sweden have burial sites prepared for Muslims, and these have become important places for families, who, through the graves of their ancestors, experience having become more strongly rooted in their new country (on Muslims burials and burial sites in Sweden, see Sorgenfrei 2021d).

3 Present Issues and the State of Academic Research on Muslims and Islam

3.1 Demographics

As a result of migration patterns, Sweden's Muslim population is very diverse. The largest groups are Turks, who began to arrive already after the Second World War; Iranian and Iraqi migrants following the wars in 1979–1989; Bosnians and West African immigrants who arrived in Sweden after wars and turmoil in the early 1990s; Somali migrants arriving since the early 1990s following the conflicts in Somalia beginning approximately at the same time; and Afghan, Syrian and other migrants from the Middle East and North Africa who have arrived in Sweden due to conflicts in the region in recent decades (Sorgenfrei 2014, p. 29). In 2015 more than 150,000 asylum seekers arrived in Sweden, many of them with a Muslim cultural background (e.g., Larsson and Sorgenfrei 2022).

3.2 Denominations

Following the great demographical variety outlined above, the Muslims of Sweden also differ denominationally. As already noted, today between 800 000 and 1 000 000 Swedes have a Muslim family background, and they identify with different Islamic traditions. Most of them come from a Sunni background, with a great variety of Sunni traditions such as different Sufi communities (Sorgenfrei 2014), branches of Salafism (Olsson 2019; Ranstorp et al. 2019) and different legal interpretations of Islam. Because of a relatively large influx of refugees from Iran and Iraq, Sweden also has a proportionally large Shia population (Larsson and Thurfjell 2013). As mentioned above, the Ahmadiyya community was already established in Sweden in the 1950s. Today the Ahmadi community has purpose-built mosques in Göteborg and Malmö, and established congregations also in Stockholm, Arvika, Luleå and Kalmar.

However, most Swedes with a Muslim cultural background are more or less secularized. Together, the national Muslim organizations mentioned above have about 200 000 members compared to the approximately 800 000 to 1 000 000 Swedes with a so-called Muslim cultural background (e.g., Thurfjell and Willander 2021). Although there is a need for more research here, this is an indication that a large majority of individuals with a Muslim cultural background are not active in a Muslim congregation. How this low interest in Muslim organizations should be interpreted is an open question, as when and why 'secular attitudes' or even anti-religious stances become manifest is not well-known. This is clearly an area for more research in the future.

3.3 Education

While it is fair to say that Islam and Muslims were almost absent from Swedish educational settings prior to the 1970s (Kittelmann Flensner and Larsson 2014), researcher Kjell Härenstam demonstrated in his doctoral thesis in pedagogy that Islam and Muslims have often been presented in a negative or stereotypical way in many of the Swedish textbooks that were in use in Swedish elementary schools during the 1980s and 1990s (Härenstam 1993; Otterbeck 2000b). According to Kittelmann Flensner (2015), pupils who express a Muslim identity today are often looked upon as deviant and different in Swedish school settings. This 'difference', however, is also shared with pupils who express any form of religious belonging. The Swedish school system is based on a non-confessional agenda and on the idea that all pupils should be treated equally, regardless of their religious, ethnic, or cultural belonging. This ideal has been criticized and Kittlemann Flensner argues, for instance, that this underpinning has contributed to the development of a secular norm that has remained unexpressed. To be religious is therefore often seen as to be different or even deviant.

Since 1992 and the so-called free school reform (*Friskolereformen* in Swedish), it has become possible to start so-called confessional schools with a specific cultural or religious profile. Following this reform, schools with an Islamic or Arabic profile were started in Sweden, and several dissertations have studied how these schools have been perceived by their pupils and how Muslim religious education has been conducted in Sweden (i.e., Aretun 2007; Berglund 2010; Brattlund 2009). Over time, confessional schools with an Arabic or Muslim profile have received heavy criticism in both public and political debates. Some

12 Muslims in Sweden: Historical Developments ...

schools have also been shut down because of problems with their management, and some have been associated with the promotion of values that are deemed to be contrary to the dominant values of Swedish society, such as equality between the sexes, gender segregation or even the promotion of a violent interpretation of Islam (Larsson and Sorgenfrei 2022).

One basis in Swedish society is the establishment of so-called study associations (*studieförbund* in Swedish) that can promote further education and *bildung* for workers and the public. Since 2001 the Muslim study association, Ibn Rushd, has been granted official status as well as economic support from the Swedish National Council of Adult Education (*Folkbildningsrådet* in Swedish). Resembling the criticisms that were voiced against confessional Muslim schools, Ibn Rushd has also received heavy criticism for promoting Islamism and for its association with the Muslim Brotherhood (Norell et al. 2018).

These accusations have been refuted by Ibn Rushd, and to put a stop to them an independent investigation was commissioned. In 2019, the political scientist Erik Amnå presented his findings in a report, and he concluded that there were some minor problems within Ibn Rushd that had to do with the fact that this was a young study association that did not enjoy the same experience as the old associations; moreover, there were some topics that were looked upon as being too sensitive to discuss within Ibn Rushd, especially concerning homosexuality. In conclusion, Amnå stressed that there was no support for the allegations that Ibn Rushd were promoting Islamism or that they were associated with the Muslim Brotherhood (Amnå 2019). Its critics were not content with this conclusion, however, and Ibn Rushd has still suffered from a negative press, causing it to lose financial support from some local municipalities (Larsson and Sorgenfrei 2022).

3.4   Majority Discourse

Resembling the discussion in most countries in Europe and the wider Western world, Islam and Muslims in Sweden have generally become associated with either violence and terrorism or migration, integration and segregation. While earlier decades have been preoccupied with questions related to the institutionalization and governance of Islam and Muslims (Mausen 2007), 9/11, the subsequent rise of Islamist violence, the global war on terrorism and the rise of the Islamic State in Syria and Iraq have led to new focuses in both public discussions and academic research. As Stefano Allievi argues, for instance (2006), the ethnic and linguistic backgrounds of migrants with a Muslim cultural background who arrived in Europe after the Second World War and in the 1960s and

1970s have been discarded and pushed to the background, 'Muslimness' often being stressed instead today (Sunier 2012). As shown by, for instance, Egdunas Racius and Göran Larsson (2010), the history of Islam and Muslims in Europe is a complex history, and it is therefore not accurate to treat Islam as a new religion in Europe. Regardless of the fact that the histories of Europe and of the larger Muslim world are entwined (e.g., Green 2020), anti-Muslim rhetoric often portrays Islam and Muslims as a new phenomenon that threatens social order (e.g., Larsson and Spielhaus 2017), including in Sweden.

3.5 Majority Attitudes

A slight majority of the Swedish population are positive about cultural and religious plurality, but there are important differences regarding attitudes towards different religions. For a long time, Islam has been the least favoured religion among Swedes, and approximately 50 percent of the population express negative views of it (Weibull 2019). After the arrival of more than 150,000 refugees and asylum-seekers in 2015, the public perception of migrants in Sweden also changed from positive to somewhat more negative (Demker 2019). In the 2022 national election, questions regarding law and order, migration and restrictions of minority rights were high on the political agenda. The Sweden Democrats, a right-wing party that for centuries has represented a political vision whereby Sweden should develop a very restricted policy towards migration and which has dubbed Islam to be one of the greatest threats to Europe in our day and age, grew to become Sweden's second largest political party.

3.6 Research on Islam in Sweden

When assessing past and present research, the number of publications and research projects on Islam and Muslims in Sweden has rapidly increased since the 1990s (Larsson 2004). Today research on Islam and Muslims includes, for instance, studies of religious, cultural and linguistic aspects (i.e., Berglund 2010; Olsson 2019; Thurfjell and Willander 2021; Sorgenfrei 2018; Willander 2019), but also of discrimination, racism and segregation (i.e., Bursell 2018; Puranen 2019, Larsson and Sorgenfrei 2018), Islamophobia (i.e., Gardell 2015; Larsson and Stjernholm 2016), Sufism in Sweden (Sorgenfrei 2014; Sorgenfrei and Stjernholm 2022), Islamism and Salafism in Sweden (Olsson 2019; Olsson, Roald, Sorgenfrei and Svensson 2022a, b; Olsson et al. 2022a, b, Sorgenfrei 2021a, b, c),

12 Muslims in Sweden: Historical Developments ...

and examinations of how to prevent violent extremism (Gustafsson and Ranstorp 2017; Nilsson and Frees Esholdt 2022; Rostami et al. 2020). There are also some more general overviews of Islam and Muslims in Sweden (Larsson 2014; Sorgenfrei 2018). An ongoing project[1] (Borevi and Sorgenfrei) also analyses relations between Islam and the state in Sweden from a longitudinal perspective. In late 2022, the Swedish Research Council decided to fund a so-called Research School that will recruit twelve PhD candidates to focus on the study of Islam.

Even though it is difficult to access and provide a fair picture of previous research on Islam and Muslims in Sweden, it is accurate to say that the field has grown over the years. Simultaneously the number of researchers in Sweden has grown, and a fair number of doctoral theses have explicitly addressed Islam and Muslims in Sweden. Examples include, for instance, Pia Karlsson Minganti's thesis (2007) on identity processes among young Muslim women; Madelene Sultán Sjövist's thesis (2006) on conversion processes to Islam; Johan Cato's thesis on parliamentary debates on Muslims in Sweden; Nina Jakku's thesis (2019) on Muslim women wearing the *niqab* (i.e., the facial veil); and Vanja Mosbach's (2022) study of Muslim women who identify as feminists. While these studies have primarily been defended within the study of religions or adjacent disciplines, there are of course other studies that address questions like, for instance, segregation, discrimination, or the legal aspects of the freedom of religion (see Arwall 1998; Larsson and Sayed 2017) or finance (Larsson and Willander 2021a, b).

3.7 Government Reports

An increasing number of government reports, explicitly or implicitly dealing with Islam and Muslims, have also been issued in recent decades (e.g. the Swedish Agency for Support to Faith Communities, the Swedish Civil Contingencies Agency, the Equality Ombudsman the Swedish National Council for Crime Prevention, or the Swedish Defence Research Agency). Some government enquiries have also dealt with questions like the slaughtering of animals (including dietary laws and slaughtering methods; Gunner 1999), imam training programs (SOU 2009, p. 53), the fight against violent extremism (SOU 2013: 81) and the state funding of religious bodies (SOU 2018, p. 18).

---

[1] The project by Karin Borevi and Simon Sorgenfrei is entitled *Muslims and the Swedish Model: A Longitudinal Study of State-Muslim Civil Society Relations*, and is funded by the Swedish Research Council (VR).

Even though some publications have been compiled and published by Muslims in Sweden in recent years (see, for instance, the journals *Salaam* or *Minaret*, the former was analysed by Otterbeck 2000a), most discussions by Muslims about Islam and Muslim affairs are today confined to the Internet or social media (e.g., Facebook, Twitter, or Instagram). Unfortunately, the Muslim presence on social media is not a well-researched topic in Sweden (some exceptions are Sorgenfrei 2021a, b; Svensson 2020).

4 Future Challenges

As indicated in the introduction to this chapter, the study of Islam and Muslims in Sweden has grown rapidly over the years. Irrespective of this positive development, there are several areas that deserves more attention, and it is possible to speak about blank spots. Most Swedish researchers with an interest in Islam and Muslims do not work on Swedish data, but rather on source material regarding the Middle East and North Africa. Resembling many other countries in Europe (Mausen 2007), most of the research focuses on the institutionalization and governmentalization of Islam and Muslims in Sweden. There are of course exceptions, and several theses have been very successful in their documentation and analysis of other aspects of Muslim affairs.

However, one major challenge is the funding of projects that stretch out over long periods of time and that include archive and field studies (i.e., interviews and participant observation) and big data research (including online media and registration data). Up until today, it has mainly been thesis projects that have conducted interviews and participant observation among Muslims. Overall these projects have all been very beneficial, but they have not continued after the termination of the doctoral projects, and they have rarely been repeated. As a result, there are still large questions that have not been addressed, as well as a lack of longitudinal studies.

For instance, the everyday lives of individuals who self-identify as Muslims have not been extensively covered, especially if we also include those that show a low or no interest in their religion, that is, the secularized or so-called 'cultural Muslims'; important exceptions are Otterbeck 2010; Thurfjell and Willander 2021).

Another aspect that, surprisingly, we have very little knowledge about is the religious life of Muslims. For instance, how do various Muslims celebrate their religious holidays (one important exception is Berglund and Sorgenfrei 2009);

12 Muslims in Sweden: Historical Developments ...

what do Muslims think about the guidance provided by imams and other religious authorities (both online and offline); to what extent are they affected by global developments (i.e., wars, migration patterns, and the general unrest that predominates in many Muslim majority countries); and to what extent do the intersectional aspects (i.e., gender, age, economy, education, 'time in Sweden', etc.) impact on Muslims and their participation in society? To what extent are Muslim groups divided along sectarian, ethnic, cultural and linguistic lines (maybe also including gender and age as important parameters), and to what degree are these differences and potential dividing lines played out in Sweden?

As in most parts of Europe, there is a need for more studies of anti-Muslim sentiments, discrimination and racism in Sweden. However, to study these burning social issues it is necessary to strive for definitions that are generally accepted and shared by scholars, government bodies and most Muslims, otherwise it is very difficult to make comparisons and measure developments over time or to suggest how to combat these social problems (Larsson and Stjernholm 2006; Larsson and Sander 2015). That said, it is also necessary to stress that Sweden has strong legislation that, at least in theory, should hinder Muslims from suffering from hate crimes or discriminations that are based on their religious identifications. Following this legislation, there is also strong protection for freedom of expression, and consequently it is also possible to voice anti-religious opinions. Although it could be legitimate to hold or voice strong criticism of Islam as a religion, such opinions might be hurtful to some Muslims.

With the last three general elections, it has become more common for Swedish political parties to voice opinions that stress the necessity of putting more pressure on migrants and asylum-seekers (not the least if they are identified as Muslims) to integrate and become part of the Swedish social fabric. Various unspecified forms of Islamism (i.e., political expressions of Islam) and symbolic expressions of Islam (e.g., clothing like the *hijab* or the *niqab*, or buildings associated with Islam, like mosques) have often been targeted in both political and public debates. Although a critical debate is part of a democratic society, it is also necessary to remember that the legislation on freedom of religion gives Muslims a legal right to express their religious beliefs as individuals or larger groups. Thus, it is important that scholars continue to study and document to what extent this so-called positive aspect of the legislation on freedom of religion is protected or not, and to what extent political debates have an impact on hate crimes and discrimination. That said, it is also essential to pay attention to the fact that migrants with a Muslim cultural background can also express anti-migration opinions and even voice criticism of certain expressions of Islam. To understand these opinions, we believe it is necessary to pay attention to, for instance, gender and age differences, as well as how long different groups of Muslims have been in Sweden. To document these questions, there is a need for both larger surveys and studies based on interviews.

However, there is a general problem with response rates for many areas that are more densely populated with migrants and asylum-seekers. To put it differently, surveys provide different response rates from different parts of society. This is a methodological problem, as the general surveys that produce aggregated results for the whole of Sweden (on, for instance, opinions and attitudes like the SOM Institute at the University of Gothenburg[2]) are not representative of the whole of Sweden and leave out important segments of the population (some of these problems are addressed in Larsson and Willander 2021a, b). So, if we want to collect large data samples from individuals and groups who self-identify as Muslims, we need to develop new methods for data collection. Instead of posting surveys via ordinary mail (or via bank applications)—which is the standard procedure for most social scientists working in Sweden—there is also a need to collect field data using assistants with local knowledge who might be able to communicate in another language than Swedish. While a potential benefit of this method of collecting data is that it provides a good opportunity to include field assistance or scholars who have a footing in local communities, it is expensive and time-consuming (for a discussion see, Esaiasson 2019).

References

Allievi, Stefano. 2006. How and why 'Immigrants' became 'Muslims.' *ISIM Review* 18(1):37.

Alwall, Jonas. 1998. *Muslim rights and plights: The religious liberty situation of a minority in Sweden.* Lund: Lund University Press.

Rostami, Amir, Joakim Sturup, Hernan Mondani, Pia Thevselius, Jerzy Sarnecki, and Christofer Edling. 2020. The Swedish Mujahideen: An exploratory study of 41 Swedish foreign fighters deceased in Iraq and Syria. *Studies in Conflict and Terrorism* 43(5):382–395.

Amnå, Erik. 2019. *När tilliten prövas. En studie av studieförbundet Ibn Rushds samhällsbidrag.* Stockholm: Folkbildningsrådet.

Aretun, Åsa. 2007. *Barns växa 'vilt' och vuxnas vilja att forma: Formell och informell socialisation i en muslimsk skola.* Linköping: Linköpings universitet.

---

[2] For more information on the SOM Institute, go to https://www.gu.se/en/som-institute (accessed 21st November 2022).

12 Muslims in Sweden: Historical Developments … 215

Arly Jacobsen, Brian, Göran Larsson, and Simon Sorgenfrei. 2014. The Ahmadiyya mission to the Nordic countries. In *Handbook of Nordic New Religions*, Eds. James R. Lewis and Inga Bårdsen Tøllefsen, 359–373. Boston: Brill.

Arne, Ture J. 1952. *Svenskarna och österlandet*. Stockholm: Natur and Kultur.

Berglund, Jenny. 2010. *Teaching Islam: Islamic Religious Education in Sweden*. Münster: Waxmann.

Berglund, Jenny, and Simon Sorgenfrei, Ed. 2009. *Ramadan. En svensk tradition*. Lund: Arcus.

Birkeland, Harris. 1954. *Nordens historie i middelalderen etter arabiske kilder: Oversettelse til norsk av de arabiske kilder med innledning, forfatterbiografier, bibliografi og merknader*. Oslo: Dybwad.

Brattlund, Åsa. 2009. *What role of God and national curriculum in school life?: A comparative study of schools with a Muslim profile in England and Sweden*. Stockholm: Department of Education, Stockholm University.

Bursell, Moa. 2018. Perceptions of discrimination against Muslims: A study of formal complaints against public institutions in Sweden. *Journal of Ethnic and Migration Studies* 47(5):1162–1179.

Demker, Marie. 2019. Migrationsfrågorna som ideologisk lots: Partipolitisering och polarisering. In *Storm och stiltje*, Eds. Ulrika Andersson, Björn Rönnerstrand, Patrik Öhberg, and Annika Bergström, 421–431. Göteborg: SOM-institutet.

Duczko, Wladyslaw. 2004. *Viking Rus: Studies on the presence of Scandinavians in Eastern Europe*. Boston: Brill.

Esaisson, Peter. 2019. *Förorten. Ett samhällsvetenskapligt reportage*. Stockholm: Timbro.

Gardell, Mattias. 2015. What's love got to do with it? Ultranationalism, Islamophobia and Hate Crimes in Sweden. *Journal of Religion and Violence* 3(1):91–115.

Gardell, Mattias. 2018. *Moskéers och muslimska församlingars utsatthet och säkerhet i Sverige 2018*. Uppsala: Centrum för mångvetenskaplig forskning om rasism.

Green, Nile. 2020. *Global Islam: A very short introduction*. Oxford: Oxford University Press.

Gunner, Göran. 1999. *Att slakta ett får i Guds namn: om religionsfrihet och demokrati*. Stockholm: Fakta info direkt.

Gustafsson, Linus, and Magnus Ranstorp. 2017. *Swedish foreign fighters in Syria and Iraq. An analysis of open-source intelligence and statistical data*. Stockholm: Swedish Defence University. https://www.diva-portal.org/smash/get/diva2:1110355/FULLTEXT01.pdf Accessed: 24. Nov. 2022.

Härenstam, Kjell. 1993. *Skolboks-islam: Analys av bilden av islam i läroböcker i religionskunskap*. Göteborg: Göteborg University.

Ibn Fadlan. 2012. *Ibn Fadlan and the land of darkness: Arab travellers in the far North*. Translated with an introduction by Paul Lunde and Caroline Stone. London: Penguin Books.

Jakku, Nina. 2019. *Muslimska kvinnors mobilitet: Möjligheter och hinder i de liberala idealens Sverige*. Lund: Lunds universitet.

Jarring, Gunnar. 1987. Sveriges diplomatiska förbindelser med tatarerna på Krim. In *Utrikespolitik och historia. Studier tillägnade Wilhelm M. Carlgren den 6 aj 1987*, Ed M. Berquist et al. 83–90. Stockholm: Militärhistoriska förlaget.

Jonsson Hraundal, Thorir. 2013. *The Rus in Arabic sources: Cultural contacts and identity*. Bergen: University of Bergen.

Minganti, Karlsson, and Pia. 2007. *Muslima: Islamisk väckelse och unga muslimska kvinnors förhandlingar om genus i det samtida Sverige.* Stockholm: Stockholms universitet.

Karlsson, Pia. 1995. *Moskéer i Sverige. En religionsetnologisk studie av intolerans och administrativ vanmakt.* Stockholm: Svenska kyrkans forskningsråd.

Flensner, Kittelmann, Karin, and Göran Larsson. 2014. Swedish religious education at the end of the 1960s: Classroom obervations, early video ethnography and the national curriculum of 1962. *British Journal of Religious Education* 36(2):202–217.

Kronberg, Klas, Per Sandin, and Åsa Karlsson, Eds.. 2016. *When Sweden was ruled from the Ottoman Empire.* Stockholm: Armémuseum.

Larsson, Göran, and Egdunas Racius. 2010. A different approach to the history of Islam and Muslims in Europe: A North-Eastern angle, or the need to reconsider the research field. *Journal of Religion in Europe* 2:350–373.

Larsson, Göran, and Sorgenfrei, Simon. 2018. *Andra antireligiösa hatbrott och diskriminerande attityder.* Stockholm: Myndigheten för stöd till trossamfund.

Larsson, Göran, and Åke. Sander. 2015. An urgent need to consider how to define Islamophobia. *Bulletin for the Study of Religion* 44(1):13–17.

Larsson, Göran, and Erika Willander. 2021a. Belonging, identification and trust among self-identified Muslims in Sweden: What we know and what We don't know. In *Muslims in the Western World: Sense of belonging and political identity,* Ed. Daniel Stockemer, 129–146. Heidelberg: Springer.

Larsson, Göran, and Erika Willander. 2021b. Muslim attitudes towards Islamic finance in Sweden: The case of loans with inerest. *Nordic Journal of Religion and Society* 34(2):76–88.

Larsson, Göran, and Riem Spielhaus. 2017. Europe with or without Muslims: Creating and maintaining cultural boundaries. In *Cultural borders of Europe: Narratives, concepts and practices in the present and the past,* Eds. Mats Andrén, Thomas Lindkvist, Ingmar Söhrman, and Katharina Vajta, 40–53. Oxford: Bergham.

Larsson, Göran, and Simon Sorgenfrei. 2022. 'Sweden'. In *Yearbook of Muslims in Europe,* Eds. Račius, Egdūnas and Müssig, Stephanie, vol. 14. Leiden: Brill.

Larsson, Göran, and Thurfjell, David. 2013. *Shiamuslimer i Sverige. En kortfattad översikt.* Stockholm: SST.

Larsson, Göran, and Mosa Sayed. 2017. *Annotated legal documents on Islam in Europe. Compiled and annotated.* Boston: Brill.

Larsson, Göran., and Simon Stjernholm. 2016. Islamophobia in Sweden: Muslim advocacy and hate-crime statistics. In *Fear of Muslims? International perspectives on Islamophobia,* Ed. Douglas Pratt and Rachel Woodlock, 153–166. Heidelberg: Springer.

Larsson, Göran. 2004. *Islam och muslimer i Sverige: En kommenterad bibliografi.* Göteborg: Makadam förlag.

Larsson, Göran. 2011. From aesthetic conflict to anti-mosque demonstrations. The institutionalisation of Islam and Muslims in Sweden. In *Mosques in Europe. Why a solution has become a problem,* Ed. Stefano Allievi, 355–372. London: Alliance publishing.

Mausen, M. 2007. *The governance of Islam in Western Europe: A state of the art report.* IMISCOE Working Paper No. 16.

Mikkelsen, Egil. 2008. The Vikings and Islam. In *The Viking world,* Ed. Stefan Brink and Niel Price, 543–549. New York: Routledge.

12 Muslims in Sweden: Historical Developments ... 217

Mosbach, Vanja. 2022. *Voices of Muslim feminists: Navigating tradition, authority and the debate about Islam.* Uppsala: Uppsala universitet.

Nilsson, Marco, and Henriette Frees Esholdt. 2022. After the Caliphate: Changing mobilization in the Swedish Salafi-Jihadist environment following the Fall of ISIS. *Studies in Conflict and Terrorism.* https://doi.org/10.1080/1057610X.2022.2104682.

Norell, Magnus. et al. 2019. *Muslimska Brödraskapet i Sverige.* Stockholm: MSB.

Olsson, Susanne. 2019. *Contemporary Puritan Salafism: A Swedish case study.* Sheffield: Equinox.

Olsson, Susanne, Anne-Sofie Roald, Simon Sorgenfrei, and Jonas Svensson. 2022. *Wahhabism i Sverige : Nätverk, praktiker och mission.* Stockholm: Myndigheten för samhällsskydd och beredskap.

Olsson, Susanne, Simon Sorgenfrei, and Jonas Svensson. 2022b. 'Puritan Salafis in a liberal democratic context. In *Salafi-Jihadism and digital media: The Nordic and international context,* Ed. Magnus Ranstorp, Linda Ahlerup, and Filip Ahlin, 92–112. New York: Routledge.

Otterbeck, Jonas. 2000a. *Islam på svenska. Tidskriften Salaam och islams globalisering.* Lund: Stockholm: Almqvist and Wiksell International.

Otterbeck, Jonas. 2000b. *Islam, muslimer och den svenska skolan.* Lund: Studentlitteratur

Otterbeck, Jonas. 2010. *Samtidsislam. Unga muslimer i Malmö och Köpenhamn.* Stockholm: Carlsson.

Puranen, Bi. 2019. *Med migranternas röst: den subjektiva integrationen.* Stockholm: Institutet för framtidsstudier.

Ranstorp, Magnus, Filip Ahlin, Peder Hyllengren, and Magnus Normark. 2019. *Between Salafism and Salafi-Jihadism Influence and Challenges for Swedish Society.* Stockholm: Försvarshögskolan.

Sorgenfrei, Simon, and Simon Stjernholm. 2022. Salafi Sufism? Islamic border-keeping in contemporary Sweden. *Approaching Religion* 12(2):77–91.

Sorgenfrei, Simon. 2016. *Sufism i Sverige—en kartläggning av sufigrupper i Stockholm, Göteborg och Malmö.* Stockholm: Myndigheten för stöd till trossamfund.

Sorgenfrei, Simon. 2018. *Islam i Sverige: De första 1300 åren.* Stockholm: Myndigheten för stöd till trossamfund.

Sorgenfrei, Simon. 2020a. Establishing Islam in Sweden. The first Tatar community and Muslim congregation in Sweden—and its Sources. *Studia Orientalia* 8(2):82–95.

Sorgenfrei, Simon. 2020b. *Muslimska begravningsseder och begravningsceremonier.* Stockholm: Myndigheten för stöd till trossamfund.

Sorgenfrei, Simon. 2021a. Branding Salafism: Salafi missionaries as social media influencers. *Method and Theory in the Study of Religion* 34(3):211–237.

Sorgenfrei, Simon. 2021b. Crowdfunding Salafism. Crowdfunding as Muslim mission method. *Religions* 12(3). https://doi.org/10.3390/rel12030209.

Sorgenfrei, Simon. 2021c. 'Perhaps we see it in negative terms, but, ultimately, it is positive': the responses of Swedish Salafis to COVID-19. *Scandinavian Journal of Islamic Studies* 15(2). https://doi.org/10.7146/tifo.v15i2.125959

Sorgenfrei, Simon. 2021d. *Muslimska begravningsseder och begravningsceremonier.* Stockholm: Myndigheten för stöd till trossamfund.

Sorgenfrei, Simon. 2022. *'De kommer att vara annorlunda svenskar': berättelsen om Sveriges första muslimer.* Stockholm: Norstedts.

SOU 2013:81: *När vi bryr oss: förslag om samverkan och utbildning för att effektivare förebygga våldsbejakande extremism : betänkande.* Fritze, Stockholm.

SOU 2018:18: *Statens stöd till trossamfund i ett mångreligiöst Sverige.* Stockholm: Norstedts juridik.

SOU 2009:52: *Staten och imamerna: Religion, integration, autonomi.* Stockholm: Fritzes.

Sultán Sjöqvist, Madeleine. 2006. *'Vi blev muslimer'. Svenska kvinnors berättar. En religionssociologisk studie av konversionsberättelser.* Uppsala: Acta Universitatis Upsaliensis.

Sunier, Thijl. 2012. Beyond the domestication of Islam in Europe: A reflection on past and future research on Islam in European societies. *Journal of Muslims in Europe* 2(1):189–208.

Svensson, Jonas. 2020. Computing Swedish Salafism: An example of a digital humanities approach to collecting, organizing, and analyzing Data on Web-based Salafi Missonary Activity in Sweden. *Journal of Religion in Europe* 13(1–2):1–22.

Thurfjell, David, and Erika Willander. 2021. Muslims by ascription: On post-Lutheran secularity and Muslim immigrants. *Numen: International Review for the History of Religions* 68:307–335.

Tweed, Thomas A. 2006. *Crossing and dwelling: A theory of religion.* Cambridge: Harvard University Press.

Weibull, Lennart. 2019. Synen på trosuppfattningar i Sverige. In *Storm och stiltje*, Eds. Ulrika Andersson, Björn Rönnerstrand, Patrik Öhberg, and Annika Bergström, 433–453. Göteborg: SOM-institutet.

Willander, Erika. 2019. *The religious landscape of Sweden: Affinity, affiliation and diversity in the 21st century.* Stockholm: The Agency for State Support to Faith Communities.

Zetterstéen, Karl Vilhelm. 1952. De krimska tatarernas diplomatiska korrespondens med den svenska regeringen. *Kungl. Humanistiska vetenskaps-samfundet i Uppsala. Årsbok.*

Göran Larsson is Professor of Religious Studies at the University of Gothenburg, Sweden. His research focuses mainly on Islam and Muslims in Europe. In 2021, he edited the book *The Legacy, Life and Work of Geo Widengren and the Study of the History of Religions after World War II* (Leiden-Boston: Brill).

Simon Sorgenfrei is Professor in the Study of Religions and Director of the Institute for the Study of Multireligiosity and Secularity (IMS) at Södertörn University, Sweden. His research focuses on Islam and Muslims in the West. His most recent publication is *"De kommer att vara annorlunda svenskar". Berättelsen om Sveriges första muslimer* (Stockholm: Nordstedt, 2022).

Printed in the United States
by Baker & Taylor Publisher Services